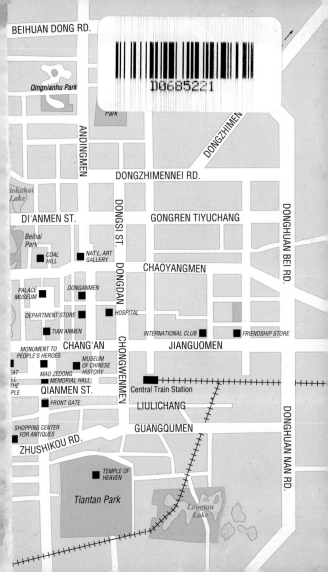

BEIHUAN DONG RD.

Qingnianhu Park

D0685221

Park

ANDINGMEN

DONGZHIMEN

DONGZHIMENNEI RD.

Beihai Lake

DI'ANMEN ST.

DONGSI ST.

GONGREN TIYUCHANG

DONGHUAN BEI RD.

Beihai Park

COAL HILL

NAT'L. ART GALLERY

CHAOYANGMEN

PALACE MUSEUM

DONGANMEN

DONGDAN

DEPARTMENT STORE

HOSPITAL

TIAN ANMEN

INTERNATIONAL CLUB

FRIENDSHIP STORE

MONUMENT TO PEOPLE'S HEROES

CHANG'AN

CHONGWENMEN

JIANGUOMEN

EAT LL THE PLE

MAO ZEDONG MEMORIAL HALL

MUSEUM OF CHINESE HISTORY

Central Train Station

QIANMEN ST.

FRONT GATE

LIULICHANG

SHOPPING CENTER FOR ANTIQUES

GUANGQUMEN

ZHUSHIKOU RD.

DONGHUAN NAN RD.

TEMPLE OF HEAVEN

Tiantan Park

Longtan Lake

MANDARIN
CHINESE
AT A GLANCE
PHRASE BOOK & DICTIONARY FOR TRAVELERS

BY SCOTT D. SELIGMAN
Director, Public Relations
Government and International Affairs
United Technologies Corporation
Washington, D.C.

and

I-CHUAN CHEN
Contract Conference Interpreter (Chinese and English)
Language Services
United States Department of State
Washington, D.C.

Third Edition

BARRON'S

All inquiries should be addressed to:
Barron's Educational Series, Inc.
250 Wireless Boulevard
Hauppauge, New York 11788
www.barronseduc.com

Library of Congress Catalog Card No. 2006045999

ISBN-13: 978-0-7641-3556-9 (book)
ISBN-10: 0-7641-3556-2 (book)
ISBN-13: 978-0-7641-7954-9 (package)
ISBN-10: 0-7641-7954-3 (package)

Library of Congress Cataloging-in-Publication Data
Seligman, Scott D.
    Mandarin Chinese at a glance : phrase book & dictionary for travellers / by
Scott D. Seligman and I-chuan Chen—3d. ed.
        p.   cm.
    Includes index.
    ISBN-13: 978-0-7641-3556-9 (bk. : alk. paper)
    ISBN-13: 978-0-7641-7954-9 (package)
    ISBN-10: 0-7641-3556-2 (bk. : alk. paper)
    ISBN-10: 0-7641-7954-3 (package)
    1. Chinese language—Conversation and phrase books–English.   I. Chen,
I-Chuan, 1940–   II. Title.
PL1125.E6S35   2006
495.1′83421—dc22   2006045999

PRINTED IN CHINA
9 8 7 6

CONTENTS

PREFACE

So you're taking a trip to one of the many fascinating countries of the world. That's exciting! This new phrase book will prove an invaluable companion that will make your stay far more interesting.

This phrase book is part of a series in which we present the phrases and words that a traveler most often needs for a brief visit to a foreign country, where the customs and language are often different. Each of the phrase books highlights the terms particular to that country, in situations that the tourist is most likely to encounter. With a specially developed key to pronunciation, this book will enable you to communicate quickly and confidently in colloquial terms. It is intended not only for beginners with no knowledge of the language, but also for those who have already studied it and have some familiarity with it.

Some of the unique features and highlights of the Barron's series are:

- Easy-to-follow *pronunciation keys* and complete phonetic transcriptions for all words and phrases in the book.
- Compact *dictionary* of commonly used words and phrases—built right into this phrase book so there's no need to carry a separate dictionary.
- Useful phrases for the *tourist*, grouped together by subject matter in a logical way so that the appropriate phrase is easy to locate when you need it.
- Special phrases for the *business traveler*, including banking terms.
- Thorough section on *food and drink*, with comprehensive food terms you will find on menus; these terms are often difficult or impossible to locate in dictionaries, but our section gives you a description of the preparation as well as a definition of what it is.
- *Emergency phrases* and terms you hope you won't need: medical problems, theft or loss of valuables, replacement or repair of watches, cameras, and the like.

▦   *Sightseeing itineraries*, shopping tips, practical travel
tips to help you get off the beaten path and into the
countryside, to the small towns and cities, and to the
neighboring areas.
▦   A *reference section* providing: important signs,
conversion tables, holidays, telling time, days of the
week, and months of the year.
▦   A brief *grammar section*, with the basic elements of the
language quickly explained.

Enjoy your vacation and travel with confidence. You
have a friend by your side.

INTRODUCTION

CHINESE DIALECTS

Spoken Chinese is divided into many different dialects. Although the written language is essentially the same throughout China, the pronunciation of the words varies tremendously in different regions. Speaking their native dialects, people from the north of China communicate verbally with southerners with about as much difficulty as French people trying to speak with Italians.

It was in order to facilitate communication that the Chinese decided to establish a standard language for themselves. The dialect they chose as the standard is called Mandarin (*pǔtōnghuà* in Chinese), and it is native to the Beijing (Peking) area. Mandarin is taught throughout the People's Republic of China (PRC), as well as in Taiwan, where it is called *guóyǔ*. It is also widely spoken in Singapore, Hong Kong, and other parts of Southeast Asia where there are large numbers of Chinese. Sometimes it is also referred to as *huáyǔ* or *hànyǔ*.

Mandarin isn't the only dialect you'll come across on a tour of China. Among the dozens of other widely spoken dialects are Cantonese, which is heard in and around Guangzhou or Canton, the capital of Guangdong Province, as well as in Hong Kong and Macao; Shanghainese, spoken in the greater Shanghai area; Hunan dialect, spoken in Hunan Province; and Sichuan (Szechuan) dialect, spoken in Sichuan Province. You'll also hear the Hokkien dialect in Fujian Province as well as in Taiwan and in many parts of Southeast Asia where Chinese people who trace their ancestry back to Fujian live. For the purposes of a tour of China, however, Mandarin is by far the best dialect to learn. You'll find plenty of Mandarin speakers no matter where you go in the mainland or Taiwan.

SPEAKING CHINESE

The Chinese are delighted when foreigners try to speak their language. They will forgive you a multitude of sins, try their best to understand you, even if your pronunciation is close to unintelligible, and probably even compliment you on your excellent command of Chinese. You needn't take such flattering compliments too seriously; they are simply the Chinese way of being polite and of expressing appreciation for your efforts.

In general, you'll have the best chance of being understood by Chinese who have had frequent contact with foreigners. They are more accustomed to, and better able to make sense of, the predictable mispronunciations. But don't let this stop you from speaking to anyone and everyone you meet. If all else fails, simply show the Chinese characters in this book for the phrase you wish to convey.

VISITING TAIWAN AND HONG KONG

Although this book has been written primarily for travelers to the PRC, most of the phrases included in it are also useful in Taiwan, where the Mandarin dialect is widely spoken. The native Taiwanese majority—those whose ancestors emigrated to Taiwan from southern Fujian Province during the nineteenth century, as opposed to the approximately 18 percent of "mainlanders" whose families arrived in the 1940s during the Communist takeover of the mainland—speak a dialect that is quite a bit different from Mandarin. But Mandarin has been taught widely in schools in Taiwan for many years, and virtually any educated person in Taiwan can understand it.

There are some linguistic differences to keep in mind, however. Though at least 98 percent of the vocabulary used in this book are understandable on both sides of the Taiwan Strait, some of the terms reflect PRC usage and are not widely used on Taiwan. A handful may not be understood at all, but in general, basic conversational vocabulary varies very little.

There are also some pronunciation differences. Generally speaking, the further you are from Beijing, the less standard the Mandarin pronunciation of the local populace. Inhabitants of Taiwan have a distinct accent when they speak Mandarin, just as Australians and Americans do when they speak English. It's not impossible to understand, but it can take some getting used to.

The native dialect of most of the residents of Hong Kong and Macao is *Guǎngdōnghuà*, or Cantonese, unintelligible to native speakers of Mandarin. Mandarin has become increasingly popular in Hong Kong and Macao since the colonies returned to Chinese sovereignty in the late 1990s. But because of Hong Kong's history as a British colony, the most widely spoken second language there is still English, and, in general, you should be able to get by in English with little difficulty. Mandarin is also spoken in Macao, which the Portuguese returned to China in 1999, but Cantonese is the native dialect and is heard far more frequently.

The written Chinese in this book is expressed in simplified characters. The Communists simplified many characters in the 1950s in order to make the language easier to learn and promote literacy among the masses. Most of these forms are not widely used in Hong Kong, however, and still less in Taiwan, so people in these places may not easily recognize some of the written characters in this book, though in most cases they'll be able to make good educated guesses.

QUICK PRONUNCIATION GUIDE

PINYIN SPELLING

The Chinese language in this book is rendered in characters as well as in a romanized system called *pīnyīn*, which translates quite simply as "spelling." The characters themselves give little or no phonetic information, and their pronunciation must normally be learned by rote. You won't be expected to learn characters to use this book effectively; we include them primarily to facilitate your communication with Chinese people when phonics fail you. Most Chinese can't read pinyin very well, even though many used it when learning Chinese in primary school. In Taiwan, it is hardly used at all.

Pinyin is the official romanization system of the People's Republic of China. It was adopted in the 1950s and has gained wide acceptance in China and abroad in recent years, essentially supplanting all previous romanization systems. Because pinyin is commonly used on street signs and storefronts in large cities, a knowledge of it can aid you as you make your way in China.

The traditional spellings of many names, such as *Peking, Tientsin, Canton,* and *Mao Tse-tung,* have been replaced with their less familiar but more phonetic pinyin forms: *Beijing, Tianjin, Guangzhou,* and *Mao Zedong.* The pinyin system is fairly accessible to native speakers of English. There are, however, a handful of notable exceptions. The table on page 3 explains pinyin pronunciation in detail.

Don't skip this section; you really need to master pinyin for this book to be useful to you. However, to help jog your memory, we include a summary of the hardest pinyin sounds to remember—both on page 10 and at the end of the book. And as an added convenience we have reprinted some of the most troublesome pinyin initials and their phonetic equivalents on the bottom of each left-hand page in the body of the book.

SYLLABLES

Syllables are the building blocks of Chinese words and phrases. In the written language, each syllable can be rendered as a distinct character. The syllable consists of three components: the *initial*, the *final*, and the *tone*. For example, in the word *táng*, which means "sugar," the initial is the *t* sound at the beginning of the syllable; the final is the *ang* sound at the end; and the tone, represented by the (´) mark, is the rising tone of voice in which the word is pronounced. All three components must generally be present for the word to be completely understandable in Chinese, though some syllables don't require initials, and sometimes they are pronounced in a neutral tone.

INITIALS

Initials are always consonants, and in pinyin most of the pronunciations are fairly intuitive to native speakers of English. Following is a table of initials with an explanation of how to pronounce them.

PINYIN INITIAL	ENGLISH EQUIVALENT	EXAMPLES	APPROXIMATE PRONUNCIATION
b, p, m, f, d, t, n, l, g, k, j, s, w, y, ch, sh	approximately the same as in English	neng tou gan	*nung* *toe* *gone*
c	like the *ts* in *rats*	can cu	*tsahn* *tsoo*
h	more guttural than the English *h*. More like the German *ch* as in *ach*	hen hao	*hun* *how*
q	like the *ch* in *cheap*	qin qu	*cheen* *chü*
r	a cross between a *j* and an *r*. No English equivalent; something like the *z* in *azure*	ren ru	*wren* *roo*
x	like the *sh* in *sheen*	xiao xin	*shee-yow* *sheen*
z	like *dz* to sound like the *ds* in *kids*	zai zu	*dzye* *dzoo*
zh	like the hard *j* in *jack*	zhang zhou	*jahng* *joe*

FINALS

Finals always begin with vowels. They may end in vowels, consonants, or diphthongs. Study the list of finals below. In many cases they can be pronounced accurately by using your intuition as a native English speaker—but there are a few surprises.

PINYIN FINAL	ENGLISH EQUIVALENT	EXAMPLES	APPROXIMATE PRONUNCIATION
a	*ah* as in *rah*	ba	*bah*
		na	*nah*
ai	like the *y* in *rye* or *my*	tai	*tie*
		lai	*lye*
an	*ahn*, to rhyme with *John*	ban	*bahn*
		can	*tsahn*
ang	*ahng*, as in *angst*	tang	*tahng*
		chang	*chahng*
ao	like the *ow* in *cow*	chao	*chow*
ar	as in *are*	nar	*nar*
e	like the *u* sound in *bush*	de	*duh*
		le	*luh*
ei	like the *a* in *pay* or *play*	fei	*fay*
		shei	*shay*
en	like the *un* in *pun*	men	*mun*
eng	like the *ung* in *hung*	deng	*dung*
er	like the *ur* in *cur*	mer	*mur*
i	like the *ee* in *flee* when following *b, p, m, d, t, n, l, j, q,* and *x*	ji	*jee*
		xi	*shee*
	like a *zz* after *z, c,* and *s*	zi	*dz*
		si	*sz*
	like an *r* after *zh, ch, sh,* and *r*	zhi	*jr*
		shi	*shr*
ia	*ya*, like the *ia* in the name *Mia*, but said in one syllable	lia	*lya*
		xia	*shya*

PINYIN FINAL	ENGLISH EQUIVALENT	EXAMPLES	APPROXIMATE PRONUNCIATION
ian	*yen*	pian	*pyen*
iang	*yahng*, with the same vowel as in the word *angst*	liang jiang	*lyahng* *jyahng*
iao	*ee-yow*, to rhyme with the cat's *meow*, but said in one syllable	biao liao	*bee-yow* *lee-yow*
ie	*yeh*	bie	*byeh*
in	*een* as in *green*	qin xin	*cheen* *sheen*
ing	as in *sing*	bing	*bing*
iong	*yawng*, to rhyme with *strong*	qiong xiong	*chyawng* *shyawng*
iu	like the *eo* in the name *Leo*, pronounced in one syllable	qiu liu	*cheo* *leo*
o	like the *aw* sound in *awe*, to rhyme with *saw*	mo po	*maw* *paw*
ong	like the *ong* in *wrong*, but with a rounder *o* sound	long zhong	*long* *jawng*
ou	like the *o* in *toe* or *ho*	mou zhou	*moe* *joe*
u	*oo* as in *boo* after most letters pronounced as *ü* (see below) after *j, q, x,* or *y*	mu du qu xu	*moo* *doo* *chü* *shü*
ü	no English equivalent; like the German *ü* or the French *eu.* Used only after *n* and *l*	nü lü	*nü* *lü*
ua	*wah*, like the *ua* in *guava*	zhua gua	*jwah* *gwah*

PINYIN FINAL	ENGLISH EQUIVALENT	EXAMPLES	APPROXIMATE PRONUNCIATION
uai	*wye*, to rhyme with *rye*	guai	*gwye*
uan	*wahn*, to rhyme with *swan* after most letters	tuan duan	*twahn* *dwahn*
	wen, to rhyme with *when* after *j, q, x*, or *y*	yuan juan	*ywen* *jwen*
uang	*wahng*, with the same vowel as the word *angst*	zhuang kuang	*jwahng* *kwahng*
ue or üe	*oo-eh*, to rhyme with *moo* and *yeh*, merged into one syllable. Written with (¨) symbol after *n* and *l*	xue lüe	*shooeh* *looeh*
ui	*way*	dui	*dway*
un	*one* is the closest sound in English, though the vowel is actually closer to the *oo* sound in *book*.	dun sun	*dwun* *swun*
	After *j, q*, and *x*, pronounced like the English *win*	jun xun	*jwin* *shwin*
uo	*waw*, to rhyme with *thaw*	duo cuo	*dwaw* *tswaw*

TONES

Each Chinese syllable also has a special intonation that must be used when it is pronounced. Spoken Mandarin has four distinct tones. They do not correspond to absolute musical pitches, but rather are spoken differently by different individuals, depending on the range of their voices.

What is important is that the tones remain relatively distinct from one another.

For example, the first tone is pronounced at a high, level pitch at the top of one's vocal range. For a woman this will generally be a higher pitch than for a man, but this makes no difference as long as it's done at the top of one's register. The second tone rises from the middle of the voice to the top, as when asking a question in English, even though a rising tone implies no interrogative in Chinese. The third tone starts in the middle of the voice and dips to the bottom before rising a bit at the end. The fourth tone starts high and ends low, as when scolding someone or emphasizing something in English. The figure below illustrates the four tones.

The tones are indicated by the use of diacritical marks above the syllables. The first tone, the even tone, is illustrated

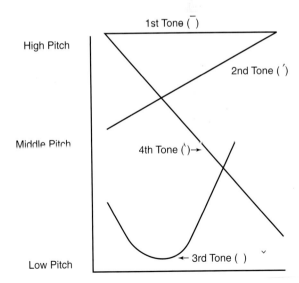

with a horizontal mark above the syllable (ˉ). The second tone, which rises, is shown with a line sloping up (ˊ). The third tone, which dips to the bottom of the voice, is indicated with a U-shaped mark (ˇ). The fourth, or falling, tone is illustrated with a line sloping down (ˋ).

The importance of the tones is clear from the example of the syllable *ma*. *Mā*, in the first tone, means "mother." In the second tone, *má* is understood to mean "hemp." The third tone form, *mǎ*, means "horse." And in the fourth tone, *mà* means "to scold." If you are careless with your tones, you are more than likely to make a serious mistake speaking Chinese, since the language is rich in homonyms. The tones help a Chinese listener distinguish different words. Asking for *táng* at the table will get you sugar, but if you pronounce it *tāng*, you'll be given a bowl of soup.

Even a syllable with a given tone can have more than one meaning. *Shī*, for example, means both "lion" and "poem" in the first tone, as well as other things. A Chinese can generally figure out what you mean from the context of your remarks, but imagine how much harder you make his or her task if you mispronounce the word. In various other tones, *shi* can mean history, a teacher, an envoy, a market, to show, a lifetime, a test, a style, the number ten, a stone, or the verb "to be."

You'll notice that in this book we have frequently omitted the tone mark over a particular syllable. This simply means that the syllable should be unstressed and pronounced in a neutral tone of voice.

One more point: We've used standard punctuation marks in this text. These are as intelligible to the Chinese as to us. But when you're speaking Chinese, don't make the all-too-common mistake of raising your pitch at the end of a question or dropping it after an exclamation, as you might in English, for this will interfere with the proper pronunciation of tones. Just keep to the tones as marked and you will get the desired results.

SOME CONVENTIONS

We've adopted a few conventions in our use of pinyin that we hope will be helpful to you. First of all, we have omitted the space between two syllables when the syllables combine to form a common word. For example, to say "already" in Chinese requires two characters: *yǐ* and *jīng*. Neither can stand alone; the meaning comes from the combination. So for the sake of clarity we render it *yǐjīng*. This technique should help you to recognize words—as opposed to just syllables—a bit more quickly. We are also capitalizing the initial letter of words that begin sentences.

Finally, spoken Chinese occasionally involves a *change* in the tone of a syllable, depending on the context. When two third tones occur together, for example, the first one is generally pronounced as a second tone. We have built such changes in for you in this book, so you needn't concern yourself with these rules. It is for this reason, however, that the same word may occasionally appear in different tones in this book. An example is *wǒ* ("I" or "me"). This occasionally shows up as *wó*, depending on the tone of the word that follows it. Just say it the way it appears in the text and you won't go wrong. If you need to know the standard tone of the word out of context, check the dictionary at the end of the book.

THE COMMON PROBLEMS OF PINYIN		
INITIALS*		
c = *ts*, as in *rats* **x** = *sh*	**q** = *ch* **zh** = *j*	**z** = *dz*, like the *ds* sound in *kids*
FINALS		
ai rhymes with *rye*	**an** = *ahn*, rhymes with *John*	**ang** = *ahng* as in *angst*
ao rhymes with *cow* **en** rhymes with *pun*	**e** = *u* as in *bush* **eng** rhymes with *hung*	**ei** rhymes with *pay* **ia** = *ya*
i sounds like *ee* after most letters, but like *zz* after *z*, *c*, and *s*, and like an *r* after *zh*, *ch*, *sh*, and *r*	**ian** = *yen* **iao** = *ee-yow*	**iang** = *yahng* **ie** = *yeh*
iu rhymes with *Leo* **u** rhymes with *boo* in most cases, but becomes the German *ü* after *j*, *q*, *x*, and *y*	**iong** = *yawng* **o** = *aw* **ua** = *wah* **uan** = *wahn*; but *wen* after *j*, *q*, *x*, and *y*	**in** rhymes with *green* **ou** rhymes with *toe* **uai** = *wye* **uang** = *wahng*; vowel as in *angst*
un = *one*, but the vowel is as in *book*	**ue** = *oo-eh* **ün** rhymes with *win*	**ui** rhymes with *way* **uo** = *waw*

*The "Initials" of this table are hereafter repeated at the bottom of every left-hand page for the reader's convenience.

THE BASICS FOR GETTING BY

MOST FREQUENTLY USED EXPRESSIONS

The expressions in this section are ones you'll use again and again—they are the fundamental building blocks of conversation. They will help you to express your wants and needs, and they include some simple question forms. We suggest that you become very familiar with these phrases.

beautiful	*piàoliàng*	漂亮
Excuse me.		
(to apologize for something)	*Duìbuqǐ.*	对不起。
(to get attention)	*Láo jià!*	劳驾！
Forget it. Never mind.	*Suàn le.*	算了。
good	*hǎo*	好
Good-bye. (see you later)	*Zài jiàn.*	再见。
Good morning.	*Zǎoshàng hǎo.*	早上好。
Good night.	*Wǎn ān.*	晚安。
Hello.	*Ní hǎo.*	你好。
I'm very sorry.	*Wó hěn bàoqiàn.*	我很抱歉。
Is it convenient?	*Fāngbiàn ma?*	方便吗？
It doesn't matter.	*Méi yǒu guānxi.*	没有关系。
Just a second.	*Děng yíxià.*	等一下。

May I trouble you?	*Máfan nǐ.*	麻烦你？
maybe	*kěnéng*	可能
No hurry.	*Bù jí.*	不急。
No problem.	*Méi wèntí.*	没问题。
not so	*bú shì*	不是
O.K.	*kéyǐ.*	可以。
please	*qǐng*	请
right	*duì*	对
See you tomorrow.	*Míngtiān jiàn.*	明天见。
Thank you.	*Xièxie.*	谢谢。
That's all right.	*Xíng.*	行。
wonderful	*hǎo jí le*	好极了
wrong	*bú duì*	不对
yes	*shì de*	是的
You're welcome.	*Bú kèqi.*	不客气。

FORMS OF ADDRESS

Traditional Chinese forms of address were used in prerevolutionary China but fell into disuse, especially during the Cultural Revolution of the 1960s and 1970s, when they were condemned as bourgeois. Since China's reopening to the West in the late 1970s, however, they have made a resounding comeback, to the extent that Communist-era terms like *tóngzhì* for "comrade" are now seldom heard. The traditional forms have been used continuously in Taiwan, Hong Kong, Macao, and Chinese communities elsewhere in the world.

c = ts; *q* = ch; *x* = sh; *z* = dz; *zh* = j

Sir	*Xiānshēng*	先生
Madame	*Fūrén*	夫人
	Tàitai	太太
Miss	*Xiáojiě*	小姐
Ms.	*Nǔshì*	女士
Master (a respectful term used to address professional people, including chefs, waiters, and craftsmen)	*Shīfu*	师傅

COMMUNICATION

Do you speak English?	*Nǐ huì shuō Yīngwén ma?* 你会说英文吗？
I speak a little Chinese.	*Wǒ huì shuō yìdiǎn Zhōngwén.* 我会说一点中文。
Do you understand?	*Ní dǒng ma?* 你懂吗？
	Ní tīngde dong ma? 你听得懂吗？
I understand.	*Wó dǒng.*　　我懂。
I don't understand.	*Wǒ bù dǒng.* 我不懂。
	Wǒ tīng bù dǒng. 我听不懂。
Let me think.	*Ràng wó xiǎng yī xiǎng.* 让我想一想。

What?	*Shénme?* 什么？
What did you say?	*Nǐ shuō shénme?* 你说什么？
How do you say ____ in Chinese?	____ *yòng Zhōngwén zěnme shuō?* ____用中文怎么说？
What does this (that) mean?	*Zhè shì shénme yìsi?* 这是什么意思？
Please speak more slowly.	*Qíng nǐ shuō màn yīdiǎn.* 请你说慢一点。
Please repeat.	*Qíng nǐ zài shuō yíbiàn.* 请你再说一遍。
That is not important.	*Nèige bú yàojǐn.* 那个不要紧。

INTRODUCTIONS

I'm American.	*Wǒ shì Měiguó rén.* 我是美国人。
My name is ____.	*Wǒ de míngzì jiào ____.* 我的名字叫____。
What's your name?	
■ (formal)	*Qǐng wèn guì xìng dà míng?* 请问贵姓大名？
■ (colloquial)	*Nǐ jiào shénme míngzì?* 你叫什么名字？
How are you?	*Nǐ hǎo?* 你好？
Very well, thanks, and you?	*Hén hǎo, xièxie. Nǐ ne?* 很好，谢谢。你呢？

c = ts; *q* = ch; *x* = sh; *z* = dz; *zh* = j

GETTING AROUND

Where is ____?	____ *zài nálǐ?*	____在哪里?
▦ a bookstore	*shūdiàn*	书店
▦ the business center	*shāngwù zhōngxīn*	商务中心
▦ a café	*kāfēitīng*	咖啡厅
▦ a convenience store	*xiǎo mài bù*	小卖部
▦ the dining room	*cāntīng*	餐厅
▦ the entrance	*rùkǒu*	入口
▦ the exit	*chūkǒu*	出口
▦ a gift store	*lǐpǐn diàn*	礼品店
▦ the gym	*jiànshēnfáng*	健身房
▦ the lobby	*dàtīng*	大厅
▦ a newsstand	*bàotān*	报摊
▦ a public telephone	*gōngyòng diànhuà*	公用电话
▦ a restaurant	*fànguǎn*	饭馆
▦ the taxi	*chūzū qìchē*	出租汽车
▦ a teahouse	*cháguǎn*	茶馆
▦ the telephone	*diànhuà*	电话
▦ the toilet	*cèsuǒ*	厕所
▦ the washroom	*xíshǒu jiān*	洗手间
May I ask you a question?	*Qǐng wèn.*	请问
Please help me.	*Qǐng bāngmáng.*	请帮忙。

I'm lost.	*Wǒ mí lù le.* 我迷路了。	
We're lost.	*Wǒmén mí lù le.* 我们迷路了。	
Where are my friends?	*Wǒ dē péngyou zài náli?* 我的朋友在哪里？	
Where is the tourist bus?	*Lǚyóu chē zài náli?* 旅游车在哪里？	
I am looking for ____.	*Wǒ zài zhǎo ____.* 我在找____。	
Which way did they go?	*Tāmén wǎng náli qù le?* 他们往哪里去了？	
to the left	*xiàng zuǒ*	向左
to the right	*xiàng yòu*	向右
straight ahead	*xiàng qián*	向前

c = ts; *q* = ch; *x* = sh; *z* = dz; *zh* = j

SHOPPING

How much does it cost?	*Duōshǎo qián?*	多少钱？
I'd like ____.	*Wó xiǎngyào ____.*	我想要____。
Please give me ____.	*Qǐng géi wǒ ____.*	请给我____。
Please show me ____.	*Qǐng géi wǒ kàn ____.*	请给我看____。
just right	*gānggāng hǎo*	刚刚好
approximately; more or less	*chà bu duō*	差不多
Too expensive!	*Tài guì le!*	太贵了！
Can you come down in price?	*Piányí dián, hǎo ma?*	便宜点好吗？
It's still too expensive.	*Háishi tài guì.*	还是太贵。
I don't want it.	*Wǒ bù xiǎngyào.*	我不想要。
The quality is not so good.	*Zhìliàng bú tài hǎo.*	质量不太好。

MISCELLANEOUS

I'm hungry.	*Wǒ è le.*	我饿了。
I'm thirsty.	*Wó kě le.*	我渴了。
I'm tired.	*Wǒ lèi le.*	我累了。
I don't feel well.	*Wǒ bù shūfu.*	我不舒服。
I'm sick.	*Wǒ bìng le.*	我病了。
What's that?	*Nà shì shénme?*	那是什么？

What's up? How's everything?	*Zěnme yàng?*	怎么样？
Do you know?	*Nǐ zhīdào ma?*	你知道吗？
I don't know.	*Wǒ bù zhīdào.*	我不知道。

QUESTIONS

How?	*Zěnme?*	怎么？
How much?	*Duōshǎo?*	多少？
What?	*Shénme?*	什么？
When?	*Shénme shíhòu?*	什么时候？
Where is ____?	*____ zài nálǐ?*	____在哪里？
Which?	*Něige?*	哪个？
Who?	*Shéi?*	谁？
Why?	*Wèishénme?*	为什么？

PROBLEMS, PROBLEMS, PROBLEMS (EMERGENCIES)

Help! (for life-threatening emergencies only)	*Jiù mìng!*	救命！
Please help me quickly!	*Qǐng kuài lái bāng wǒ!*	请快来帮我！
Be careful! Watch out!	*Xiǎo xīn!*	小心！
Look!	*Kànkan!*	看看！

c = ts; *q* = ch; *x* = sh; *z* = dz; *zh* = j

Listen!	*Tīng!*	听！
Wait!	*Děng yī děng!*	等一等！
Wait a moment!	*Děng yí xià!*	等一下！
Fire!	*Qí huǒ le!*	起火了！
Stop him!	*Zhuāzhù tā!*	抓住他！
I have lost ____.	*Wǒ diū le ____.*	我丢了____。
▥ my suitcase	*wǒ de tíbāo*	我的提包
▥ my watch	*wǒ de shóubiǎo*	我的手表

He has stolen ____.	*Tā tōu le ____.*	他偷了____。
▥ my passport	*wǒ de hùzhào*	我的护照
▥ my wallet; purse	*wǒ de qiánbāo*	我的钱包
Where is a policeman?	*Nálí yóu jǐngchá?*	哪里有警察

COMPLICATIONS

I haven't done anything wrong.	*Wǒ méi fàn cuò.*	我没犯错。
I want to go to ____.	*Wǒ yào qù ____.*	我要去____。
▨ the American consulate	*Měiguó Shíguǎn*	美国使馆
▨ the police station	*jǐngchá jú*	警察局
Can you help me, please?	*Nǐ kéyǐ bāng wǒ ma?* 你可以帮我吗？	
Who speaks English?	*Shéi néng shuō Yīngwén?* 谁能说英文？	
I need an interpreter.	*Wǒ xūyào fānyì.* 我需要翻译。	

NUMBERS

You will use numbers the moment you arrive in China, whether to exchange money at the airport, pay a taxi driver, or describe the length of your stay to an immigration official or hotel clerk. Here we list the cardinal numbers, give the rule for converting a cardinal to an ordinal number, and also specify fractions and other useful measures.

CARDINAL NUMBERS

0	*líng*	零
1	*yī*	一
2		

c = ts; *q* = ch; *x* = sh; *z* = dz; *zh* = j

▓ (the numeral)	*èr*	二
▓ (when used in collaboration with measure words)	*liǎng*	两
3	*sān*	三
4	*sì*	四
5	*wǔ*	五
6	*liù*	六
7	*qī*	七
8	*bā*	八
9	*jiǔ*	九
10	*shí*	十
11	*shí yī*	十一
12	*shí èr*	十二
13	*shí sān*	十三
14	*shí sì*	十四
15	*shí wǔ*	十五
16	*shí liù*	十六
17	*shí qī*	十七
18	*shí bā*	十八
19	*shí jiǔ*	十九
20	*èr shí*	二十
21	*èr shí yī*	二十一
22	*èr shí èr*	二十二

30	*sān shí*	三十
31	*sān shí yī*	三十一
40	*sì shí*	四十
50	*wǔ shí*	五十
60	*liù shí*	六十
70	*qī shí*	七十
80	*bā shí*	八十
90	*jiǔ shí*	九十
100	*yì bǎi*	一百
101	*yì bǎi líng yī*	一百零一
102	*yì bǎi líng èr*	一百零二
103	*yì bǎi líng sān*	一百零三
110	*yì bǎi yì shí*	一百一十
120	*yì bǎi èr shí*	一百二十
130	*yì bǎi sān shí*	一百三十
200	*liǎng bǎi*	两百
201	*liǎng bǎi líng yī*	两百零一
300	*sān bǎi*	三百
400	*sì bǎi*	四百
500	*wú bǎi*	五百
600	*liù bǎi*	六百
1,000	*yì qiān*	一千

c = ts; *q* = ch; *x* = sh; *z* = dz; *zh* = j

1,001	*yì qiān líng yī*	一千零一
1,100	*yì qiān yì bǎi*	一千一百
1,200	*yì qiān èr bǎi*	一千二百
1,350	*yì qiān sān bái wǔ shí*	一千三百五十
2,000	*liǎng qiān*	两千
5,000	*wǔ qiān*	五千
10,000	*yí wàn*	一万
100,000	*shí wàn*	十万
1,000,000	*yì bǎi wàn*	一百 万
10,000,000	*yì qiān wàn*	一千万
100,000,000	*yí yì*	一亿
1,000,000,000	*shí yì*	十亿
1,000,000,000,000	*wàn yì*	万亿
199____ (year)	*yì jiǔ jǔ ____ nían*	一九九____年
200____ (year)	*èr líng líng ____ nían*	二零零____年

ORDINAL NUMBERS

Making cardinal numbers into ordinal numbers is a simple task in Chinese. You simply add the prefix **dì** to the number. Note the following examples:

first	*dì yī*	第一
second	*dì èr*	第二
third	*dì sān*	第三

fourth	*dì sì*	第四
tenth	*dì shí*	第十
fiftieth	*dì wǔ shí*	第五十
one hundredth	*dì yì bǎi*	第一百
one thousandth	*dì yì qiān*	第一千

FRACTIONS AND QUANTITIES

a half	*yí bàn*	一半
half a	*bàn ge*	半个
a quarter	*sì fēn zhī yī*	四分之一
three-quarters	*sì fēn zhī sān*	四分之三
a third	*sān fēn zhī yī*	三分之一
two-thirds	*sān fēn zhī èr*	三分之二
a cup of	*yì bēi*	一杯
a dozen of	*yì dǎ*	一打
a gram of	*yí kè*	一克
a kilogram of	*yì gōng jīn*	一公斤
a catty of (Chinese measurement)	*yì jīn*	一斤
a liter of	*yì shēng*	一升
a little bit of	*yì diǎn*	一点
a lot of	*hěn duō*	很多

c = ts; *q* = ch; *x* = sh; *z* = dz; *zh* = j

a pair of	*yí duì*	一对
enough of	*gòu le*	够了
too much of	*tài duō le*	太多了
ratio	*bǐ lì*	比例
____ percent	*bǎi fēn zhī* ____	百分之____
▨ twenty	*èr shí*	二十
▨ seventy-five	*qī shí wǔ*	七十五
____ times as much	____ *bèi*	____倍
▨ six	*liù*	六
▨ one hundred	*yì bǎi*	一百

WHEN YOU ARRIVE

PASSPORT AND CUSTOMS

You need a visa to enter China. Normally this is a stamp on your passport issued before you arrive, though visas can sometimes be arranged at the port of entry. Group visas are also sometimes issued to tour groups traveling together. The visa specifies dates between which you are permitted to remain in China; if you wish to stay longer, it is necessary to extend your visa officially in order to avoid a fine.

Customs, once very stringent, have now become routine or even virtually nonexistent for most tourists and business travelers. Visitors may bring most items into China duty free, though large electronic appliances such as stereos, desktop computers, and television sets are dutiable. Smaller items such as cameras, watches, radios, jewelry, and calculators are technically supposed to be declared upon arrival and noted on the Customs form; if they are carried out at the end of your stay in China, no duty is assessed. This rule is honored in the breach; however, in practice, such items are rarely declared and rarely taxed.

My name is ___.	*Wǒ de míngzì jiào ___.*	我的名字叫___。
I'm ___.	*Wǒ shì ___.*	我是___。
American	*Měiguó rén*	美国人
Canadian	*Jiānádà rén*	加拿大人
British	*Yīngguó rén*	英国人
Australian	*Àozhōu rén*	澳洲人
New Zealander	*Xīn Xīlán rén*	新西兰人
My address is ___.	*Wǒ de dìzhǐ shì ___.*	我的地址是___。

c = ts; *q* = ch; *x* = sh; *z* = dz; *zh* = j

I'll be staying at ____.	*Wǒ huì zhù zài ____.*	我会住在____。
Here is (are) my ____.	*Zhè shì wǒ de ____.*	这是我的____。
▨ arrival card	*rùjìng dēngjì kǎ*	入境登记卡
▨ Customs certificate	*hǎiguān shēnbào dān*	海关申报单
▨ departure card	*chūjìng dēngjì kǎ*	出境登记卡
▨ documents	*wénjiàn*	文件
▨ health certificate	*jiànkāng shēnmíng kǎ*	健康申明卡
▨ passport	*hùzhào*	护照
▨ residence permit	*jūliúzhèng*	居留证
▨ visa	*qiānzhèng*	签证
I've come ____.	*Wǒ lái ____.*	我来____。
▨ on a business trip	*zuò shēngyì*	做生意
▨ to participate in a conference	*cānjiā huìyì*	参加会议
▨ to participate in an exhibition	*cānjiā zhǎnlǎn*	参加展览
▨ to participate in a delegation	*cānjiā dàibiǎo tuán*	参加代表团
▨ on a visit	*lǚxíng*	旅行
▨ on vacation	*dùjià*	度假
▨ to visit relatives	*tànqīn*	探亲
I'm here with a group.	*Wǒ shì suí tuán lái de.*	我是随团来的____。
I'll be staying ____.	*Wǒ yào zhù ____.*	我要住____。

a few days	*jǐ tiān*	几天
a few weeks	*jǐge xīngqī*	几个星期
a week	*yíge xīngqī*	一个星期
a month	*yíge yuè*	一个月

I'm traveling ____.	*Wǒ ____ lǚxíng.*	我____旅行。
alone	*dāndú*	单独
with my husband	*gēn wǒ zhàngfu*	跟我丈夫
with my wife	*gēn wǒ tàitai*	跟我太太
with my family	*gēn wǒ jiārén*	跟我家人
with my friend	*gēn wǒ de péngyou*	跟我的朋友
with my colleague	*gēn wǒ de tóngshì*	跟我的同事
with a tour group	*gēn lǚyóu tuán*	跟旅游团

These are my bags.	*Zhè shì wǒ de xíngli.* 这是我的行李。
checked luggage	*tuōyùn de xínglǐ*	托运的行李
hand luggage	*shǒutí xínglǐ*	手提行李

Where shall I go to claim my luggage?	*Dào nálǐ qù qǔ xínglǐ?* 到哪里去取行李？
Shall I open my bag?	*Xíngli yào dǎkāi ma?* 行李要打开吗？
Must you x-ray my bag?	*Zhèijiàn xínglǐ yídìng yào jīngguò X guāng jiǎnchá ma?* 这件行李一定要经过X光检查吗？

c = ts; *q* = ch; *x* = sh; *z* = dz; *zh* = j

Will the X ray damage my film?	*X guāng huì sǔnhuài wǒde jiāojuǎn ma?* X光会损坏我的胶卷吗？
I have very high-speed film.	*Gāo gǎn guāngdù jiāo juǎn.* 高感光度胶卷。
I have nothing to declare.	*Wǒ méi shénme yào bàoguān de.* 我没什么要报关的。
I have only a carton of cigarettes.	*Wǒ zhǐ yǒu yì tiáo xiāngyān.* 我只有一条香烟。
I have only a bottle of whiskey.	*Wǒ zhǐ yǒu yì píng wēishìjì.* 我只有一瓶威士忌。
They're gifts.	*Zhèixiē shì lǐpǐn.* 这些是礼品。
They're samples.	*Zhèixiē shì yàngpǐn.* 这些是样品。
This is for my personal use.	*Zhè shì zìjǐ yòng de.* 这是自己用的。
Do I have to pay duty?	*Wǒ yào fù shuì ma?* 我要付税吗？
I expect to take this out of China when I leave.	*Wǒ jiāng dài zhèige chūjìng.* 我将带这个出境。
Are you finished with your inspection?	*Jiǎnchá wánle ma?* 检查完了吗？
May I close my bag now?	*Xíngli kéyǐ shōu qǐlái ma?* 行李可以收起来吗？

LOST LUGGAGE

My luggage is lost.	*Wǒde xínglǐ bújiàn le.* 我的行李不见了。

Where do I report lost luggage?	*Dào nálǐ qù shēnbào yíshī de xínglǐ?* 到哪里去申报遗失的行李？
When will my luggage arrive?	*Wǒde xínglǐ shénme shíhòu dào?* 我的行李什么时候到？
Must I come back to the airport to claim it?	*Yídìng yào wǒ huí fēijīchǎng qǔ ma?* 一定要我回飞机场取吗？
Will you deliver it to my hotel?	*Nǐmén néng sòng dào lǚguǎn ma?* 你们能送到旅馆吗？

BAGGAGE AND PORTERS

Porters are hard to find at Chinese airports, but major airports are equipped with baggage carts. You can usually wheel the carts through Customs right to the street.

baggage (luggage)	*xíngli*　行李
Where can I find a baggage cart?	*Nálǐ yǒu xíngli chē?* 哪里有行李车？
Who can help me carry my bags?	*Shéi néng bāng wǒ bān xíngli?* 谁能帮我搬行李？
I need a porter.	*Wǒ xūyào fúwùyuán.* 我需要服务员。
These are my (our) bags.	*Zhè shì wǒ (wǒmén) de xíngli.* 这是我（我们）的行李。
that big one	*nèi jiàn dà de*　那件大的
these two little ones	*zhèi liǎng jiàn xiǎo de*　这两件小的

c = ts; *q* = ch; *x* = sh; *z* = dz; *zh* = j

| Please put them here. | *Qǐng fàng zhèli.*
请放这里。 |
| Please bring these to
the car. | *Qǐng bān dào chē shàng.*
请搬到车上。 |

Please be careful.	*Qǐng xiǎoxīn yìdiǎn.* 请小心一点。
I'll carry this one myself.	*Zhèi jiàn wǒ zìjǐ ná.* 这件我自己拿。
This is for you.	*Zhè shì géi nǐde.* 这是给你的。
Thank you very much for your help.	*Duō xiè nǐ de bāngmáng.* 多谢你的帮忙。

AIRPORT TRANSPORTATION

Where is the information desk?	*Xúnwèn chù zài nálǐ?* 询问处在哪里？
Where is the hotel desk?	*Lǚguǎn fúwù chù zài nálǐ?* 旅馆服务处在哪里？
Where is the representative from ____?	____ *dàibiǎo zài nálǐ?* ____代表在哪里？
▓ the ____ Hotel	____ *Fàndiàn*　　____饭店
▓ my host organization	*jiēdài dānwèi*　　接待单位
▓ my travel service	*lǚxíng shè*　　旅行社
▓ my school	*xuéxiào*　　学校
No one has come to meet me.	*Méi rén lái jiē wǒ.* 没人来接我。
Where do I wait for a hotel shuttle bus?	*Zài nǎlǐ děng lǚguǎn de bāshì?* 在哪里等旅馆的巴士？
How do I pay?	*Zěnme fù qián?* 怎么付钱？
I need a taxi.	*Wǒ xūyào chūzū qìchē.* 我需要出租汽车
Where can I get a taxi?	*Nǎlǐ yǒu chūzū qìchē?* 哪里有出租汽车？
Is this the line for taxis?	*Zài zhèlǐ páiduì děng chūzū chē ma?* 在这里排队等出租汽车吗？

c = ts; *q* = ch; *x* = sh; *z* = dz; *zh* = j

BANKING AND MONEY MATTERS

EXCHANGING MONEY

Chinese currency is called **rénmínbì**, which means, literally, "the people's money." It is denominated in the **yuán**, which is also known colloquially as the **kuài**. The yuán breaks down into 10 **máo** (also called **jiǎo**), or 100 **fēn**. Paper certificates come in 1, 5, 10, 20, 50, and 100 yuán denominations, and there are also 10- and 5-jiǎo notes, as well as seldom-encountered 1-, 2-, and 5-fēn notes. One-yuán coins are in circulation, as are 1- and 5-jiǎo coins and 1-, 2-, and 5-fēn coins, but the latter are of so little value that they are sometimes ignored when change is made. Taxi drivers, in particular, seldom give back such small change unless it is demanded of them.

Foreign currency, which can be imported in unlimited quantities, can be converted into rénmínbì throughout China at branch offices of the Bank of China (found at all airports), and also at stores with foreign clientele, nearly all hotels where foreigners stay, and at some other banks. Unlike the practice in other countries, the exchange rate is exactly the same whether you convert your money in a hotel, a shop, or a bank. By law, no commission other than the standard bank rate may be charged. Traveler's checks, however, fetch a slightly higher exchange rate than cash. Be sure to bring your passport with you when you change money, and remember your hotel room number if you do it at your hotel.

Rénmínbì is also available from ATM machines by using foreign ATM cards, but this can be spotty. Your best bet is to bring enough traveler's checks for your trip, since you can't always count on getting cash on a credit card guarantee.

There is some black market money exchanging activity, but this is not recommended because it is illegal, because it's easy to be cheated with counterfeit bills, and because it can cause complications upon exiting China. Since the yuán is not freely convertible, reconverting unused Chinese money on departure requires that one produce the official exchange memo issued in the initial conversion of foreign currency.

Where can I exchange ____?	*Náli kéyǐ duìhuàn ____?*	哪里可以兑换?
cash	*xiànkuǎn*	现款
money	*qián*	钱
rénmínbì (Chinese currency)	*rénmínbì*	人民币
traveler's checks	*lǚxíng zhīpiào*	旅行支票
U.S. dollars	*Měi yuán*	美元
Hong Kong dollars	*Gǎng bì*	港币
Japanese yen	*Rì yuán*	日元
English pounds sterling	*Yīng bàng*	英镑
Australian dollars	*Àodàlìyà yuán*	澳大利亚元
a personal check	*gèrén zhīpiào*	个人支票
a money order	*huìkuǎn dān*	汇款单

c = ts; *q* = ch; *x* = sh; *z* = dz; *zh* = j

▨ a cashier's check	*yínháng běnpiào*	银行本票

Where is there a bank?	*Yínháng zài náli?* 银行在哪里？
exchange rate	*duìhuàn lǜ* 兑换率
At what time do they ____?	*Jí diǎn ____?* 几点？

▨ open	*kāi mén*	开门
▨ close	*guān mén*	关门

office hours	*yíngyè shíjiān*	
	营业时间	
Where is the cashier's counter?	*Náli yǒu chūnà guìtái?*	
	哪里有出纳柜台？	
What is today's exchange rate for U.S. dollars?	*Jīntiān Měi yuán duìhuàn lǜ duōshǎo?*	
	今天美元兑换率多少？	
I'd like to cash this check.	*Wǒ xiǎng yòng zhèizhāng zhīpiào duìxiàn.*	
	我想用这张支票兑现。	
Where do I sign?	*Zài náli qiān zì?*	
	在哪里签字？	
Where do I endorse it?	*Bèimiàn qiān zì xiě zài náli?*	
	背面签字写在哪里？

Please give me ____.	*Qǐng géi wǒ ____.*		请给我____。
▓ large bills	*dà é chāopiào*	大额钞票	
▓ small bills	*xiǎo é chāopiào*	小额钞票	
▓ coins	*yìngbì*	硬币	

Please give me two fifty-yuan bills.	*Qǐng géi wó liǎng zhāng wǔshi yuán de.*	
	请给我两张五十元的。	
Please give me one hundred-yuan bill.	*Qǐng géi wǒ yì zhāng yìbǎi yuán de.*	
	请给我一张一百元的。	
Do you accept credit cards?	*Nǐmen shōu xìnyòng kǎ ma?*	
	你们收信用卡吗？

c = ts; *q* = ch; *x* = sh; *z* = dz; *zh* = j

May I guarantee my check with a credit card?	*Wǒ kéyǐ yòng xìnyòng kǎ dānbǎo wǒ de zhīpiào ma?*	
	我可以用信用卡担保我的支票吗？	
Where is there an automatic teller machine?	*Nálǐ yǒu tíkuǎn jī?*	
	哪里有提款机？	
Does it accept foreign bank cards?	*Shōu wàiguó yínháng kǎ ma?*	
	收外国银行卡吗？	

CREDIT CARDS

Can I use my credit card to get cash?	*Wǒ néng yòng xìnyòng kǎ duìhuàn xiànkuǎn ma?*	
	我能用信用卡兑换现款吗？	
Which credit cards do you accept?	*Nǐmén jiēshòu nǎxiē xìnyòng kǎ?*	
	你们接受哪些信用卡？	
Do you need to ____ my credit card?	*Nǐ xūyào ____ wǒ de xìnyòng kǎ ma?*	
	你需要____我的信用卡吗？	
▓ swipe	*shuā*	刷
▓ check	*chá*	查
Do you need another form of identification?	*Nǐ xūyào wǒ biéde zhèngjiàn ma?*	
	你需要我别的证件吗？	
This is the only credit card I have.	*Zhè shì wǒ wéiyī de xìnyòng kǎ.*	
	这是我唯一的信用卡。	
I don't have any other credit cards.	*Wǒ méiyǒu biéde xìnyòng kǎ.*	
	我没有别的信用卡。	

BUSINESS BANKING TERMS

amount	*jīn é*	金额
bad check	*wúxiào zhīpiào*	无效支票
bank	*yínháng*	银行
Bank of China	*Zhōngguó Yínháng*	中国银行
bill (currency note)	*chāopiào*	钞票
bond	*Zhàiquàn*	债券
borrow	*jiè*	借
cash	*xiànkuǎn*	现款
cash a check	*zhīpiào duìxiàn*	支票兑现
cashier	*chūnàyuán*	出纳员
capital	*zīběn*	资本
check	*zhīpiào*	支票
close an account	*qǔxiāo zhànghù*	取消帐户
counter	*guìtái*	柜台
credit	*xìndài*	信贷
deposit	*cún kuǎn*	存款
dollar (U.S.)	*Měiyuán*	美元
endorse	*bèishū*	背书
equity	*gǔquán*	股权
exchange rate	*duìhuàn lǜ*	兑换率

c = ts; *q* = ch; *x* = sh; *z* = dz; *zh* = j

futures	*qīhuò*	期货
income	*shōurù*	收入
income tax	*suǒdé shuì*	所得税
insurance	*báoxiǎn*	保险
interest	*lìxi*	利息
interest rate	*lìlǜ*	利率
investment; invest	*tóuzī*	投资
lend (to)	*jiè (gěi)*	借（给）
letter of credit	*xìnyòng zhèng*	信用证
loan	*dàikuǎn*	贷款
loss	*sǔnshī*	损失
make change	*zhǎo língqián*	找零钱
money order	*huìkuǎn dān*	汇款单
note	*piàojù*	票据
open an account	*kāilì zhànghù*	开立帐户
▦ foreign exchange account	*wàihuì zhànghù*	外汇帐户
▦ local currency account	*rénmínbì zhànghù*	人民币帐户
personal check	*sīrén zhīpiào*	私人支票
principal	*běnjīn*	本金
processing fee	*shǒuxù fèi*	手续费
profit	*lìrùn*	利润
safe	*báoxiǎn guì*	保险柜
savings	*chǔxù*	储蓄

securities	*zhèngquàn*	证券
service charge	*fúwù fèi*	服务费
sign	*qiān zì*	签字
share	*gǔfèn*	股份
stock	*gǔpiào*	股票
stockbroker	*gǔpiào jīngjì rén*	股票经纪人
stock exchange	*zhèngquàn jiāoyì suǒ*	证券交易所
tax	*shuì*	税
tax rate	*shuì lǜ*	税率
traveler's check	*lǚxíng zhīpiào*	旅行支票
withdrawal	*tíkuǎn*	提款
Have you received my wire transfer?	*Nǐ shōudào wǒ de diànbào zhuǎnzhàng ma?*	你收到我的电报转帐吗？

TIPPING AND GIFT GIVING

Although the Chinese government does not officially condone tipping, the practice has become commonplace on the mainland, and it has always been acceptable in Taiwan, Hong Kong, and Macao. While a gratuity is not always expected in China today, it is seldom refused.

Tips are both appropriate and welcome in hotels, for example, when a bellhop carries your luggage to your room or an enthusiastic travel guide or service person goes out of his or her way to help you. You may also tip a hairdresser, barber, or manicurist, or anyone else who performs a

c = ts; *q* = ch; *x* = sh; *z* = dz; *zh* = j

personal service. Chinese taxi drivers do not generally solicit tips directly, but sometimes they are slow to make change if they believe a client is likely to let them keep it. Depending on the quality of service, you may request the change or not, as you wish.

Larger eating establishments that cater to foreigners, on the other hand, increasingly follow the practice of adding a service charge to their bills. In these situations you need not leave a tip. Nor are gratuities expected in smaller eating establishments that serve predominantly local clientele. Since local Chinese still do not tip as a regular practice, foreigners who patronize these establishments are not expected to do so either.

Many formal occasions in China call for an exchange of gifts. A guest who visits a school or a factory, for example, may leave a souvenir of his or her visit. One generally accepts a gift graciously in China—refuse only if you suspect the gift would obligate you too much. Accept with both hands; this is the polite and customary way. As a rule, the Chinese do not open gifts in front of the gift giver, but it is not wrong to do so or to ask a Chinese recipient to open a gift immediately if you wish.

Don't be surprised if a Chinese refuses a gift from you the first time you offer it. This is a traditional polite gesture and may not mean that the gift is unwelcome. Try again; if you are repeatedly rebuffed, then by all means stop offering.

tip	*xiǎofèi* 小费
This is for you.	*Zhè shì géi nǐ de.* 这是给你的。
Is tipping ____ here?	*Zhèlǐ ____ géi xiǎofèi ma?* 这里____给小费吗？
▨ expected	*xūyào* 需要
▨ permitted	*kéyǐ* 可以

How much should I tip?	*Yīnggāi gěi dūosháo xiǎofèi?* 应该给多少小费？
Is it all right to tip in foreign currency?	*Kéyǐ yòng wàibì gěi ma?* 可以用外币给吗？
I would like to give a tip.	*Wó xiáng gěi yìdiǎn xiǎofèi.* 我想给一点小费。
Is there a service charge on the bill?	*Zhàngdān bāokuò fúwùfèi ma?* 帐单包括服务费吗？

c = ts; *q* = ch; *x* = sh; *z* = dz; *zh* = j

AT THE HOTEL

GETTING TO YOUR HOTEL

There are a few ways of referring to hotels in Chinese, and they are mostly interchangeable. **Fàndiàn** (literally, "place for taking meals") and **lǚguǎn** ("place for travelers") are most commonly used in China, together with **bīnguǎn** ("place for guests"), which generally refers more to a guest house than a hotel. A guest house may also be called a **zhàodàisuǒ** ("place for reception or entertainment"). In Hong Kong and Taiwan you are more likely to hear the term **jiǔdiàn** ("place for liquor").

Which hotel is our group staying at?	*Wǒmén de tuán zhù zài něige lǚguǎn?* 我们的团住在哪个旅馆？
Will I stay in a guest house?	*Wǒ huì zhù bīnguǎn ma?* 我会住宾馆吗？
I'm looking for the _____ Hotel.	*Wó zhǎo _____ Fàndiàn.* 我找_____饭店。
Is it near?	*Hěn jìn ma?* 很近吗？
Where can I get a taxi?	*Náli yǒu chūzū qìchē?* 哪里有出租汽车？
How much is the fare?	*Duōshǎo qián?* 多少钱？
How long is the trip?	*Yào dūoshǎo shíjiān?* 要多少时间？
Can I walk there?	*Zǒu de dào ma?* 走得到吗？

CHECKING IN

I have a room reservation.	*Wǒ yǐjīng yùdìng le fángjiān.* 我已经预定了房间。
Please check for my name.	*Qǐng chá wǒ de míngzì.* 请查我的名字。
My last name is ____.	*Wǒ xìng ____.* 我姓_____。
My first name is ____.	*Wǒ de míngzì jiào ____.* 我的名字叫_____。
My host organization is ____.	*Wǒ de jiēdài dānwèi shì ____.* 我的接待单位是_____。
I don't have a reservation.	*Wǒ méi yǒu yùdìng.* 我没有预定。
Please check for me which other hotels have vacancies.	*Qǐng bāng wǒ dǎtīng něi jiā fàndiàn yǒu kōng fángjiān.* 请帮我打听哪家饭店有空房间。

c = ts; *q* = ch; *x* = sh; *z* = dz; *zh* = j

I would like ____.	*Wǒ xiǎngyào*	我想要_____。
■ a single room	*dānjiān*	单间
■ a double room	*shuāng rén fáng*	双人房
■ a suite	*tàojiān*	套间

I will be staying for ____.	*Wǒ yào zhù ____.*	我要住_____。
■ one night	*yì tiān*	一天
■ two nights	*liǎng tiān*	两天
■ a week	*yì xīngqī*	一个星期

I would like a room ____.	*Wǒ yào yǒu ____ de fángjiān.*	我要有_____的房间。
■ with a bath	*sīrén xízǎo jiān*	私人洗澡间
■ with a balcony	*yángtái*	阳台
■ with a double bed	*shuāng rén chuáng*	双人床
■ with two single beds	*liǎngge dānrén chuáng*	两个单人床。
■ with a nice view	*fēngjǐng hǎo*	风景好

Does it have ____?	*Yǒu méi yǒu ____.*	有没有_____。
■ air conditioning	*kōngtiáo*	空调
■ a coffeepot	*kāfēi hú*	咖啡壶
■ heat	*nuǎnqì*	暖气
■ hot water	*rè shuǐ*	热水
■ an in-room fax	*kèfáng nèi de chuánzhēnjī*	客房内的传真机
■ a refrigerator	*bīngxiāng*	冰箱
■ a telephone	*diànhuà*	电话
■ television	*diànshì*	电视

I don't like this room.	*Wǒ bù xǐhuān zhèi jiān.* 我不喜欢这间。
May I change to another room?	*Kéyǐ huàn yì jiān ma?* 可以换一间吗？
This room is too noisy.	*Zhèige fángjiān tài chǎole.* 这个房间太吵了。
Do you have a nonsmoking room?	*Yǒu méiyǒu bù xīyān de fángjiān?* 有没有不吸烟的房间？
Do you have something ____?	*Yǒu méi yǒu ____ de?* 有没有_____的？

■ better	*bǐjiào hǎo*	比较好
■ brighter	*bǐjiào liàng*	比较亮
■ cheaper	*bǐjiào piányi*	比较便宜
■ larger	*bǐjiào dà*	比较大
■ quieter	*bǐjiào ānjìng*	比较安静
■ smaller	*bǐjiào xiǎo*	比较小

What floor is the room on?	*Fángjiān zài jǐ lóu?* 房间在几楼？
Where is the elevator?	*Diàntī zài náli?* 电梯在哪里？
Do you have a room that is equipped for handicapped people?	*Yǒu fāngbiàn cánjī rén de fángjiān ma?* 有方便残疾人的房间吗？
Please carry my bags up to my room.	*Qíng bǎ xínglǐ sòng dào wǒ de fángjiān.* 请把行李送到我的房间。

c = ts; q = ch; x = sh; z = dz; zh = j

HOTEL SERVICES

I would like to see ____. *Wó xiǎng jiàn ____.*
我想见_____ 。

▓ the assistant manager	*zhùlǐ jīnglǐ*	助理经理
▓ the bell captain	*fúwùyuán lǐngbān*	服务员领班
▓ the concierge	*fúwùtái jīnglǐ*	服务台经理
▓ the general manager	*zǒngjīnglǐ*	总经理
▓ the room attendant	*fúwùyuán*	服务员
front desk	*qiántái*	前台
service desk	*fúwùtái*	服务台

May I have my room key please? *Qǐng géi wǒ fángjiān yàoshi.*
请给我房间钥匙。

Shall I return the key to the service desk? *Yàoshi yào huán gěi fúwùtái ma?*
钥匙要还给服务台吗？

I have lost my key. *Wǒ diū le wǒ de yàoshi.*
我丢了我的钥匙。

What is my room number? *Wǒ de fángjiān hàoma duōshǎo?*
我的房间号码多少？

I am staying in room number ____. *Wǒ zhù ____ hào fáng.*
我住_____号房。

405 *sì líng wǔ*
四零五

NOTE: Room and telephone numbers are read digit by digit in Chinese, so room 436 is not room *sìbǎi sānshíliù* (four hundred thirty-six) but rather room **sì sān liù** (four three six).

I have laundry to ____.	*Wó yǒu yīfu yào ____*	我有衣服要_____。
■ dry clean	*gānxǐ*	干洗
■ iron	*tàng*	烫
■ wash	*xǐ*	洗

I need this done immediately.	*Wó mǎshàng jiù yào.* 我马上就要。
My shirt is missing a button.	*Wǒde chènshān shǎole ge kòuzi.* 我的衬衫少了个扣子。
When will you return this?	*Shénme shíhòu sònglái?* 什么时候送来？
Where can I get my shoes shined?	*Zài nálí kéyǐ cā xié?* 在哪里可以擦鞋？

Where is ____?	*____ zài nálǐ?*	____ 在哪里？
■ the bathroom	*Cèsuǒ*	厕所
■ the restaurant	*Cāntīng*	餐厅
■ the telephone	*Diànhuà*	电话

I need ____.	*Wǒ xūyào ____.*	我需要_____。
■ a towel	*máojīn*	毛巾
■ a blanket	*yì chuáng tǎnzi*	一床毯子
■ a light bulb	*dēngpào*	灯泡
■ a pillow	*yíge zhěntóu*	一个枕头
■ soap	*féizào*	肥皂
■ some hangers	*yīxiē yījià*	一些衣架

Please send ____ to my room.	*Qǐng sòng ____ dào wǒde fángjiān.*	请送_____到我的房间。

c = ts; *q* = ch; *x* = sh; *z* = dz; *zh* = j

an ashtray	*yānhuī gāng*	烟灰缸
some cold (preboiled) drinking water	*lěng kāishuǐ*	冷开水
some glasses	*jǐge bōlí bēi*	几个玻璃杯
some hot water	*rè shuǐ*	热水
some ice cubes	*yīxiē bīngkuài*	一些冰块
some tea	*cháyè*	茶叶
some toilet paper	*wèishēng zhǐ*	卫生纸

What's the voltage here?	*Zhèli diànyā duōshǎo?*	这里电压多少？
Please wake me tomorrow morning at ___ o'clock.	*Míngtiān zǎoshàng ___ diǎn qǐng jiào wǒ.*	明天早上＿＿＿点请叫我。
I don't wish to be disturbed.	*Qǐng bú yào dáráo wǒ.*	请不要打扰我。

AT THE DOOR

Who is it?	*Shéi?*	谁？
Just a minute.	*Děng yí xià.*	等一下。
Come in.	*Qǐng jìn.*	请进。
Please come back later.	*Qíng wǎn yìdiǎn zài lái.*	请晚一点再来。

COMPLAINTS

My room ____.	*Wǒ de fángjiān ____.* 我的房间_____。	
■ has no air conditioning	*méiyǒu lěngqì*	没有冷气
■ has no electricity	*méi yǒu diàn*	没有电
■ has no heat	*méiyǒu nuǎnqì*	没有暖气
■ has no hot water	*méi yǒu rè shuǐ*	没有热水
■ has a strange odor	*yǒu guài wèidào*	有怪味道
■ is dirty	*zāng le*	脏了
■ is too cold	*tài lěng*	太冷
■ is too dark	*tài àn*	太暗
■ is too humid	*tài cháoshī*	太潮湿
■ is too noisy	*tài chǎo*	太吵

NOTE: China runs on a 220-volt, 50-cycle electrical system, so you can't just plug any appliance into the outlet in your hotel room and expect it to work efficiently. Furthermore, rooms in older hotels may contain electrical outlets in a number of different plug configurations. A good idea for those who expect to spend a fair amount of time in China is to buy appliances, such as electric razors, hair dryers, and portable tape recorders able to be used at either 110 or 220 volts.

c = ts; *q* = ch; *x* = sh; *z* = dz; *zh* = j

At what time is there hot water?	*Shénme shíhòu cái yǒu rè shuǐ?* 什么时候才有热水？	
When will the heat be turned on?	*Shénme shíhòu cái yǒu nuǎnqì?* 什么时候才有暖气？	
The _____ is stuck.	_____*dǎ bu kāi.*	_____打不开。
▨ curtain	*Chuānglián*	窗帘
▨ door	*Mén*	门
▨ window	*Chuāngzi*	窗子
The _____ is broken.	_____*huài le.*	_____坏了。
▨ air conditioning	*Kōngtiáo*	空调
▨ doorbell	*Ménlíng*	门铃
▨ faucet	*Shuǐlóngtóu*	水龙头
▨ lamp	*Dēng*	灯
▨ plug	*Chātóu*	插头
▨ radio	*Shōuyīn jī*	收音机
▨ remote control	*Yáokòng qì*	遥控器
▨ shower	*Línyùqì*	淋浴器
▨ telephone	*Diànhuà*	电话
▨ television set	*Diànshì*	电视
▨ toilet	*Mátǒng*	马桶
This bulb is burned out.	*Dēngpào huài le.* 灯泡坏了	
The drain is clogged.	*Páishuíguǎn sāizhù le.* 排水管塞住了。	
The _____ is leaking.	_____*lòu shuǐ.*	_____漏水。
▨ bathroom	*Cèsǔo*	厕所
▨ bathtub	*Zǎopén*	澡盆
▨ toilet	*Mátǒng*	马桶

Can you fix it?	*Nǐ néng xiū ma?* 你能修吗？
Can you make a phone call for me?	*Nǐ néng wèi wó dǎ ge diànhuà ma?* 你能为我打个电话吗？

ROOM SERVICE

What number do I dial for room service?	*Kèfáng yòngcān fúwùbù de diànhuà shì shénme?* 客房用餐服务部的电话是什么？
Where is the room service menu?	*Kèfáng yòngcān càidān zài nálǐ?* 客房用餐菜单在哪里？
Do you have any Western food?	*Yǒu Xīcān ma?* 有西餐吗？
Do you have any Japanese food?	*Yǒu Rìběn liàolǐ ma?* 有日本料理吗？
I would like to eat ____.	*Wó xiǎng chī ____.* 我想吃_____。

▨ breakfast	*zǎocān*	早餐
▨ lunch	*wǔcān*	午餐
▨ dinner	*wǎncān*	晚餐
▨ a late night snack	*yèxiāo*	夜宵

Do you have any ____?	*Yǒu méi yǒu ____?* 有没有_____？	
▨ bacon	*xūnròu*	熏肉
▨ coffee	*kāfēi*	咖啡
▨ donuts	*zhámiàn bǐngquān*	炸面饼圈

c = ts; *q* = ch; *x* = sh; *z* = dz; *zh* = j

▓ French toast	*fǎshì tǔsī*	法式吐司
▓ fried eggs	*jiān dàn*	煎蛋
▓ fried potatoes	*zhá shǔtiáo*	炸薯条
▓ ham	*huótuǐ*	火腿
▓ hot chocolate	*rè qiǎokèlì*	热巧克力
▓ milk	*niúnǎi*	牛奶
▓ oatmeal	*mài piàn*	麦片
▓ orange juice	*júzi zhī*	橘子汁
▓ pancakes	*báojiān bǐng*	薄煎饼
▓ poached eggs	*zhǔ dàn*	煮蛋
▓ sausage	*xiāngcháng*	香肠
▓ scrambled eggs	*chǎo jīdàn*	炒鸡蛋
▓ tea	*chá*	茶
▓ waffles	*huáfū bǐng*	华夫饼
▓ yogurt	*suān nǎi*	酸奶

I would like some more ____.	*Wǒ hái yào ____.* 我还要_____。	
▓ bread or rolls	*miànbāo*	面包
▓ butter	*huángyóu*	黄油
▓ cream	*nǎiyóu*	奶油
▓ honey	*fēngmì*	蜂蜜
▓ jam	*guǒjiàng*	果酱
▓ pepper	*hújiāo*	胡椒
▓ salt	*yán*	盐
▓ sugar	*táng*	糖
▓ syrup	*tángjiāng*	糖浆
▓ toast	*kǎo miànbāo*	烤面包

I think I'll have a Chinese breakfast.	*Wó xiǎng chī Zhōngshì zǎocān.* 我想吃中式早餐	
■ crullers	*yóutiáo*	油条
■ dried minced fish	*yúsōng*	鱼松
■ dried minced meat	*ròusōng*	肉松
■ peanuts	*huāshēngmǐ*	花生米
■ pickles; pickled vegetables	*pàocài*	泡菜
■ rice gruel; congee	*xīfàn*	稀饭
■ salty soybean milk	*xián dòujiāng*	咸豆浆
■ sesame seed cake	*shāobǐng*	烧饼
■ steamed bread	*mántóu*	馒头
■ steamed stuffed buns	*bāozi*	包子
■ sweet soybean milk	*tián dòujiāng*	甜豆浆
■ thousand-year eggs	*pídàn*	皮蛋

DEPARTURE

We are leaving ____.	*Wǒmén ____ zǒu.* 我们____走。	
■ tomorrow	*míngtiān*	明天
■ today	*jīntiān*	今天

c = ts; *q* = ch; *x* = sh; *z* = dz; *zh* = j

Please send a porter to my room.	*Qǐng pài fúwùyuán lái qǔ xíngli.* 请派服务员来取行李。
I have two large bags.	*Wó yóu liǎng dà jiàn.* 我有两大件。
May I leave my bags in the room?	*Wǒ kéyí bǎ xíngli liú zài fángjiān li ma?* 我可以把行李留在房间里吗？
Please send our baggage down to the lobby.	*Qíng bǎ xíngli sòng dào lóuxià dàtīng.* 请把行李送到楼下大厅。
I would like to pay the bill.	*Wǒ yào fù zhàng.* 我要付帐。
Where shall I pay?	*Zài náli fù zhàng?* 在哪里付帐？
May I use my credit card?	*Wǒ kéyǐ yòng xìnyòng kǎ ma?* 我可以用信用卡吗？
What cards do you accept?	*Nǐmén jiēshòu shénme kǎ?* 你们接受什么卡？
May I check the bill a moment?	*Wǒ kéyǐ chákàn yíxià zhàngdān ma?* 我可以察看一下帐单吗？
This is not my bill.	*Zhè búshì wǒde zhàngdān.* 这不是我的帐单。
There must be a mistake.	*Zhèli yǒu cuò.* 这里有错。
What is this charge?	*Zhèi xiàng shì shénme?* 这项是什么？
This charge is incorrect.	*Zhèi xiàng bú duì.* 这项不对。

I should not be charged for that.	*Wǒ bù yīnggāi fù zhèi xiàng.* 我不应该付这项。
I refuse to pay for that.	*Wǒ jùjué fù zhèi xiàng.* 我拒绝付这项。
How much is the room tax?	*Fángjiān shuì duōshǎo?* 房间税多少？
Please give me a separate bill for telephone calls.	*Qǐng lìngwài géi wǒ yífèn dǎ diànhuà de zhàngdān.* 请另外给我一份打电话的帐单。
Where shall I sign?	*Wǒ zài náli qiān zì?* 我在哪里签字？
I had a very comfortable stay.	*Wǒ zhù de hěn shūfu.* 我住得很舒服。
Your service was ____.	*Nǐ mén de fúwù ____.* 你们的服务_____。
▨ very good	*hén hǎo*	很好
▨ passable	*hái kéyǐ*	还可以
▨ not so good	*bú tài hǎo*	不太好
▨ very bad	*hěn chà*	很差

Travel Tips   It is possible, through diet and habit, to ease the transition to a new time zone, commonly referred to as "jet lag." Up to four days prior to your departure, begin accustoming your body to its future schedule by gradually changing the times you eat until they more closely match that of your destination. Eat lightly and avoid carbohydrates. If you are taking a night flight, eat very little the day of your departure and avoid alcohol and even dinner on the plane if it is offered. Instead, ask to have your breakfast earlier, then rest until it is served. When you arrive, you will have had your breakfast about the same time as people in that country, and be ready for your next meal at the appropriate time. When you do have your next meal, try to eat a lot of protein, followed in the next meal by a high-carbohydrate diet. Avoid taking a nap during your first day, and instead, go to bed a little earlier than usual.

GETTING AROUND TOWN

THE BUS

Buses are a very common means of transportation in China. They run nearly everywhere in the major cities, and the fares are extremely low. Foreigners seldom ride public buses in China, though a trip can be a real adventure. Because service personnel on public buses rarely speak English and stops are seldom marked in pinyin, be sure first to get someone to write down your destination in characters if you wish to take a bus.

At least two service personnel are assigned to each bus: a driver and one or two conductors, depending on the size of the bus (some buses have two coaches joined accordion-style). The conductor accepts fares, gives out tickets, yells out stops as they are passed, and is posted by the door of the bus to collect money. If you hand him or her a slip of paper with your destination in Chinese characters, he or she will let you know when it's time to get off.

One word of warning: Crowded buses are more the rule than the exception in urban China. Be prepared to be pushed and even squeezed if you board a bus in Beijing or Shanghai during rush hour.

Where is the bus terminal?	*Gōnggòng qìchē zhàn zài náli?* 公共汽车站在哪里？
Which bus do I take to get to ____?	*Dào ____ zuò jǐ lù chē?* 到___坐几路车？
How much is the fare?	*Piàojià duōshǎo?* 票价多少？
In which direction should I go?	*Zóu něige fāngxiàng?* 走哪个方向？

c = ts; *q* = ch; *x* = sh; *z* = dz; *zh* = j

How often do the buses come?	*Qìchē duōjiǔ yì bān?* 汽车多久一班？
Does the bus go to ____?	*Chēzi dào ____ qù ma?* 车子到____去吗？
Is it far from here?	*Lí zhèli yuǎn ma?* 离这里远吗？
How many stops are there?	*Yǒu duōshǎo zhàn?* 有多少站？
Must I change buses?	*Yào huàn chē ma?* 要换车吗？
Where do I have to get off?	*Zài náli xià chē?* 在哪里下车？
Please tell me where to get off.	*Qǐng gàosù wǒ zài náli xià chē.* 请告诉我在哪里下车。

TAXIS

If you are not part of a group traveling on a tourist bus, chances are you will find taxis a reasonably priced and efficient means of getting around most of China's major cities.

Taxis can be hailed just about anywhere. Different car models fetch different rates, however, and the better the car, the more expensive the ride. Most Chinese taxis have meters, and drivers will willingly issue receipts to those who request them.

It's an excellent idea to get someone to write down your destination in Chinese characters before you take a taxi; this can help a lot in preventing mishaps.

Where can I find a taxi?	*Náli yǒu chūzū qìchē?* 哪里有出租汽车？

Please call me a taxi.	*Qǐng gěi wǒ jiào chē.* 请给我叫车。	
Driver! Can you take me?	*Sījī, nǐ néng dài wǒ ma?* 司机，你能带我吗？	
I want to go to ____.	*Wǒ yào qù ____.* 我要去____。	
■ the airport	*fēijī chǎng*	飞机场
■ the hotel	*lǚguǎn*	旅馆
■ the railroad station	*huǒchē zhàn*	火车站
■ Please take me to____.	*Qǐng dài wǒ dào ____.*	请带我到____。
■ the bus station	*gōnggòng qìchē zhàn*	公共汽车站
■ this address	*zhèige dìzhǐ*	这个地址
Do you know where it is?	*Nǐ zhīdào zài nǎli ma?* 你知道在哪里吗？	
How much is it?	*Yào duōshǎo qián?* 要多少钱？	
I will pay what is on the meter.	*Wǒ huì àn biǎo fù kuǎn.* 我会按表付款。	
Please turn on the meter.	*Qǐng dá biǎo.* 请打表。	
Please take the ____ route.	*Qíng zǒu ____ de lù.* 请走____的路。	
■ fastest	*zuì kuài*	最快
■ most scenic	*fēngjǐng hǎo*	风景好
I'm in a hurry.	*Wǒ yào gǎn shíjiān.* 我要赶时间。	

c = ts; *q* = ch; *x* = sh; *z* = dz; *zh* = j

Please drive a little faster.	*Qǐng kāi kuài yìdiǎn.* 请开快一点。	
I think you are going the wrong way.	*Wó xiǎng ní zǒu cuò le.* 我想你走错了。	
Please drive a little more slowly.	*Qǐng kāi màn yìdiǎn.* 请开慢一点。	
Please stop a moment _____.	*Qǐng tíng yíxià.* 请停一下。	
■ at the corner	*zài lùkǒu*	在路口
■ at the next block	*zài xià yìtiáo jiē*	在下一条街
■ in front of that building	*zài dà lóu qiánmiàn*	在大楼前面。
Can you wait for me?	*Nǐ néng déng wǒ ma?*	你能等我吗？
I'll be right back.	*Wǒ mǎshàng jiù huílái.*	我马上就回来。
I expect to be back _____.	*Wǒ _____ jiù huílái.*	我___就回来。
■ in a few minutes	*jǐ fēn zhōng*	几分钟
■ in an hour or two	*yì liáng xiǎoshí*	一两小时
■ as soon as I'm through sightseeing	*kàn wán*	看完
How much do I owe you?	*Wǒ gāi fù nǐ duōshǎo?*	我该付你多少？
Do not try to cheat me.	*Búyào qīpiàn wǒ.* 不要欺骗我。	

I refuse to pay so much money.

Wǒ jùjué fù zènme duō.
我拒绝付这么多。

You took a circuitous route.

Nǐ ràole tài duō wānlù.
你绕了太多弯路。

I will report you to the authorities.

Wǒ yào xiàng dāngjú tóusù nǐ.
我要向当局投诉你。

Please give me a receipt.

Qǐng gěi wǒ kāi shōujù.
请给我开收据。

SIGHTSEEING AND TOURS

Where is a travel agency?

Nǎli yǒu lǚxíngshè?
哪里有旅行社？

I need an English-speaking guide.

Wǒ xūyào shuō Yīngwén de dǎoyóu.
我需要说英文的导游。

How much will it cost ____?

____ yào dūoshǎo?
____要多少？

■ per day

Yì tiān
一天

■ per hour

Yíge xiǎoshí
一个小时

Where do they sell guidebooks?

Nǎli yǒu mài lǚyóu shǒucè?
哪里有卖旅游手册？

Where do they sell local maps?

Nǎli yǒu mài běndì dìtú?
哪里有卖本地地图？

What are the sights of interest here?

Zhèli yǒu shénme míngshèng?
这里有什么名胜？

Can you arrange a tour of the area?

Nǐ néng ānpái běndì de lǚyóu ma?
你能安排本地的旅游吗？

c = ts; *q* = ch; *x* = sh; *z* = dz; *zh* = j

How long is the tour?	*Lǚyóu yào duōjiǔ?*	旅游要多久？
We would like to see_____.	*Wǒmén xiǎng qù kàn.*	我们想去看____。
■ an antique market	*gúdǒng shìchǎng*	古董市场
■ an aquarium	*shuǐzúguǎn*	水族馆
■ an art museum	*měishùguǎn*	美术馆
■ a botanical garden	*zhíwùyuán*	植物园
■ a Catholic church	*Tiānzhǔ jiàotáng*	天主教堂
■ a department store	*bǎihuò shāngdiàn*	百货商店
■ the downtown area	*shì zhōngxīn*	市中心
■ a flower garden	*huāyuán*	花园
■ a foreign language bookstore	*wàiwén shūdiàn*	外文书店
■ a fruit and vegetable market	*cài shìchǎng*	菜市场
■ a library	*túshūguǎn*	图书馆
■ a museum	*bówùguǎn*	博物馆
■ a park	*gōngyuán*	公园
■ a Protestant church	*Jīdū jiàotáng*	基督教堂
■ a scenic area	*fēngjǐng qū*	风景区
■ a shopping center	*gòuwù zhōngxīn*	购物中心

■ a sporting arena   *tíyùguǎn*   体育馆

■ a stadium   *yùndòng chǎng*   运动场

■ a supermarket   *chāojí shìchǎng*   超级市场

■ a temple   *miào*   庙

■ a university   *dàxué*   大学

■ a zoo   *dòngwùyuán*   动物园

ADMISSIONS

Is it all right to go in now?   *Xiànzài kéyǐ jìnqù ma?*
现在可以进去吗？

Is it open?   *Kāi le ma?*
开了吗？

At what time does it ____?   *Jí diǎn zhōng ____?*
几点钟____？

■ open   *kāi mén*   开门

■ close   *guān mén*   关门

Where can I buy tickets?   *Dào nálí mǎi piào?*
到哪里买票？

What is the admission?   *Piàojià duōshǎo?*
票价多少？

Are children's tickets ____?   *Xiǎohái ____ ma?*
小孩____吗？

■ free   *miǎnfèi*   免费

■ half price   *bànpiào*   半票

Is it all right to take pictures?   *Kéyǐ zhàoxiàng ma?*
可以照相吗？

Do you have an English-language brochure?   *Yǒu Yīngwén zīliào ma?*
有英文资料吗？

c = ts; *q* = ch; *x* = sh; *z* = dz; *zh* = j

A SIGHTSEEING ITINERARY

China is just too vast and too varied for anyone to expect to see it all in one or two trips. Even a three-week tour of eight or nine cities is at best a whirlwind tour, what the Chinese would call *zóu mǎ kàn huā*, meaning "gazing at flowers from horseback." Here are some—but by no means all—of the important places and sights you should try not to miss.

BEIJING

Beijing is a "must see," since so many of China's cultural treasures and landmarks can be seen there, and since it figures so prominently in Chinese history, having served as the capital over many centuries. It's also one natural starting point for a journey into China, since it is the terminus of most of the international air routes into the PRC.

In the geometric center of the city is the *Gùgōng*, or **Forbidden City**, the Imperial Palace during the Ming and Qing Dynasties. A labyrinth of courtyards, formal halls, gardens and ceremonial gates, it is now a museum open to the public that can take a day or two to explore thoroughly. The southern gate of the Forbidden City is called **Tiān'ānmén**, or the "Gate of Heavenly Peace." It was from the top of this gate that Mao Zedong announced the founding of the People's Republic in 1949, and it bears his likeness today. It is the symbol of the new China.

To the south of the gate is **Tiān'ānmén Square**, a vast plaza even larger than Moscow's Red Square, said to accommodate as many as half a million people. This was the site where student protesters were killed in 1989.

Tiān'ānmén Square is bounded on the west by the *Rénmín Dàhuìtáng*, the **Great Hall of the People**. The Great Hall, seat of the National People's Congress, is a mammoth structure built in the late 1950s that contains enormous reception rooms, auditoriums, and banquet halls. To the east are the **Museums of Chinese History and the Chinese Revolution**, best left for a rainy day. In the center of the square is the **Monument to the People's Heroes**, a memorial dedicated to those who died during the Chinese Revolution, and just to its south is the **Chairman Mao Memorial Hall**, which contains an exhibit devoted to a few prominent Communist revolutionaries and the remains of Mao Zedong himself, on view in a glass sarcophagus.

Completing the perimeter of the square at its south end is **Qiánmén**, the "front gate," which originally was connected to an earth and stone wall that surrounded the entire city.

Southeast of the square is *Tiāntán*, the **Temple of Heaven**, a complex of beautiful ceremonial buildings and an altar at which the Ming and Qing emperors made sacrifices to heaven to ensure a good harvest. The complex dates to the fifteenth century, and is well worth visiting.

Northeast of the square is the **Lama Temple**, or *Yōnghé Gōng*, formerly the residence of an emperor's son, and later home to a Tibetan lamasery. Near it is the **Confucius Temple**, a thirteenth-century structure, and not too far away is **Rìtán Park**, the gardens surrounding the Altar of the Sun.

Just across the street from the Forbidden City to the north is a park surrounding **Coal Hill** (*Méi Shān* or *Jǐng Shān*), an artificial hill created with earth excavated when the moat surrounding the Forbidden City was dug. The last emperor of the Ming Dynasty hanged himself on this hill. Nearby is **Zhōngnánhǎi**, the compound in which the State Council's offices are located and in which China's highest-ranking leaders live. Chairman Mao lived there. It is closed to the public, but foreign dignitaries are occasionally received there. North of Zhongnanhai is **Běihǎi Park**, a public park with a lovely lake and a Tibetan-style Dagoba.

OUTSIDE BEIJING

The greater Beijing area also includes *Shísānlíng*, the **Ming Tombs**, the mausolea of 13 Ming emperors set in a picturesque valley. The sacred way leading to the tombs begins with a marble gate of five archways and is guarded by a regimen of stone animals and statues of warriors and officials. One of the tombs has been excavated, and visitors may descend into it.

c = ts; q = ch; x = sh; z = dz; zh = j

Yíhéyuán, the **Summer Palace**, is also on most itineraries. It is a compound on the shores of Lake Kūnmíng less than ten miles northwest of the city that was built in the late nineteenth century for the notorious Empress Dowager. Funds intended for China's imperial navy were appropriated for this purpose, and were used by the Empress in particular to construct a large marble pleasure boat on the edge of the lake that should not be missed. Not too far away you can still see some of the ruins of **Yuánmíngyuán**, an earlier palace destroyed by foreign troops in 1860. Beyond the summer palace is Xiāngshān, **Fragrant Hill**, a lovely park that contains the **Temple of the Sleeping Buddha** and the **Temple of the Azure Clouds**. The latter includes a memorial to Dr. Sun Yat-sen, the father of modern China.

About 40 miles north of Beijing is **Bādálǐng**, the most popular site for viewing the Chángchéng, or **Great Wall**. The wall is often seen together with the Ming Tombs on one trip outside of town. Its reputation precedes it and it is no disappointment—the Great Wall is well worth the trip. Other locations for visiting the wall are **Mùtiányù**, a bit less crowded and built up than Badaling, and, somewhat further away, **Sīmǎtái**, where you can see unrestored sections of the wall.

About nine miles southwest of Beijing you can visit the **Marco Polo Bridge** (Lúgōuqiáo), an arched stone bridge said to have been admired by Marco Polo when he visited China in the thirteenth century. The bridge has two balustrades on which more than 400 white stone lions, no two exactly alike, are perched. It is most famous as the site where, in 1937, Chinese forces shot at advancing Japanese troops and the Sino-Japanese war began. Further down the road is **Zhōukǒudiàn**, the site at which the fossilized bones of Peking Man were unearthed in the 1920s.

Further outside of Beijing—a few hours in either direction by car—are *Dōnglíng*, the **Eastern Qing Tombs**, and *Xīlíng*, the **Western Qing Tombs**, where the Qing emperors rest. They are in better condition than the Ming tombs, and there are a number of avenues of stone figures and animals to enjoy. The mausoleums of the Emperor Qianlong and of the Empress Dowager are located at the

Eastern tombs; the latter was opened in the early twentieth century and one may descend into its inner chamber.

OVERNIGHT TRIPS FROM BEIJING

A number of places within striking distance of Beijing are good choices for overnight and weekend trips. Among these are **Chéngdé**, a mountain resort in northern Héběi Province that was used as a summer retreat for the Manchu court during the Qing (Manchu) Dynasty. To strengthen ties with Tibet, the Emperor Kāngxī built a series of Tibetan-style temples in this city, including a replica of Lhasa's famous Potala Palace. A popular seaside resort located about four and one-half hours by train from Beijing is **Běidàihé**. It was a small fishing village until the early twentieth century, when it became a favorite retreat of foreigners who lived in Beijing during the hot summer months. They constructed many villas there, buildings now owned by the Chinese government and used by the senior party leaders every summer. Nearby is **Shānhǎiguān**, the gateway to Manchuria and the eastern terminus of the Great Wall, the point at which the wall meets the sea.

Dàtóng is another convenient destination, about ten hours by train from Beijing in northern Shanxi Province. The town is known for the magnificent Buddhist shrines that can be seen at the nearby **Yúngāng Grottoes**, and for its many monasteries. Also accessible from Beijing is **Luòyáng**, an ideal place to stop if you happen to be traveling by train between Beijing and Xī'ān. Luòyáng, known as the location where Buddhism was first introduced into China, boasts the White Horse Temple, reputed to be the first Buddhist Temple in China, as well as much Buddhist sculpture in the nearby Longmen caves.

THE NORTHEAST

Northeast China, familiarly known as Manchuria, is heavily industrialized due to historical occupation by the

c = ts; q = ch; x = sh; z = dz; zh = j

Japanese and the Russians. The Japanese invaded officially in 1932 and stayed until 1945. The region is known for its bitter cold weather with winter temperatures falling as low as −22°F. Cities of interest in this region include **Harbin** (*Hāěrbīn*), the capital of distant Heilongjiang Province, 700 miles northeast of Beijing, a 19-hour train ride. Russian influence is apparent from the architecture here, and the city is known for its annual ice festival in late January, when beautiful ice sculptures are displayed. **Shěnyáng**, formerly called Mukden, is the capital of Liaoning Province. The Manchus originated here before they conquered China in 1644, and Manchu tombs, plus an Imperial Palace used by them for the first eight years of their rule, are popular attractions. Also of interest in the Northeast is **Dàlián** (formerly Dairen), a heavily industrialized manufacturing center an hour and a half by plane from Beijing.

EASTERN CHINA

Easily accessible from Beijing, **Shànghǎi** is China's most populous city, and it has a rich history. It was a nineteenth-century treaty port and a major foreign enclave until 1949, and its skyline bears this out. Tall European-style buildings line the Wàitān, or "**Bund**" area between the Huangpu River and Zhongshan Road—a must for an evening stroll. Shanghai is a manufacturing and shipping center and is one of the leading commercial and cultural centers of China. Places to visit include the new **Shanghai Museum**, a world-class facility that is one of the most celebrated and successful examples of modern architecture in China today. It houses an internationally renowned collection of Chinese art and artifacts, including bronze, ceramics, painting, and calligraphy. Also of interest are Yú Yuán, the gardens of the Yu family, and **Chénghuángmiào**, a temple dedicated to the local gods, a short distance away. Other temples worth a visit include **Lónghuá Sì,** which includes a wooden, seven-story pagoda, and **Yùfó Sì**, the Temple of the Jade Buddha. Don't forget a walk down crowded **Nánjīng Dōng Lù**, a major shopping plaza and an important Chinese fashion center.

Old Shanghai was built on the west bank of the Huangpu River; the east bank, called the **Pǔdōng** area, was accessible from the city only by ferryboat and remained undeveloped until the 1990s. After the State Council approved a plan for its development, and two suspension bridges were built over the river, Pudong began to commercialize quite rapidly. It is one of China's principal foreign investment zones, and its symbol—indeed, the symbol of the new Shanghai—is the **Oriental Pearl Tower**, at just over 1,500 feet the highest television tower in Asia and the third-tallest in the world.

Sūzhōu, 50 miles west of Shanghai in Jiangsu Province, is aptly nicknamed "the Venice of the Orient" because of the many canals that crisscross the town. Suzhou is most famous for its landscape gardens, which number more than 150, some being more than 1,000 years old. Among the more famous: **Tiger Hill, the Pavilion of the Surging Waves, the Garden of the Humble Administrator**, and the **Lion Grove**. Since the 1980s Suzhou has also become one of China's most important manufacturing centers.

Hángzhōu, a city in Zhejiang Province three and one-half hours by train from Shanghai, is renowned as one of the loveliest in all of China. An old Chinese saying goes, "There is paradise in heaven, and then there are Suzhou and Hangzhou on earth." Hangzhou is located near **West Lake**, which boasts lovely hills, stone bridges, pagodas, temples, pavilions, and many varieties of bamboo. Hangzhou is noted for its cuisine and for its silk and embroidery.

Also easily accessible from Shanghai are the cities of **Nánjīng** and **Wúxī**, both in Jiangsu Province. Nanjing, 186 miles up the **Chángjiāng** (Yangtse River) from Shanghai, was China's capital during many dynasties. Don't miss the **Mausoleum of Dr. Sun Yat-sen** (1866–1925), the founder of modern China, in the **Purple Mountains** east of the city. Also nearby is the **Tomb of the Emperor Tàizǔ** (Hóng Wǔ), the founder of the Ming Dynasty. **Wúxī**, located on **Lake Tài**, is 87 miles west of Shanghai and is known as an industrial and resort center.

c = ts; q = ch; x = sh; z = dz; zh = j

Also of interest is the city of **Qīngdǎo** (Tsingtao), a seaport on the coast of Shandong Province occupied by Germany between the end of the nineteenth century and World War I, and later by Japan. Qingdao is a pleasant seaside resort with interesting European architecture. It is known worldwide for the excellent beer produced in a factory first set up by Germans.

THE SOUTHEAST

Guǎngzhōu, formerly known as Canton, is one of China's gateway cities due to its proximity to Hong Kong, only three hours away by rail and even closer by hovercraft. The "City of Rams," as it is known, was where the Opium War began in 1839, and it was one of the treaty ports opened to the British at the end of that war in 1842. At the beginning of the twentieth century Guangzhou was also the site of early revolutionary activities that led ultimately to the overthrow of the Qing Dynasty (1644–1911). Guangzhou, heavily urbanized and relatively lacking in charm, is nonetheless home to monuments, museums, and temples, and of course to Cantonese cuisine, which is among China's finest.

Scenic spots near Guangzhou include the **Seven Star Rocks**, seven peaks standing in the formation of the Big Dipper, and **Cōnghuá Hot Springs**, a health spa. Also not to be missed is the nearby town of **Fóshān**, famous for the last 800 years as a center for pottery, porcelain, textiles, and other handicrafts. Of special interest are the tiny thumb-sized figurines crafted nearby.

Abutting Hong Kong is the city of **Shēnzhèn**, which was a quiet fishing village until the 1980s when it was designated by the central government as a "special economic zone" in order to absorb foreign investment. Shenzhen took maximum advantage of its proximity to Hong Kong and established itself as one of China's key manufacturing and financial centers. It has since become a metropolis where residents enjoy a much higher standard of living than do many others in China.

Without a doubt, one of China's loveliest landscapes, **Guìlín** (Kweilin) has been attracting tourists for hundreds of years. The town, located in Guangxi Zhuang Autonomous Region, is a short hop by plane from Guangzhou. A visit to Guilin is convincing evidence that traditional Chinese landscape paintings are not only symbolic but, in fact, can be completely realistic in their portrayal of exquisite scenery. Take a boat trip down the Li River to nearby Yangshuo and view the weathered limestone outcroppings for which the region is most famous.

Hǎinán, once part of Guangdong Province, was declared a province in its own right in 1988. It is China's second largest island and boasts a year-round tropical maritime climate. The authorities have successfully promoted Hainan, with its pleasant weather and pristine beaches, as a tourism destination. The island also boasts nature preserves where its lush tropical forests and rare animals and plants can be enjoyed.

CENTRAL CHINA

Xī'ān, the capital of Shaanxi Province, is located more than 500 miles southwest of Beijing and about 1,000 miles inland from Shanghai. Xi'an shows China's ancient history more vividly than any other city. The first Emperor of China, **Qín Shǐhuáng**, is buried nearby in a still-unexcavated tomb, guarded by an army of more than 6,000 terra-cotta warriors with horses and chariots that were discovered quite by accident in 1974 and subsequently unearthed. The **Terra-Cotta Warriors and Horses Museum** constructed on the site is a must-see in Xi'an.

Other sites of interest include the old city wall (one of the few in China still basically intact), the **Bell Tower**, and the two **Wild Goose Pagodas**, as well as the Shaanxi Provincial Museum, which houses a collection of important cultural relics, among them the "Forest of Tablet Stones" more than 1,000 steles that are calligraphic treasures dating back as far as the Han Dynasty.

Outside of town, don't miss **Bànpō Village**, an excavation of a 6,000-year-old neolithic village, the **Huáqīng Pool**, a hot spring that dates back to the Tang Dynasty, and

c = ts; *q* = ch; *x* = sh; *z* = dz; *zh* = j

the **Qiánlíng Tomb**, the joint mausoleum of Tang Emperor Gaozong and his consort, Empress Wǔ Zétiān.

A favorite trek through central China begins in **Sìchuān** Province and takes the traveler down the mighty Changjiang (Yangtse River) by boat. Sichuan, China's most populous province, is known for its lush vegetation, tremendous agricultural output, and of course its fiery cuisine. **Chéngdū**, the provincial capital, is an industrial and agricultural center. Not too far away is **Éméi Mountain**, known for spectacular scenery and for its famous Buddhist temple, traditionally a center for martial arts training in China. And don't miss **Chóngqìng** (Chunking), the other major city in Sichuan, which is also an industrial base. It was the provisional capital of the Chinese Nationalists during World War II.

THE FAR WEST AND SOUTHWEST

A number of destinations in China's Far West and Southwest are often omitted from tours but are worth visiting if time allows. Due west of Beijing is **Gānsū** Province, which boasts the famous **Mógāo Grottoes**, hundreds of caves containing Buddhist carvings dating from the Jin Dynasty (265–420). The grottoes are in the town of **Dūnhuáng**, which sits astride the ancient Silk Road near the border of **Xīnjiāng** Autonomous Region. Further down the **Silk Road** in Xinjiang is **Turpan** (Turfan), an oasis located in a geological depression about 500 feet below sea level. And half a day by car from Turpan is **Urumqi**, the capital of Xinjiang and home to 13 of China's many minority groups. The residents of Urumqi are principally Muslems.

Relatively few tourists are lucky enough to visit **Tibet** (Xīzàng). It is difficult to get there, but it is a fascinating journey nonetheless. **Lhasa**, the capital of the Autonomous Region, is 12,000 feet above sea level, and most visitors find that the altitude takes some getting used to. The most famous sight in Lhasa is the **Potala Palace**, a 13-story building on a cliff first built in the seventh century and since restored.

Visitors to **Kūnmíng**, the capital of Yunnan Province, are generally impressed by the climate—perpetual springtime, according to the Chinese. Yunnan sits astride China's border with Burma, Laos, and Vietnam. Kumning was the terminus of the Burma Road, and American pilots flew there over the "Burma hump" to carry supplies to China during World War II. The Western Hills of Kunming boast temples and pavilions, and offer a magnificent view of the entire area.

One pleasant day trip from Kunming is to **Shílín**, the **Stone Forest**, a veritable thicket of slender limestone outcroppings that are compared to trees. A longer excursion will take the traveler to **Xishuang Banna**, a tropical paradise that is home to many minority peoples, the largest number of whom are of the Dai nationality.

HONG KONG

Hong Kong (pronounced *Xiānggǎng* in Mandarin) has certainly earned the sobriquet "the pearl of the Orient." This gleaming metropolis adjacent to Guangdong Province was nothing more than a fishing port when, in the middle of the nineteenth century, the British acquired it in a series of treaties with China's Qing Dynasty government and turned it into a prosperous entrepôt.

After more than 150 years as a British crown colony, Hong Kong reverted to Chinese sovereignty in 1997 in a ceremony televised throughout the world. The reintegration was accomplished under a "one country, two systems" formula created by Deng Xiaoping whereby the Chinese government pledged to preserve Hong Kong's capitalist system for a period of 50 years and grant the region "a high degree of autonomy" in managing its internal affairs.

The "special administrative region" of Hong Kong consists of the island of Hong Kong, the adjacent **Kowloon** (*Jiǔlóng* in Mandarin) peninsula, the "New Territories," which abut the city of Shenzhen, and more than 260 outlying islands.

Hong Kong is more of a shopper's paradise than a tourist destination, but there are some sights of interest worth visiting. Highest on the list is a trip to **Victoria Peak**, the summit of Hong Kong island from which the panoramic view

c = ts; *q* = ch; *x* = sh; *z* = dz; *zh* = j

of the colony is truly breathtaking. The Peak is reachable by taxi, but the better way to go is to take the Peak Tram, which climbs up the side of the mountain and offers some dramatic views of its own.

Other places of interest on the island include the **Aw Boon Haw (Tiger Balm) Gardens**, the **Flagstaff House Museum of Tea Ware**, and **Stanley Market**, where you can buy clothing and souvenirs.

You can get to **Kowloon** from Hong Kong island by subway, but many prefer to take the venerable Star Ferry instead. It's worth the ride for the harbor view alone. Kowloon is an excellent place to shop for electronics, jewelry, clothing, souvenirs, and just about everything else Hong Kong has to offer. Haggling is commonplace at the small stores, though not the custom at the larger department stores. If you have an evening free, visit the outdoor **Temple Street Market**, which features heavily discounted clothing and a wide variety of souvenirs and miscellaneous housewares. Or else, find your way to **Lei Yu Mun**, where you can pick out fresh seafood from any of several vendors and carry it down the road to a restaurant that will be only too happy to prepare it for you.

If you have a little more time to spend in Hong Kong, visit the New Territories, which have wonderful hiking trails, or take an inexpensive ferry ride from Hong Kong island to one of the outlying islands such as **Lantau**, **Cheung Chau**, or **Lamma Island**. There you can find Buddhist Temples, good hiking trails, and excellent seafood restaurants. On Lantau you can see the world's largest, outdoor, seated, bronze Buddha.

MACAO

When the Portuguese government lowered its flag over the enclave of Macao in December 1999 it returned to China the first—and last—European colony in Asia. The handover marked the end of nearly 450 years of Portuguese rule over this six-square-mile territory that was once part of Guangdong Province and is now a special administrative region of China.

Macao, far smaller in both size and population than Hong Kong, its neighbor to the east, consists of a peninsula that is connected to China and two islands, **Taipa** and **Coloane**, all linked by causeways. While it never enjoyed the larger colony's commercial success, its economy has relied primarily on tourism and, in particular, casino gambling, for many years. Known as "the Monte Carlo of the East," it is still the gambling capital of Asia.

Macao is also notable for its historic colonial-style European architecture, Chinese temples, and traces of Portuguese fortresses. Don't miss the plaza on which the **Church of St. Paul** (São Paulo) used to stand. Only the front of this richly decorated Baroque façade of this seventeenth-century building remains, but it is quite beautiful and has, in fact, become the symbol of Macao. For a bird's-eye view of the entire colony, visit its highest point, **Lighthouse Hill**.

You are likely to be well rewarded if you take the time to sample Macanese cuisine, an interesting blend of East and West. You can get pure Cantonese and classical Portuguese dishes there, of course, but make an effort to try some of the more exotic fare that features spices from Europe, Africa, Brazil, and Malaya.

TAIWAN

Known in the West for many years by the Portuguese name "Formosa," Taiwan has a varied colonial past. All or part of it has been held, at one point or another in its history, by the Dutch, the Spanish, the French, and the Japanese. Its history has thus often set it apart from the rest of the China mainland.

The island became a province in China in the late nineteenth century, and was ceded to Japan in 1895, together with the **Pescadore (Pénghú) Islands**. Taiwan and the Pescadores were restored to Chinese rule in 1945 at the end of World War II. In 1949, after years of civil strife between the Nationalist government and the upstart Communist Party, the Nationalists were forced to retreat to Taiwan, thus

c = ts; q = ch; x = sh; z = dz; zh = j

paving the way for the founding of the People's Republic by the Communists on the mainland during that year.

For many years after that, the Nationalists and Communists put forth rival claims to sovereignty, each purporting to be the sole, legitimate government of all of China, even though the Communists held the mainland and the Nationalists controlled only Taiwan and several other islands. The PRC government views Taiwan as a renegade province of China whose reunification with the mainland is a high priority and is only a question of time. For their part, the authorities on Taiwan have renounced their claim to the mainland in recent years, but they have insisted on their legitimacy as the government of Taiwan.

Taiwan has much to offer the tourist. When the Nationalists beat their hasty retreat to Taiwan in 1949, they took with them the finest jade, porcelain, paintings, and bronzes from the Imperial Palace in Beijing. They deposited these in a museum they constructed in the capital city, **Taipei** (*Táiběi*). As a result, Taipei is home to a treasure trove of some of the most breathtaking examples of Chinese art and artifacts that exist in the world today. A visit to the **National Palace Museum**, home to more than 620,000 of these objects from the imperial collection, is thus a "must-see" on a visit to Taipei. Because exhibit space is limited, however, only a small portion of the collection is on view at any given time.

Taipei's development has been quite rapid. What was rice paddies 30 short years ago is now boulevard after boulevard of gleaming office towers, apartment blocks, and department stores. But there are still hints of the past, as a visit to **Lungshan Temple**, the city's oldest and most famous, can testify. It is a fine example of traditional Chinese temple architecture. For a modern twist on these traditional Chinese forms, you can also visit the **Sun Yat-sen** and **Chiang Kai-shek Memorial Halls**.

Taipei's cultural life centers around the **National Theater** and **National Concert Hall**, which produce Chinese and Western operas, dramas, symphonies, and ballets, and feature famous performers from around the world. And you'll find some of the world's finest Chinese cuisine—representative of all parts of China—in Taipei's restaurants.

If you have time for a trip around the island, there are many places worth a visit. A volcanically formed island, Taiwan has a spine of mountains at its center that gradually—and in some cases not so gradually—levels off into the sea. This makes it a fun place for mountain climbing. And don't miss sunrise over **Alishan**, Taiwan's most famous mountain.

A trip down the narrow **Suao-Hualian Highway** is a breathtaking experience. The winding highway is carved into the sides of steep mountains, and is perched as much as 2,600 feet above the Pacific Ocean. From **Hualian**, at the southern end of this road, you can travel inland to **Tienhsiang** via **Taroko Gorge**, a narrow ravine cut into solid granite mountains over the years by a river. Pagodas, temples, and waterfalls complete the exceptional experience. Tienhsiang itself is at the eastern end of the **Cross-Island Highway**, also carved into solid rock and well worth the journey.

It's not by chance that **Sun Moon Lake** in central Taiwan was Chiang Kai-shek's favorite retreat from the heat of Taipei. A beautiful lake in a natural setting with Chinese pavilions and temples perched on the slopes nearby, the lake today is one of Taiwan's most popular honeymoon destinations.

Historic **Tainan**, in the south of Taiwan, is Taiwan's oldest city. It features lots of reminders of the city's past, including dozens of temples, some of which date back to the seventeenth century, as well as the remains of Dutch forts that are equally old. Further south is **Kenting National Park**, where you can see interesting rock and coral formations. And at the very southern tip of the island you can visit **Oluanpi**, where you can see Taiwan's oldest lighthouse and visit a tropical recreation area.

c = ts; q = ch; x = sh; z = dz; zh = j

PLANNING A TRIP

LEAVING TOWN

During your stay in China, you'll probably want to visit several cities. Air travel in particular is far more common and easier than ever, with travel agents and ticket offices in abundance and several airlines competing on specific air routes. But there are still formalities, such as producing your passport at the airport, even when traveling domestically, that you don't necessarily see in other countries.

I would like to visit ____.	*Wǒ xiǎng qù ____.*	
	我想去____。	
How can I get to ____?	*Wǒ zěnmé qù ____?*	
	我怎么去____？	
You can go ____.	*Nǐ kéyǐ ____.*	
	你可以____。	
■ by bicycle	*qí zìxíngchē*	骑自行车
■ by boat	*zuò chuán*	坐船
■ by bus	*zuò bāshì*	坐巴士
■ by car	*zuò qìchē*	坐汽车
■ by city bus	*zuò gōnggòng qìchē*	坐公共汽车
■ by plane	*zuò fēijī*	坐飞机
■ by taxi	*zuò chūzū qìchē*	坐出租汽车
■ by train	*zuò huǒchē*	坐火车
■ on foot	*zǒu lù*	走路

CHINESE PLACE NAMES

SPELLING COMPARISON CHART

PINYIN SPELLING	CHINESE CHARACTER	TRADITIONAL SPELLING
Ānhuī	安徽	Anhwei
Aòmén	澳门	Macao; Macau
Běidàihé	北戴河	Peitaiho
Běijīng	北京	Peking; Peiping
Chángchūn	长春	Changchun
Chángjiāng	长江	Yangtse River
Chángshā	长沙	Changsha
Chéngdé	承德	Chengteh
Chéngdū	成都	Chengtu
Chóngqìng	重庆	Chungking
Dàlián	大连	Dairen
Dàtóng	大同	Tatung
Dūnhuáng	敦煌	Tunhuang
Fújiàn	福建	Fukien
Fúzhōu	福州	Foochow
Gānsù	甘肃	Kansu
Gāoxióng	高雄	Kaohsiung
Guǎngdōng	广东	Kwangtung
Guǎngxī	广西	Kwangsi
Guǎngzhōu	广州	Canton; Kwangchow
Guìlín	桂林	Kweilin
Guìyáng	贵阳	Kweiyang
Guìzhōu	贵州	Kweichow
Hāěrbīn	哈尔滨	Harbin
Háikǒu	海口	Haikow
Hǎinán	海南	Hainan
Hángzhōu	杭州	Hangchow
Hànkǒu	汉口	Hankow
Héběi	河北	Hopeh
Héféi	合肥	Hofei
Hēilóngjiāng	黑龙江	Amur River
Hénán	河南	Honan
Húhéhàotè	呼和浩特	Huhehot
Huáng Hé	黄河	Hwang Ho; Yellow River
Húběi	湖北	Hupeh

c = ts; q = ch; x = sh; z = dz; zh = j

CHINESE PLACE NAMES

SPELLING COMPARISON CHART

PINYIN SPELLING	CHINESE CHARACTER	TRADITIONAL SPELLING
Húnán	湖南	Hunan
Jiāngsū	江苏	Kiangsu
Jiāngxī	江西	Kiangsi
Jílín	吉林	Kirin
Jīlóng	基隆	Keelung
Jǐnán	济南	Tsinan
Jīnmén	金门	Quemoy; Kinmen
Kāifēng	开封	Kaifeng
Kāshí	喀什	Kashgar
Kūnmíng	昆明	Kunming
Lánzhōu	兰州	Lanchow
Lāsà	拉萨	Lhasa
Liáoníng	辽宁	Liaoning
Luòyáng	洛阳	Loyang
Nánchāng	南昌	Nanchang
Nánjīng	南京	Nanking
Nánníng	南宁	Nanning
Níngbō	宁波	Ningpo
Níngxià	宁夏	Ningsia
Pǔdōng	浦东	Putung
Qīngdǎo	青岛	Tsingtao
Qīnghǎi	青海	Tsinghai
Qínhuángdǎo	秦皇岛	Chinhuangtao
Qǔfù	曲阜	Chufu
Shǎanxī	陕西	Shensi
Shāndōng	山东	Shantung
Shànghǎi	上海	Shanghai
Shàntóu	汕头	Swatow
Shānxī	山西	Shansi
Shěnyáng	沈阳	Mukden
Shēnzhèn	深圳	Shumchun
Shíjiāzhuāng	石家庄	Shihchiachuang
Sìchuān	四川	Szechuan
Sūzhōu	苏州	Soochow
Táiběi	台北	Taipei
Tàiyuán	太原	Taiyuan
Táiwān	台湾	Taiwan; Formosa
Táizhōng	台中	Taichung

CHINESE PLACE NAMES

SPELLING COMPARISON CHART

PINYIN SPELLING	CHINESE CHARACTER	TRADITIONAL SPELLING
Táinán	台南	Tainan
Tiānjīn	天津	Tientsin
Tǔlǔfān	吐鲁番	Turfan; Turpan
Wūlǔmùqí	乌鲁木齐	Urumchi
Wǔhàn	武汉	Wuhan
Wúxī	无锡	Wuhsi; Wusih
Xī'ān	西安	Sian
Xiàmén	厦门	Amoy
Xiānggǎng	香港	Hong Kong
Xīníng	西宁	Hsining
Xīnjiāng	新疆	Sinkiang
Xīzàng	西藏	Tibet
Yán'ān	延安	Yenan
Yángzhōu	扬州	Yangchow
Yāntái	烟台	Cheefoo; Yentai
Yúnnán	云南	Yunnan
Zhèjiāng	浙江	Chekiang
Zhèngzhōu	郑州	Chengchow
Zhūhǎi	珠海	Chuhai

BOOKING A FLIGHT

I would like to book a flight to ____.

Wǒ xiǎng zuò fēijī dào ____.
我想坐飞机到____。

When is there a flight to ____?

Shénme shíhòu yǒu fēijī dào ____?
什么时候有飞机到____?

c = ts; *q* = ch; *x* = sh; *z* = dz; *zh* = j

Which airlines fly to that city?	*Nǎjiā hángkōng gōngsī fēi nèige chéngshì?* 哪家航空公司飞那个城市？	
Do I have a choice?	*Yóu xuǎnzé ma?* 有选择吗？	
Can I fly directly from here?	*Néng zhí fēi ma?* 能直飞吗？	
Do I have to change planes?	*Yào zhuǎn jī ma?* 要转机吗？	
Where must I change planes?	*Zài nǎli zhuǎn jī?* 在哪里转机？	
Is it a nonstop flight?	*Shì zhídá de hángbān ma?* 是直达的航班吗？	
I would like a ____ ticket.	*Wǒ yào yìzhāng ____ piào.* 我要一张____票。	
▨ business class	*gōngwù cāng*	公务舱
▨ economy class	*pǔtōng cāng*	普通舱
▨ first class	*tóuděng cāng*	头等舱
▨ one-way	*dānchéng*	单程
▨ round-trip	*láihuí*	来回
I would like a ticket on ____ Airlines (Airways).	*Wó xiǎng mǎi ____ Hángkōng Gōngsī de piào.* 我想买____航空公司的票。	
▨ Aeroflot	*Éguó*	俄国
▨ Air China	*Zhōngguó Guójì*	中国国际
▨ Air France	*Fǎguó*	法国
▨ All Nippon	*Quán Rì Kōng*	全日空
▨ British	*Yīngguó*	英国

■ Cathay Pacific	*Guótài*	国泰
■ China Eastern	*Zhōngguó Dōngfāng*	中国东方
■ China Northern	*Zhōngguó Běifāng*	中国北方
■ China Southern	*Zhōngguó Nánfāng*	中国南方
■ Dragonair	*Gǎnglóng*	港龙
■ El Al	*Yǐsèliè*	以色列
■ Japan	*Rìběn*	日本
■ Korean	*Hánguó*	韩国
■ Lufthansa	*Déguó Hànshā*	德国汉莎
■ Malaysia	*Mǎláixīyǎ*	马来西亚
■ Northwest	*Měiguó Xīběi*	美国西北
■ Shanghai	*Shànghǎi*	上海
■ Singapore	*Xīnjiāpō*	新加坡
■ United	*Měiguó Liánhé*	美国联合
I would like a seat ____.	*Wó xiǔngyào ____ de wèizi.*	我想要____的位子。
■ on the aisle	*kào guòdào*	靠过道
■ by the window	*kào chuāng*	靠窗
■ in the smoking section	*néng chōuyān*	能抽烟
■ in the nonsmoking section	*bù xǔ chōuyān*	不许抽烟

c = ts; *q* = ch; *x* = sh; *z* = dz; *zh* = j

What is the fare?	*Piàojià duōshǎo?* 票价多少？
Are meals served?	*Yǒu cāndiǎn ma?* 有餐点吗？
At what time does the plane take off?	*Fēijī jídiǎn qǐfēi?* 飞机几点起飞？
What time will we arrive?	*Wǒmén jídiǎn dào?* 我们几点到？
When will we land in ____?	*Jídiǎn dào ____?* 几点到____？
What is my flight number?	*Wǒ de hángbān hàomǎ duōshǎo?* 我的航班号码多少？
I want to ____ my reservation.	*Wǒ yào ____ wǒ yùdìng de wèizi.* 我要____我预定的位子。
▮ confirm	*quèrèn*　　　确认
▮ cancel	*qǔxiāo*　　　取消
What time shall I check in?	*Jídiǎn yào dēngjì?* 几点要登记？
Do I need to show my passport?	*Xūyào chūshì hùzhào ma?* 需要出示护照吗？
How long must we wait for departure?	*Yào tuīchí duōjiǔ cái qǐfēi?* 要推迟多久才起飞？
Will you provide a meal while I wait?	*Děng de shíhòu, gěi cāndiǎn chī ma?* 等的时候，给餐点吃吗？
Where shall I collect my meal?	*Dào nǎlǐ qù qǔ cāndiǎn?* 到哪里去取餐点？

AT THE AIRPORT

Which gate do we leave from?	*Zài jǐ hào mén hòujī?* 在几号门候机？
I'd like to check my bags.	*Wó xiǎng tuōyùn xíngli.* 我想托运行李。
I have only carry-on baggage.	*Wǒ zhí yóu shǒutíbāo.* 我只有手提包。

NOTE: Some high-speed film can be damaged by airport security X rays. It is best to pack your film in your suitcase, protected by a lead-insulated bag. If you have film in your camera or carry-on baggage, avoid problems by asking the guard to examine it by hand.

Please don't let the camera and film go through the machine.	*Qǐng búyào bǎ zhàoxiàng jī hé dǐpiàn tōngguò jīqì.* 请不要把照相机和底片通过机器。
Please examine my film (camera) by hand.	*Qǐng yòng shóu jiǎnchá dǐpiàn (zhàoxiàngjī).* 请用手检查底片（照相机）。
Where can I get a snack?	*Náli yóu xiǎochī diàn?* 哪里有小吃店？
Is there time for lunch?	*Yǒu shíjiān chī wǔfàn ma?* 有时间吃午饭吗？

c = ts; *q* = ch; *x* = sh; *z* = dz; *zh* = j

ON BOARD THE PLANE

flight attendant	*chéngwùyuán*	乘务员
pilot	*zhèng jiàshǐ*	正驾驶
copilot	*fù jiàshǐ*	副驾驶
Please fasten your seat belts.	*Xì hǎo ānquándài.*	系好安全带。
My seat belt is already fastened.	*Wǒ de ānquándài yǐjīng xìhǎole.*	我的安全带已经系好了。
My _____ is (are) broken.	*Wǒ de _____ yǒu máobìng.*	我的____有毛病。
▨ earphones	*ěrjī*	耳机
▨ seat	*yǐzi*	椅子
▨ seat belt	*ānquándài*	安全带
▨ television	*diànshì*	电视
May I use my _____ now?	*Xiànzài néng yòng wǒ de _____ ma?*	现在能用我的____吗？
▨ CD player	*jīguāng chàng jī*	激光唱机
▨ cell phone	*shǒujī*	手机
▨ electronic game	*diànzi yóuxì*	电子游戏
▨ laptop computer	*biànxié shì diànnǎo*	便携式电脑
▨ tape recorder	*lùyīnjī*	录音机
I would like some _____.	*Wó xiǎngyào _____.*	我想要____。
▨ beer	*píjiǔ*	啤酒
▨ white wine	*bái pútáojiǔ*	白葡萄酒

■ red wine	*hóng pútáojiǔ*	红葡萄酒
■ cola	*kělè*	可乐
■ juice	*guǒzhī*	果汁
■ water	*kāishuǐ*	开水
■ tea	*chá*	茶
■ coffee	*kāfēi*	咖啡
■ milk	*niúnǎi*	牛奶
■ peanuts	*huāshēngmǐ*	花生米
■ potato chips	*tǔdòupiàn*	土豆片

Please bring me (a, an)____	*Qǐng géi wǒ ____.*	请给我____。
■ air sickness bag	*wèishēng dài*	卫生袋
■ blanket	*tǎnzi*	毯子
■ comb	*shūzi*	梳子
■ napkin	*cānjīn zhǐ*	餐巾纸
■ playing cards	*pǔkè pái*	扑克牌
■ postcards	*míngxìn piàn*	明信片
■ stationery	*xìn zhǐ*	信纸
■ toothbrush	*yáshuā*	牙刷
■ toothpaste	*yágāo*	牙膏
■ towel	*máojīn*	毛巾

Please ask that passenger not to smoke.	*Qǐng gàosu nèiwèi chèngkè búyào chōu yān.* 请告诉那位乘客不要抽烟。
Is the toilet occupied?	*Cèsuó yǒu rén ma?* 厕所有人吗？

c = ts; *q* = ch; *x* = sh; *z* = dz; *zh* = j

There is no toilet paper in the bathroom.	*Cèsuǒ méiyǒu wèishēng zhǐ.* 厕所没有卫生纸。

TRAIN SERVICE

Train travel in China is a good way to see parts of the countryside you would never get to see otherwise, even if you can't stop to appreciate the local color. Long-distance trains are generally very comfortable, especially if, like most foreign guests, you travel "soft class." This often means a cabin with four comfortable berths and a small table and reasonably good food service. "Hard class," a more spartan option, is also available, but it's a lot more crowded and much less comfortable. Don't be surprised if your Chinese hosts balk at your traveling that way; they are thinking only of your comfort.

The service person on the train will tell you when it is time to eat and will escort you to your assigned seat in the dining car.

Where is the train station?	*Huǒchē zhàn zài nálí?*	火车站在哪里？
I want to travel to ____.	*Wǒ yào qù ____.*	我要去____。
I would like a ____ ticket.	*Wǒ yào yì zhāng ____ piào.*	我要一张____票。
■ hard-class	*yìng wò*	硬卧
■ soft-class	*ruǎn wò*	软卧
When does the train ____?	*Huǒchē jídiǎn ____?*	火车几点____？
■ leave	*kāi*	开
■ arrive	*dào*	到
Which platform?	*Něige yuètái?*	哪个月台？

Does this train stop at ____?	*Zhèi bān chē zài ____ tíng ma?* 这班车在____停吗？
How long does it stop?	*Tíng duōjiǔ?* 停多久？
Can I get off the train for a while?	*Kéyǐ xià chē kànkan ma?* 可以下车看看吗？
All aboard!	*Shàng chē le!* 上车了！
Where is the dining car?	*Cānchē zài nálǐ?* 餐车在哪里？
Where shall I put my luggage?	*Xínglǐ yào fàng nálǐ?* 行李要放哪里？
Will you help me store my luggage?	*Nǐ néng bāng wǒ fàng xínglǐ ma?* 你能帮我放行李吗？
Will my luggage be safe there?	*Fàng zài nàlǐ fàngxīn ma?* 放在那里放心吗？
Where is the toilet?	*Cèsuǒ zài nálǐ?* 厕所在哪里？
Do you have a Western-style toilet?	*Yǒu xīshìde cèsuǒ ma?* 有西式的厕所吗？
Is it a(n) ____?	*Shì ____ ma?* 是____吗？
▓ local train	*màn chē*	慢车
▓ express	*kuài chē*	快车
Where are we now?	*Wǒmén xiànzài zài nálǐ?* 我们现在在哪里？
Is it time to eat yet?	*Kéyǐ chīfàn le ma?* 可以吃饭了吗？

c = ts; *q* = ch; *x* = sh; *z* = dz; *zh* = j

Will we arrive on time?	*Wǒmén huì zhǔnshí dào ma?* 我们会准时到吗？
Is this seat taken?	*Zhè wèizi yǒu rén zuò ma?* 这位子有人坐吗？
Excuse me, this is my seat.	*Duì bù qǐ, zhè shì wǒ de wèizi.* 对不起，这是我的位子。

SHIPBOARD TRAVEL

Going by boat is a pleasant, relaxing way to see various parts of China. In many cities, such as Shanghai and Guilin, you can take a short pleasure tour on a boat and see a good deal of the local scenery. The half-day trip down the Lijiang (Li River) in Guilin offers one of the most spectacular views in all of China. One can also take longer boat tours—a favorite route is down the Changjiang (Yangtse River).

Chinese boats vary greatly as far as quality of accommodations. The best rooms are staterooms with two or four fairly comfortable beds. There are usually no private baths, but the common bathrooms do afford some privacy, and some boats have sinks in the higher-priced rooms. First-class passengers also generally have the use of a private lounge at the front of the boat. Other accommodations are more spartan; they are on the lower level of the boat and are noisier. There are eight bunk beds to a room and the toilets are common and often not well maintained.

Where is the dock?	*Mǎtóu zài nǎli?* 码头在哪里？
When does the next boat leave for ____?	*Xià yì bān dào ____ de chuán jídiǎn kāi?* 下一班到____的船几点开？
I'd like to go by ship.	*Wó xiǎng zuò chuán qù.* 我想坐船去。

Does it take much longer by ship?	*Zuò chuán qù màn de duō ma?*	坐船去慢得多吗？
How long does it take?	*Yào duō jiǔ?*	要多久？
Do we stop anywhere?	*Zhōngtú tíng ma?*	中途停吗？
How long will the ship remain?	*Chuán yào tíng duōjiǔ?*	船要停多久？
When do we land?	*Shénme shíhòu xià chuán?*	什么时候下船？

At what time do we have to be back on board?	*Shénme shíhòu zài shàng chuán?*	什么时候再上船？
I'd like a ____ ticket.	*Wǒ xiǎngyào ____ piào.*	我想要___票。
▨ first-class	*tóuděng cāng*	头等舱
▨ cabin-class	*èrděng cāng*	二等舱

c = ts; *q* = ch; *x* = sh; *z* = dz; *zh* = j

I don't feel well.	*Wǒ bú tài shūfu.*	我不太舒服。
I'm a little seasick.	*Wǒ yǒu diǎn yūnchuán.*	我有一点晕船。
Is there any medicine to cure seasickness?	*Yǒu méi yǒu zhì yūnchuán de yào?*	有没有治晕船的药？

AVERAGE TEMPERATURES OF MAJOR CHINESE CITIES

CITY	PROVINCE	SUMMER (° Fahrenheit)	WINTER (° Fahrenheit)
Beijing	—	80	23
Changsha	Hunan	85	42
Chengdu	Sichuan	85	45
Chongqing	—	82	47
Dalian	Liaoning	72	21
Fuzhou	Fujian	82	51
Guangzhou	Guangdong	84	57
Guilin	Guangxi	84	48
Hangzhou	Zhejiang	83	39
Haerbin	Heilongjiang	72	−3
Hohhot	Nei Menggu	70	20
Kunming	Yunnan	72	48
Lanzhou	Gansu	70	47
Lhasa	Xizang	63	32
Nanjing	Jiangsu	82	39
Qingdao	Shandong	77	28
Shanghai	—	80	38
Shenyang	Liaoning	75	10
Suzhou	Jiangsu	83	39
Taiyuan	Shanxi	77	17
Tianjin	—	79	24
Urumqi	Xinjiang	90	19
Wuhan	Hubei	85	40
Wuxi	Jiangsu	82	39
Xiamen	Fujian	86	55
Xi'an	Shaanxi	86	33

CAR RENTALS

Though many long-term foreign residents drive their own cars in China, it's not common for tourists to rent a car and drive it themselves, and given the casual approach to obeying traffic regulations on the part not only of drivers but also of bicyclists and pedestrians, it's probably not advisable, either. What is possible, and recommended, is to rent a car with its driver for a day or two. This is a good way to see a lot of the sights at your own pace, without a large tour group to slow you down, and without auto repairs and similar headaches.

You can check with your local guide or your hotel to see about renting a private car for the day, but you can often rent a taxi for this purpose as well.

Where can I rent ____?	*Náli kéyǐ zūdào*	哪里可以租到____?
a bicycle	*zìxíng chē*	自行车
a car	*chūzū qìchē*	出租汽车
a minibus	*miànbāo chē*	面包车
I want a(n) ____.	*Wó xiǎngyào yíliàng ____.*	我想要一辆____。
American car	*Měiguó chē*	美国车
domestic car	*guóchǎn chē*	国产车
European car	*Ōuzhōu chē*	欧洲车
imported car	*jìnkǒu chē*	进口车
Japanese car	*Rìběn chē*	日本车
van	*Miànbāo chē*	面包车
car with air conditioning	*yǒu kōngtiáo de chē*	有空调的车

c = ts; *q* = ch; *x* = sh; *z* = dz; *zh* = j

How much does it cost ____?	____ *yào duōshǎo?*	____要多少？
■ per day	*Yì tiān*	一天
■ per week	*Yì xīngqī*	一星期
■ per kilometer	*Yì gōnglǐ*	一公里

How many kilometers per day do I get for the basic fee?
Měitiān jīběn de gōnglǐshù shì duōshǎo?
每天基本的公里数是多少？

Does the price include gasoline?
Jiàqián bāokuò qìyóu fèi ma?
价钱包括汽油费吗？

Does the car come with a driver?
Zūchē bāokuò sījī ma?
租车包括司机吗？

Can the driver speak English?
Sījī néng shuō Yīngwén ma?
司机能说英文吗？

Will the driver stay with me all day?
Sījī zhěngtiān dōu dài wǒ ma?
司机整天都带我吗？

Shall I take care of the driver's meals?
Wǒ yào fùzé sījī de fànqián ma?
我要负责司机的饭钱吗？

I will settle up with the driver at the end of the day.
Wǒ zuìhòu zài gěi sījī fùzhàng.
我最后再给司机付帐。

Does the price include insurance?
Fèiyòng bāokuò báoxiǎn ma?
费用包括保险吗？

I'd like to buy insurance.
Wó xiáng mái báoxiǎn.
我想买保险

Please tell the driver ____.	*Qǐng gàosu sījī ____.* 请告诉司机____。	
■ the car is to cold	*chēlǐ tài lěngle*	车里太冷了
■ the car is too hot	*chēlǐ tài rèle*	车里太热了
■ not to smoke	*búyào xīyān*	不要吸烟
■ to turn on the heat	*dǎkāi nuǎnqì*	打开暖气
■ to turn down the radio	*bǎ shōuyīnjī guān dī yìdiǎn*	把收音机关低一点
■ to turn off the radio	*bǎ shōuyīnjī guāndiào*	把收音机关掉
■ to close the window	*bǎ chuāng guānshàng*	把窗关上
■ not to drive so fast	*búyào kāi de zhème kuài*	不要开得这么快
■ not to drive so slowly	*búyào kāi de zhème màn*	不要开得这么慢
■ I need to arrive by 3:00	*wó déi zài sāndiǎn zhīqián dào*	我得在三点之前到
■ to wait for me here	*yào zài zhèlǐ déng wǒ*	要在这里等我
■ to take me back to my hotel	*sòng wǒ huí fàndiàn*	送我回饭店

c = ts; *q* = ch; *x* = sh; *z* = dz; *zh* = j

Travel Tips When you are packing to leave home, leave a little space in your suitcase to hold the small purchases you will make while you are away. If you can't manage this, then pack a collapsible tote bag in your suitcase, to be filled up and carried separately on your return trip.

ENTERTAINMENT AND DIVERSIONS

NIGHTLIFE

In the past, China was not known for its nightlife, but in recent years a surprising variety of after-hours options have proliferated throughout the country. One can find bars, discos, karaoke parlors, bowling alleys, movie theaters, restaurants, Internet cafés, and coffee shops. If you have energy left over after early-to-rise sightseeing trips to temples, pagodas, and other scenic and historic locations, there are plenty of late-night diversions.

There are also evening performances meant for tourists—and some aimed at locals as well—in major cities every night. It's not always easy to find out by yourself exactly what is being performed, and it's harder still to buy your own tickets, so let your guide or hotel help you. You might want to try to get in to see a martial arts or acrobatic performance, a sporting event, a concert, or a song-and-dance show. You don't need to speak Chinese to appreciate these activities, and they can be very entertaining. If you don't mind a little ambiguity, go to see a Chinese movie or a play. There will probably not be English subtitles or program notes provided, however, so you'll have to guess at the plot if you don't have an interpreter handy.

The Beijing Opera and regional operas of other provinces are also sights to behold. The Chinese love them for their portrayal of famous historic dramas and folk tales, for the symbolic and highly stylized makeup worn by the actors, and for the bright, colorful costumes. Westerners often find the singing rather shrill and unmelodious, however, and many report that without a clear idea of the plot, it is difficult to sit through an entire performance.

c = ts; q = ch; x = sh; z = dz; zh = j

MOVIES

Let's go see a movie.	*Wŏmén qú kàn diànyíng hăo bú hăo?*	
	我们去看电影好不好？	
What are they showing today?	*Jīntiān yăn shénme?*	
	今天演什么？	
It's a(n) ____ movie.	*Shì ge ____ piān.*	
	是个____片。	
■ American	*Měiguó*	美国
■ Chinese	*guóchăn*	国产
■ Hong Kong/ Taiwan	*Găngtái*	港台
■ Japanese	*Rìběn*	日本
Is it in English?	*Shì shuō Yīngwén de ma?*	
	是说英文的吗？	
Are there English subtitles?	*Yŏu méi yŏu Yīngwén zìmù?*	
	有没有英文字幕？	
Where is the movie theater?	*Diànyǐng yuàn zài nálǐ?*	
	电影院在哪里？	
Where can I buy tickets?	*Zài nálǐ kéyǐ măi piào?*	
	在哪里可以买票？	
How much for a ticket?	*Duōshăo qián yìzhāng?*	
	多少钱一张？	
action film	*dǎdòu piān*	打斗片
adventure film	*jīngxiăn piān*	惊险片
cartoon	*dònghuà piān*	动画片
documentary	*jìlù piān*	记录片

feature film	*gùshi piān*	故事片
horror film	*kǒngbù piān*	恐怖片
kung fu	*wǔxiá piān*	武侠片
mystery	*zhēntàn piān*	侦探片
romance	*yánqíng piān*	言情片
spy film	*jiāndié piān*	间谍片
war film	*zhànzhēng piān*	战争片

| Is there a refreshment stand? | *Yǒu xiǎomài bù ma?*
有小卖部吗？ |
| Where is the toilet? | *Cèsuǒ zài nálǐ?*
厕所在哪里？ |

THEATER

I'd like to see a play.	*Wó xiǎng kàn huàjù.* 我想看话剧
Where can one buy tickets?	*Zài nálǐ kéyǐ mǎidào piào?* 在哪里可以买到票？
What time does the show begin?	*Shénme shíhòu kāiyǎn?* 什么时候开演？
What time does the show end?	*Shénme shíhòu yǎn wán?* 什么时候演完？
I would like to buy tickets for tonight.	*Wó xiǎng mǎi jīnwǎn de piào.* 我想买今晚的票。
I need two ____ tickets.	*Wǒ yào liǎng zhāng piào.* 我要两张票。

c = ts; *q* = ch; *x* = sh; *z* = dz; *zh* = j

■ orchestra seats	*lóuxià de wèizi*	楼下的位子
■ balcony seats	*lóushàng de wèizi*	楼上的位子

MUSICAL/CULTURAL PERFORMANCES

We would like to go to ____.	*Wǒmén xiǎng qù ____.*	我们想去____。
■ an acrobatic performance	*kàn zájì biáoyǎn*	看杂技表演
■ a ballet	*kàn bāléi wǔ*	看芭蕾舞
■ a Cantonese opera	*kàn yuèjù*	看粤剧
■ a classical Chinese music concert	*tīng guóyuè yǎnzòu*	听国乐演奏
■ a comic dialogue performance	*tīng xiàngshēng*	听相声
■ a concert	*tīng yīnyuè huì*	听音乐会
■ a local folk opera	*kàn dìfāng xì*	看地方戏
■ a magic show	*kàn móshù biáoyǎn*	看魔朮表演
■ a martial arts performance	*kàn wǔshù biáoyǎn*	看武朮表演
■ a Peking opera	*kàn jīngjù*	看京剧
■ a singing recital	*tīng gē chàng huì*	听歌唱会

▨ a song-and-dance show	*kàn gē wǔ biáoyǎn*	看歌舞表演
Is there ____ here?	*Zhèli yǒu méi yǒu ____?*	这里有没有____？
▨ an auditorium	*lǐtáng*	礼堂
▨ a concert hall	*yīnyuè tīng*	音乐厅
▨ a movie theater	*diànyǐng yuàn*	电影院
What are they performing?	*Tāmén zài yǎn shénme?* 他们在演什么？	
I enjoy ____.	*Wó xǐhuān ____.* 我喜欢____。	
▨ chamber music	*shìnèi yuè*	室内乐
▨ classical music	*gúdiǎn yīnyuè*	古典音乐
▨ folk dances	*mínjiān wúdǎo*	民间舞蹈
▨ folk songs	*míngē*	民歌
▨ instrumental music	*qì yuè*	器乐
▨ jazz	*juéshì yīnyuè*	爵士音乐
▨ modern music	*xiàndài yīnyuè*	现代音乐
▨ revolutionary model operas	*gémìng yàngbǎnxì*	革命样板戏
▨ rock and roll	*yáogǔn yuè*	摇滚乐
▨ symphonic music	*jiāoxiǎng yuè*	交响乐
▨ vocal music	*shēng yuè*	声乐
▨ Western opera	*xīyáng gējù*	西洋歌剧

c = ts; *q* = ch; *x* = sh; *z* = dz; *zh* = j

| Are there any tickets for tonight's performance? | *Yǒu méi yǒu jīnwǎn de piào?* |
| | 有没有今晚的票？ |

| Must tickets be purchased in advance? | *Yídìng yào tíqián mǎi piào ma?* |
| | 一定要提前买票吗？ |

| How much are front row seats? | *Qiánpái zuòwèi duōshǎo qián?* |
| | 前排座位多少钱？ |

| How much are the least expensive seats? | *Zuì piányi de zuòwèi duōshǎo qián?* |
| | 最便宜的座位多少钱？ |

| May I have a program? | *Qǐng géi wǒ yì zhāng jiémùdān.* |
| | 请给我一张节目单。 |

| Is that performer famous in China? | *Nèi wèi yǎnyuán zài Zhōngguó yǒumíng ma?* |
| | 那位演员在中国有名吗？ |

| What is the play being performed tonight? | *Jīnwǎn yǎn shénme huàjù?* |
| | 今晚演什么话剧？ |

BARS AND DISCOS

| Where is the bar? | *Jiǔbā zài nǎli?* |
| | 酒吧在哪里？ |

| Please bring me a bottle of ___. | *Qǐng géi wǒ lái yìpíng ___.* |
| | 请给我来一瓶___。 |

| ▥ local beer | *běndì píjiǔ* | 本地啤酒 |
| ▥ imported beer | *jìnkǒu píjiǔ* | 进口啤酒 |

| I'd like a glass of whiskey. | *Wó xiǎngyào yì bēi wēishìjì.* | 我想要一杯威士忌。 |

■ straight   *bùjiā bīngkuài*   不加冰块

■ on the rocks   *jiā bīngkuài*   加冰块

Please bring me a glass of ____.   *Qǐng géi wǒ lái yìbēi ____.*   请给我来一杯____。

■ cold beer   *lěngdòng de píjiǔ*   冷冻的啤酒

■ red wine   *hóng pútáo jiǔ*   红葡萄酒

■ white wine   *bái pútáo jiǔ*   白葡萄酒

Please bring me ____.   *Qǐng géi wǒ lái diǎn ____.*   请给我来点____。

■ cashew nuts   *yāoguǒ*   腰果

■ peanuts   *huāshēngmǐ*   花生米

■ potato chips   *tǔdòupiàn*   土豆片

Shall we go to a nightclub?   *Wǒmén qù yèzǒnghuì, hǎo ba?*   我们去夜总会，好吧？

Is there a disco here?   *Zhèlǐ yǒu dísīkē wǔtīng mā?*   这里有迪斯科舞厅吗？

Where can we go to dance?   *Dào nálǐ qù tiàowǔ?*   到哪里去跳舞？

Is there any cover charge?   *Yǒu rùchǎng fèiyòng ma?*   有入场费用吗？

How much is it to get in?   *Rùchǎng duōshǎo qián?*   入场多少钱？

Where is the checkroom?   *Zài nálǐ cún yīfu?*   在哪里存衣服？

At what time does the show begin?   *Shénme shíhòu kāishǐ biáoyǎn?*   什么时候开始表演？

c = ts; *q* = ch; *x* = sh; *z* = dz; *zh* = j

May I buy you a drink?	*Wǒ kéyǐ qíng nǐ hē jiǔ ma?* 我可以请你喝酒吗？
What would you like to drink?	*Nǐ xiǎng hē shénme?* 你想喝什么？
Would you like to dance?	*Nǐ xiǎng gēn wǒ tiàowǔ ma?* 你想跟我跳舞吗？
Would you like to take a walk outside?	*Wǒmén dào wàimiàn qù guàngguang hǎo ma?* 我们到外面去逛逛好吗？
Would you like to go back to my hotel?	*Nǐ gēn wǒ yīqǐ huí fàndiàn, hǎo ma?* 你跟我一起回饭店好吗？

KARAOKE

Karaoke, invented by the Japanese in the late 1980s, has taken China—and indeed, most of the rest of Asia—by storm. It provides the sound track and the lyrics that enable you to give your best imitation of Frank Sinatra or Barbra Streisand in front of an entire bar, or simply to entertain your fellow banquet guests in a private room. Karaoke machines seem to be omnipresent in restaurants, bars, banquet rooms, dining halls, dance halls, and nearly everywhere people in China relax.

Many karaoke establishments offer songs from various cultures. You can usually find Mandarin, Cantonese, Japanese, and English song titles. You may be called upon to perform with little notice and no opportunity for rehearsal. But the good news is that enthusiasm counts for more than perfect pitch when you're singing karaoke.

Does this place have a karaoke lounge?	*Zhèlǐ yǒu kǎlāōukèi tīng ma?* 这里有卡拉OK厅吗？

Where can we go to sing karaoke?	*Dào nálǐ qù chàng kǎlāōukèi?* 到哪里去唱卡拉OK？
Do you have individual rooms?	*Yǒu dānjiān ma?* 有单间吗？
How much is an individual room?	*Dānjiān duōshǎo qián?* 单间多少钱？
Do you charge by the hour or by the song?	*Àn zhōngdiǎn háishi àn gēqǔ suàn?* 按钟点还是按歌曲算？
How much per hour?	*Yì xiǎoshí duōshǎo qián?* 一小时多少钱？
How much per song?	*Yìshǒu gē duōshǎo qián?* 一首歌多少钱？
Do you have ____ songs?	*Nǐmén yǒu ____ gē ma?* 你们有____歌吗？

■ Cantonese	*Yuèyǔ*	粤语
■ Chinese	*Zhōngguó*	中国
■ English	*Yīngwén*	英文
■ Hong Kong	*Xiānggǎng*	香港
■ Japanese	*Rìběn*	日本
■ Western	*Xīyáng*	西洋
■ Taiwanese	*Táiwān*	台湾

How do I ____?	*Zěnmé ____?* 怎么____？	
■ adjust the volume	*tiáojié yīnliàng*	调节音量
■ adjust the pitch	*tiáojié gāodī yīn*	调节高低音

c = ts; *q* = ch; *x* = sh; *z* = dz; *zh* = j

- adjust the speed | *tiáozhěng kuàimàn* 调整快慢

- change a song | *huàn lìngwài yìshǒu gē* 换另外一首歌

- cancel a song | *qǔxiāo yìshǒu gē* 取消一首歌

The room is too ____. | *Shìnèi guāngxiàn tài ____.* 室内光线太____。

- bright | *liàng* 亮

- dim | *àn* 暗

Is there a hostess? | *Yǒu xiáojiě ma?* 有小姐吗？

Please sing a song for me. | *Qǐng wèi wǒ chàng yìshǒu gē.* 请为我唱一首歌。

You sing beautifully. | *Nǐ chàng de zhēn hǎo.* 你唱得真好。

Please sing another one. | *Qǐng zài chàng yìshǒu.* 请再唱一首。

How late are you open? | *Nǐmén kāi dào jídiǎn?* 你们开到几点？

We'd like to order ____. | *Wǒmén xiáng diǎn ____.* 我们想点____。

- drinks | *yǐnliào* 饮料

- snacks | *xiǎochī* 小吃

Is the service charge included? | *Fúwùfèi zài nèi ma?* 服务费在内吗？

How much is the service charge? | *Fúwùfèi duōshǎo?* 服务费多少？

We would like a private room. | *Wǒmén yào dānjiān.* 我们要单间。

We would like a private room with karaoke.	*Wǒmén yào yǒu kǎlāōukèi de dānjiān.* 我们要有卡拉OK的单间。
We would like a room that can seat___ people.	*Wǒmén yào néng zuò ___ rén de dānjiān.* 我们要能坐___人的单间。

SPECTATOR SPORTS

I'd like to see a ballgame.	*Wó xiǎng qù kàn qiúsài.* 我想去看球赛。
Where's the stadium?	*Tǐyù chǎng zài náli?* 体育场在哪里？
When does the game begin?	*Bǐsài shénme shíhòu kāishǐ?* 比赛什么时候开始？
Which teams are going to play?	*Něixiē dùi cānjiā bǐsài?* 哪些队参加比赛？
What is the score?	*Bǐfēn duōshǎo?* 比分多少？
Can we go to see a ___ game?	*Wǒmén kéyǐ qù kàn ___ bǐsài ma?* 我们可以去看___比赛吗？

■ baseball	*bàngqiú*	棒球
■ basketball	*lánqiú*	篮球
■ hockey	*bīngqiú*	冰球
■ Ping-Pong	*pīngpāng qiú*	乒乓球
■ soccer	*zúqiú*	足球
■ softball	*lěiqiú*	垒球

c = ts; *q* = ch; *x* = sh; *z* = dz; *zh* = j

■ swimming	*yóuyǒng*	游泳
■ tennis	*wǎngqiú*	网球
■ volleyball	*páiqiú*	排球

ACTIVE SPORTS

Do you play volleyball?	*Ní dǎ páiqiú ma?* 你打排球吗？	
I don't play very well.	*Wó dǎ de bù tài hǎo.* 我打得不太好。	
I need practice.	*Wǒ xūyào liànxí.* 我需要练习。	
I win.	*Wǒ yíng le.*	我赢了。
You lose.	*Nǐ shū le.*	你输了。
It's a tie.	*Dǎchéng píngshǒu.*	打成平手。
Where can I rent a bicycle?	*Náli kéyǐ zū zìxíngchē?* 哪里可以租自行车？	

BEACH OR POOL

Swimming is by no means the most popular leisure activity in China, probably due in part to Chinese modesty about the body, and in part to their preference for maintaining a light complexion. There are, however, many public swimming pools in the cities and some lovely bathing beaches along China's coast.

A favorite summer retreat for people who live in Beijing—and indeed, for China's senior leadership—is **Beidaihe**, a bathing beach on the coast of Hebei Province, four and one-half hours by train from the capital. Another popular spot is **Qingdao**, a city on the Shandong Province seacoast famous for its beer (Tsingtao beer). And in recent years, **Hainan** Province has become very popular with bathers from China, Hong Kong, and elsewhere in Asia.

Chinese beaches offer most of the amenities of beaches around the world. There are lifeguards on duty, and you can rent rafts, inner tubes, paddleboats, and umbrellas. Bring your own suntan lotion, however, because it won't necessarily be available for purchase.

Where is there a swimming pool?	*Nǎli yǒu yóuyǒng chí?*	哪里有游泳池？
Can we go swimming?	*Wǒmén kéyǐ qù yóuyǒng ma?*	我们可以去游泳吗？
Can we go to the beach?	*Wǒmén kéyǐ dào hǎitān qù ma?*	我们可以到海滩去吗？
Is it safe to swim here?	*Zài zhèli yóuyǒng ānquán ma?*	在这里游泳安全吗？
Are there ____?	*Yǒu ____ ma?*	有___吗？
■ sharks	*shāyú*	鲨鱼
■ jellyfish	*shuǐmǔ*	水母
Is there a lifeguard?	*Yǒu jiùshēngyuán ma?*	有救生员吗？
Where can I get ____?	*Nǎli yǒu ____?*	哪里有___？
■ a bathing suit	*yóuyǒng yī*	游泳衣
■ a beach ball	*hǎitān wán de qiú*	海滩玩的球
■ a beach umbrella	*tàiyáng sǎn*	太阳伞

c = ts; *q* = ch; *x* = sh; *z* = dz; *zh* = j

■ a chair	*yǐzi*	椅子
■ a towel	*máojīn*	毛巾

Where can I take a shower?	*Náli kéyǐ línyù?* 哪里可以淋浴？

IN THE COUNTRYSIDE

I'd like to visit the countryside.	*Wó xiǎng dào xiāngxià qù kànkan.* 我想到乡下去看看。
Where can I rent a car?	*Náli kéyǐ zū qìchē?* 哪里可以租汽车？
Can we go camping?	*Wǒmén kéyǐ qù lùyíng ma?* 我们可以去露营吗？
Where can we go for a picnic?	*Wǒmén dào náli qù yěcān?* 我们到哪里去野餐？
What a beautiful landscape!	*Fēngjǐng háo měi!* 风景好美！
Look at ____.	*Kànkan ____ ba.* 看看____吧。
■ the bridge	*qiáo*	桥
■ the farmers	*nóngmín*	农民
■ the hill	*xiǎo shān*	小山
■ the lake	*hú*	湖
■ the mountain	*shān*	山
■ the pagoda	*báotǎ*	宝塔
■ the rice paddies	*dàotián*	稻田
■ the temple	*miào*	庙
■ the tractor	*tuōlājī*	拖拉机

■ the water buffalo	*shuǐniú*	水牛
Isn't _____ beautiful?	_____ *duō piàoliang!*	____多漂亮！
■ the ocean	*Hǎi*	海
■ the pond	*Chítáng*	池溏
■ the river	*Hé*	河
■ the stream	*Xiǎo xī*	小溪
■ the trees	*Shù*	树
■ the valley	*Shāngǔ*	山谷
■ the village	*Cūnzhuāng*	村庄
■ the waterfall	*Pùbù*	瀑布
Where does this road lead?	*Zhèi tiáo lù tōng dào nálǐ qù?* 这条路通到哪里去？	
How far away is ____?	_____ *hái yǒu duōyuǎn?* ____还有多远？	
■ the city	*Shìqū*	市区
■ the hotel	*Lǚguǎn*	旅馆
How long does it take to get to ____?	*Dào ____ qù yào duōjiǔ?* 到____去要多久？	
I'm lost.	*Wǒ mí lù le.* 我迷路了。	
Please tell me how to get to ____.	*Qǐng gàosu wǒ dào ____ zěnme zǒu?* 请告诉我到____怎么走？	

c = ts; *q* = ch; *x* = sh; *z* = dz; *zh* = j

RELIGIOUS SERVICES

Where can I find a(an) ____?	*Nǎlí yǒu* ____. 哪里有____。	
■ Buddhist temple	*Fójiào miào*	佛教庙
■ Catholic church	*Tiānzhǔ jiàotáng*	天主教堂
■ Confucian temple	*Kǒng miào*	孔庙
■ Daoist temple	*Dào guàn*	道观
■ Lama temple	*Lǎmā miào*	喇嘛庙
■ Mormon church	*Mómén jiàotáng*	摩门教堂
■ Mosque	*Qīngzhēn sì*	清真寺
■ Orthodox church	*Dōng zhèng jiào jiàotáng*	东正教教堂
■ Protestant church	*Jīdū jiàotáng*	基督教堂
■ Synagogue	*Yóutàijiào huìtáng*	犹太教会堂
At what time do services begin?	*Shénme shíhòu kāishǐ zuò lǐbài?* 什么时候开始作礼拜？	
Do you celebrate ____ mass here?	*Zhèlǐ zuò* ____ *mísā ma?* 这里做____弥撒？	
■ Chinese	*Zhōngwén*	中文
■ English	*Yīngwén*	英文
■ Latin	*Lādīng*	拉丁
Is there an empty seat?	*Yǒu kōng wèi ma?* 有空位吗？	

May I make a contribution?	*Wǒ kéyǐ juānxiàn ma?* 我可以捐献吗？	
Where is your collection box?	*Fēngxiàn xiāng zài náli?* 奉献箱在哪里？	
How old is this church?	*Zhèige jiàotáng duō lǎo le?* 这个教堂多老了？	
I would like to meet a(n) ____.	*Wó xiǎng jiàn ____.* 我想见___。	
■ abbot (Buddhist)	*fāngzhàng*	方丈
■ abbot (Daoist)	*zhùchí*	住持
■ archbishop	*dà zhǔjiào*	大主教
■ bishop	*zhǔjiào*	主教
■ cantor	*lǐngchàngzhě*	领唱者
■ cardinal	*shūjī zhǔjiào*	枢机主教
■ clergy member	*shénzhi rényuán*	神职人员
■ elder	*zhánglǎo*	长老
■ imam	*āhōng*	阿訇
■ lama	*lǎmā*	喇嘛
■ metropolitan	*dū zhǔjiào*	都主教
■ minister; pastor	*mùshī*	牧师
■ monk (Buddhist)	*héshàng*	和尚
■ monk (Christian)	*xiūshì*	修士
■ monk (Daoist)	*dàoshì*	道士
■ nun (Buddhist)	*nígū*	尼姑

c = ts; *q* = ch; *x* = sh; *z* = dz; *zh* = j

■ nun (Christian)   *xiūnǚ*   修女
■ priest   *jiàoshī; shénfù*   教士；神父
■ rabbi   *lābǐ*   拉比

EASTERN WORSHIP

Buddha   *Fó*   佛

burn incense   *shào xiāng*   烧香

chant   *niàn jīng*   念经

Goddess of Mercy *Guānyīn*   观音

hymn   *shèng gē*   圣歌

pray   *qídǎo*   祈祷

worship   *zuò lǐbài*   作礼拜

FOOD AND DRINK

MAKING DINING ARRANGEMENTS

It wasn't too many years ago that you could get any kind of food you wanted in China—as long as it was Chinese food! Today, however, a variety of cuisines are available, especially in China's larger cities. This includes food from other Asian countries such as Japan, Korea, and Thailand, as well as, increasingly, French, Italian, American, and other Western cuisines. In Hong Kong and Taiwan, food from all over the world has long been available.

If you are willing to experiment a little, and if you are amenable to exploring small establishments whose atmosphere and sanitary conditions don't necessarily measure up to international standards, you can taste some of the best Chinese food in the world. Lots of family-owned establishments are to be found in the alleyways of virtually all Chinese cities, and there is a variety of delicacies available from street vendors as well. Prices are generally extremely reasonable.

Most foreigners feel more comfortable in the higher-end restaurants where service is good, facilities are clean, and yes, the prices are higher. The good news is that with the exception of a relatively small number of very pricey and pretentious establishments, even in the better restaurants food is still a bargain in China.

If you have a large party, or if you are staging a formal banquet, it is usually necessary to make arrangements ahead of time. This involves calling ahead to the restaurant and telling the proprietor how many people will be in your party and what time you plan to arrive. If you intend to leave the menu selections to the discretion of the restaurant, you will also need to specify how much you wish to spend per person, exclusive of beverages. The restaurant may quote a minimum charge per head. The price is often negotiable to a point.

c = ts; q = ch; x = sh; z = dz; zh = j

There is seldom an upward limit, should you decide to go all out, but after a certain point the management doesn't add more courses to the meal, just more expensive ingredients.

If you've booked ahead of time, a table will be all set up for your group when you arrive, your entire menu will be planned, and one or two service people may be assigned exclusively to your table.

This section gives you the necessary vocabulary for making dining arrangements.

I would like to make a reservation for ____.	*Wǒ yào dìng* ____. 我要定____。	
■ dinner this evening	*jīntiān de wǎnfàn*	今天的晚饭
■ dinner tomorrow evening	*míngtiān de wǎnfàn*	明天的晚饭
■ lunch today	*jīntiān de wǔfàn*	今天的午饭
■ lunch tomorrow	*míngtiān de wǔfàn*	明天的午饭
■ lunch the day after tomorrow	*hòutiān de wǎnfàn*	后天的晚饭
There are ____ people in our party.	*Wǒmén yǒu* ____ *wèi.* 我们有____位。	
We would like to pay ____ per head.	*Wǒmén yào dìng* ____ *yīge rén.* 我们要定____一个人。	
■ fifty yuan	*wǔshí yuán*	五十元
■ two hundred yuan	*liángbǎi yuán*	两百元
Can you make it a little cheaper please?	*Nǐ kéyǐ suàn piányi yīdiǎn ma?* 你可以算便宜一点吗？	
That doesn't include drinks, does it?	*Jíushuǐ zài wài, shì ma?* 酒水在外，是吗？	

We would like to arrive at ____.	*Wǒmén xiǎng ____ dào.* 我们想____到。	
■ 6:00 P.M.	*xiàwǔ liù diǎn*	下午六点
■ 7:30 P.M.	*xiàwǔ qī diǎn bàn*	下午七点半
■ exactly noon	*zhèngwǔ*	正午
We will order à la carte.	*Wǒmén yào língdiǎn.* 我们要零点。	

THE CHINESE BANQUET

The chances are excellent that some time during your stay in China you will find yourself the guest at a Chinese banquet. Whether your tour operator wants to give your tour group a taste of local cuisine, your business partner wants to celebrate a contract, or your government host simply wants to make you feel welcome, a banquet is usually in order when you visit the PRC.

The Chinese follow fairly predictable norms of behavior at banquets. They won't expect you to be completely schooled in banquet etiquette and will forgive you most of your errors. But they will be delighted at any attempt by you to follow their customs, so it's worth your while to learn a bit of the routine.

Your host will probably be there to greet you when you arrive at the restaurant. Generally, tea is served first, often before the guests actually sit down at the table. After small talk, the host will give the signal for all to take their seats. At formal banquets, seats are assigned according to a fairly orderly protocol pattern and placecards signal the arrangement; in less structured situations, the host may simply point you toward a particular seat. The guest of honor is usually seated to the right of the host.

The meal typically begins with a platter of cold appetizers. The Chinese hosts—or the restaurant staff—will serve these to you. It isn't polite to help yourself at first, and

c = ts; *q* = ch; *x* = sh; *z* = dz; *zh* = j

this is true of *each* dish as it is served. After the host has started a dish, however, you may begin to serve yourself. Bear in mind that the Chinese consider it their duty to see that your plate always has some food on it, so if you keep cleaning it, they will keep filling it up. Also be sure to pace yourself: if you eat the first two dishes to satiation, you won't have room for the eight to ten dishes that may follow. A meal will generally continue through sweet, sour, salty, and spicy dishes—four of the five basic Chinese tastes—and your signal that the end is drawing near is the fish dish and perhaps a bowl of rice. After these, there will likely be a soup and a dessert.

EATING OUT

Where is a good restaurant?	*Nǎli yóu hǎo de fànguǎn?*	哪里有好的饭馆？
Is it very expensive?	*Hěnguì ma?*	很贵吗？
Which restaurant serves local dishes?	*Něige fànguǎn yóu běndì de míngcài?*	哪个饭馆有本地的名菜？
I would like to go to a _____ restaurant.	*Wó xiǎng qù yíge _____ guǎn.*	我想去一个___馆。
▓ Cantonese	*Guǎngdōng*	广东
▓ French	*Fǎguó cài*	法国菜
▓ Fujian	*Fújiàn cài*	福建菜
▓ German	*Déguó cài*	德国菜
▓ Hunan	*Húnán*	湖南
▓ Indian	*Yìndù cài*	印度菜
▓ Indonesian	*Yìnní cài*	印尼菜

	Italian	*Yìdàlì cài*	意大利菜
	Japanese	*Rìběn liàolǐ*	日本料理
	Korean	*Hánguó cài*	韩国菜
	Mandarin	*Běifāng*	北方
	Mexican	*Mòxīgē cài*	墨西哥菜
	Middle Eastern	*Zhōngdōng cài*	中东菜
	Mongolian	*Měnggǔ cài*	蒙古菜
	Moslem	*Qīngzhēn cài*	清真菜
	Peking duck	*Běijīng kǎoyā*	北京烤鸭
	Russian	*Éguó cài*	俄国菜
	seafood	*hǎixiān*	海鲜
	Shandong	*Shāndōng*	山东
	Shanghai	*Shànghǎi*	上海
	Sichuan (Szechuan)	*Sìchuān*	四川
	Southeast Asian	*Dōngnányà cài*	东南亚菜
	Taiwan	*Táiwān cài*	台湾菜
	Thai	*Tàiguó cài*	泰国菜
	vegetarian	*sùcài*	素菜
	Vietnamese	*Yuènán cài*	越南菜
	Western	*Xīcān*	西餐
	Xinjiang	*Xīnjiāng cài*	新疆菜
	Waiter! (younger man)	*Fúwùyuán!*	服务员！
	Waiter! (older man)	*Shīfu!*	师傅！

c = ts; *q* = ch; *x* = sh; *z* = dz; *zh* = j

Miss!	*Xiǎojiě!*	小姐！
A table for two, please.	*Liǎng wèi.*	两位。
We'd like to have lunch (dinner) now.	*Wǒmén xiànzài xiǎng chī zhōng (wǎn) fàn.*	我们现在想吃中（晚）饭。
The menu, please.	*Qǐng géi wǒ càidān.*	请给我菜单。
Where is the toilet?	*Cèsuǒ zài nálǐ?*	厕所在哪里？
Where can I wash my hands?	*Nálǐ kéyǐ xí shǒu?*	哪里可以洗手？
Can you recommend some dishes?	*Nǐ géi wǒmén jièshào cài hǎo ma?*	你给我们介绍菜好吗？
What is the chef's specialty?	*Dà shīfu náshǒu cài shì shénme?*	大师傅拿手菜是什么？
Please bring us ____.	*Qǐng géi wǒmén ____.*	请给我们____。
▩ an appetizer	*kāiwèi de xiǎocài*	开胃的小菜
▩ a beer	*píjiǔ*	啤酒
▩ a bottle of mineral water	*yì píng kuàngquán shuǐ*	一瓶矿泉水
▩ some cold (preboiled) water	*lěng kāishuǐ*	冷开水
▩ some tea	*chá*	茶
May I order now?	*Xiànzài kéyí diǎn cài ma?* 现在可以点菜吗？	

I'd like ____.	*Wó xiǎngyào* ____.	
	我想要____。	
Please also bring us ____.	*Qǐng lìngwài géi wǒmén* ____.	
	请另外给我们____。	

▨ a bowl	*yíge wǎn*	一个碗
▨ chopsticks	*kuàizi*	筷子
▨ a fork	*yíge chāzi*	一个叉子
▨ a glass	*yíge bēizi*	一个杯子
▨ a hot towel	*rè máojīn*	热毛巾
▨ a knife	*xīcān dāo*	西餐刀
▨ a napkin	*yì zhāng cānjīn*	一张餐巾
▨ noodles	*miàntiáo*	面条
▨ a plate	*yíge pánzi*	一个盘子
▨ rice	*mǐfàn*	米饭
▨ a spoon	*yíge tiáogēng*	一个调羹
▨ steamed bread	*mántóu*	馒头
▨ a toothpick	*yì gēn yáqiān*	一根牙签
▨ a wet towel	*shī máojīn*	湿毛巾

NOTE: Chinese table manners dictate that one cover one's mouth with one's hand while using a toothpick. The teeth should not be visible to others.

c = ts; q = ch; x = sh; z = dz; zh = j

SAUCES, SEASONINGS, AND CONDIMENTS

大蒜	*dàsuàn*	garlic
姜	*jiāng*	ginger
辣椒酱	*làjiāo jiàng*	hot pepper sauce
辣油	*làyóu*	hot sauce (oil)
芥末	*jièmò*	mustard
胡椒	*hújiāo*	pepper
盐	*yán*	salt
香油；蔴油	*xiāngyóu; máyóu*	sesame oil
酱油	*jiàngyóu*	soy sauce
蕃茄酱	*fānqié jiàng*	tomato sauce (also ketchup)
醋	*cù*	vinegar

CHINESE DISHES

APPETIZERS

叉烧肉	*chāshāo ròu*	barbecued pork
油焖笋	*yóumèn sǔn*	braised bamboo shoots
冷盘	*lěngpán*	cold platter
豆腐干	*dòufu gān*	dried bean curd
辣白菜	*là báicài*	hot pickled cabbage
海蜇皮	*hǎizhé pí*	jellyfish

酱牛肉	*jiàng niúròu*	marinated beef
锅贴	*guōtiē*	pan-fried pork dumplings
花生米	*huāshēng mǐ*	peanuts
腌黄瓜	*yān huángguā*	pickled cucumber
泡菜	*pàocài*	pickled vegetables
芝蔴鸡	*zhīmá jī*	sesame chicken
熏鸡	*xūn jī*	smoked chicken
春卷	*chūnjuǎn*	spring roll (egg roll)

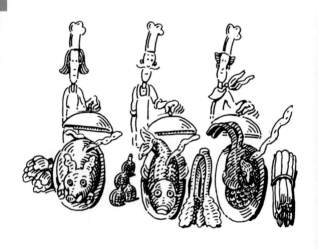

c = ts; *q* = ch; *x* = sh; *z* = dz; *zh* = j

MEAT DISHES

肉	*ròu*	meat
■ 牛肉	*niúròu*	beef
■ 猪肉	*zhūròu*	pork
■ 羊肉	*yángròu*	lamb
扣肉	*kòuròu*	braised pork
宫保肉丁	*gōngbǎo ròu dīng*	diced pork with hot peppers
回锅肉	*huíguō ròu*	double-cooked pork
鱼香肉丝	*yúxiāng ròu sī*	spicy shredded pork
木须肉	*mùxū ròu*	stir-fried pork with egg and black fungus (generally served with thin pancakes)
糖醋排骨	*tángcù páigǔ*	sweet-and-sour spareribs
糖醋里脊	*tángcù lǐjī*	sweet-and-sour boneless pork
牛肉丸	*niúròu wán*	beef meatballs
蚝油牛肉	*háoyóu niúròu*	beef with oyster sauce
红烧牛肉	*hóngshāo niúròu*	braised beef
蒙古烤肉	*Ménggú kǎo ròu*	Mongolian barbecue (beef and fresh vegetables grilled in a barbecue sauce)

干煸牛肉丝	*gānbiān niúròu sī*	sautéed shredded beef
青椒牛肉丝	*qīngjiāo niúròu sī*	shredded beef with peppers
芥兰牛肉	*gàilán niúròu*	sliced beef with Chinese broccoli
雪豆牛肉	*xuědòu niúròu*	stir-fried beef with snow peas
羊肉串	*yángròu chuàn*	lamb shish kabob
涮羊肉	*Shuàn yángròu*	Mongolian hot pot (slices of lamb and assorted vegetables in a cauldron of boiling water, then dipped in sauce)
葱爆羊肉	*cōngbào yángròu*	quick-fried lamb with scallions

POULTRY

鸡	*jī*	chicken
鸭	*yā*	duck
鹅	*é*	goose
鸽子	*gēzi*	pigeon
醉鸡	*zuì jī*	chicken in wine
陈皮鸡	*chénpí jī*	chicken with orange peel

c = ts; *q* = ch; *x* = sh; *z* = dz; *zh* = j

棒棒鸡	*bàngbang jī*	cold chicken with spicy sesame sauce
脆皮鸡	*cuìpí jī*	crispy-skin chicken
腰果鸡丁	*yāoguǒ jīdīng*	diced chicken with cashew nuts
宫保鸡丁	*gōngbǎo jīdīng*	diced chicken with hot peppers
柠檬鸡	*níngméng jī*	lemon chicken
纸包鸡	*zhǐbāo jī*	paper-wrapped chicken
怪味鸡	*guàiwèi jī*	strange-tasting chicken (cooked chicken slices marinated in garlic and soy sauce)
樟茶鸭	*zhāngchá yā*	camphor and tea smoked duck
香酥鸭	*xiāngsū yā*	crispy duck
卤鸭	*lǔ yā*	duck braised in soy sauce
南京板鸭	*Nánjīng bǎn yā*	Nanjing steamed duck cutlets
北京烤鸭	*Běijīng kǎo yā*	Peking roast duck
咸水鸭	*xiánshuǐ yā*	saltwater duck
红烧鸭	*hóngshāo yā*	stewed duck
炸鸽子	*zhá gēzi*	deep-fried pigeon

| 炒鸽松 | *chǎo gē sōng* | fried minced pigeon |

SEAFOOD

鲍鱼	*bàoyú*	abalone
红烧鱼	*hóngshāo yú*	braised fish
红烧鱼肚	*hóngshāo yúdǔ*	braised fish maw
红烧海参	*hóngshāo hǎishēn*	braised sea cucumber
蛤蜊	*géli*	clams
螃蟹	*pángxiè*	crab
脆皮鱼	*cuìpí yú*	crispy-skin fish
墨鱼	*mòyú*	cuttlefish
炸虾球	*zhá xiā qiú*	deep-fried shrimp balls
鳗鱼	*mányú*	eel
鱼	*yú*	fish
豆瓣鱼	*dòubàn yú*	fish with hot bean sauce
炒螃蟹	*chǎo pángxiè*	fried crab
青豆虾仁	*qīngdòu xiārén*	fried shrimp with green peas
海蜇皮	*hǎizhé pí*	jellyfish
龙虾	*lóngxiā*	lobster
蚝	*háo*	oysters
明虾	*míngxiā*	prawns

c = ts; *q* = ch; *x* = sh; *z* = dz; *zh* = j

干炒明虾	*gānchǎo míngxiā*	sautéed prawns
干贝	*gānbèi*	scallops
海参	*hǎishēn*	sea cucumber (sea slug)
虾	*xiā*	shrimp
腰果虾仁	*yāoguǒ xiārén*	shrimp with cashew nuts
芙蓉虾仁	*fúróng xiārén*	shrimp with egg white
宫保虾仁	*gōngbǎo xiārén*	shrimp with hot peppers
熏鱼	*xūn yú*	smoked fish
鱿鱼	*yóuyú*	squid
清蒸鳗鱼	*qīngzhēng mányú*	steamed eel
清蒸全鱼	*qīngzhēng quán yú*	steamed whole fish
炒鱼片	*chǎo yú piàn*	stir-fried sliced fish
糖醋鱼	*tángcù yú*	sweet-and-sour fish
糖醋虾	*tángcù xiā*	sweet-and-sour shrimp
西湖脆鱼	*Xīhú cuì yú*	West Lake crispy fish
松子黄鱼	*sōngzǐ huángyú*	yellow croaker with pine nuts

VEGETABLES

竹笋	*zhúsǔn*	bamboo shoot
豆腐	*dòufu*	bean curd
豆芽	*dòuyá*	bean sprout
苦瓜	*kǔguā*	bitter melon
西兰花	*xīlánhuā*	broccoli
洋白菜	*yáng báicài*	cabbage
胡萝卜	*hú luóbo*	carrot
菜花	*càihuā*	cauliflower
腰果	*yāoguǒ*	cashew nut
芹菜	*qíncài*	celery
粟子	*lìzi*	chestnut
芥兰	*gàilán*	Chinese broccoli
韭菜	*jiǔcài*	Chinese chives
玉米	*yùmǐ*	corn
黄瓜	*huángguā*	cucumber
茄子	*qiézi*	eggplant
青椒	*qīngjiāo*	green pepper
生菜	*shēngcài*	lettuce
莲藕	*liánǒu*	lotus root
蘑菇	*mógū*	mushroom
■ 草菇	*cǎogū*	straw mushroom
■ 香菇	*xiānggū*	black mushroom

c = ts; *q* = ch; *x* = sh; *z* = dz; *zh* = j

洋葱	*yángcōng*	onion
花生	*huāshēng*	peanut
土豆；洋芋；马铃薯	*tǔdòu; yángyù; mǎlíngshǔ*	potato
豌豆；雪豆	*wāndòu; xuědòu*	snow pea
黄豆；大豆	*huángdòu; dàdòu*	soybean
菠菜	*bōcài*	spinach
葱	*cōng*	spring onion (scallion)
扁豆；四季豆	*biǎndòu; sìjìdòu*	string bean
芋头	*yùtóu*	taro
西红柿；番茄	*xīhóngshì; fānqié*	tomato
萝卜	*luóbo*	turnip
核桃	*hétáo*	walnut
荸荠	*bíqí*	water chestnut
冬瓜	*dōngguā*	winter melon

VEGETABLE DISHES

沙锅豆腐	*shāyuō dòufu*	bean curd in casserole
麻婆豆腐	*mápó dòufu*	bean curd with minced pork in hot sauce
红烧豆腐	*hóngshāo dòufu*	braised bean curd in soy sauce
家常豆腐	*jiācháng dòufu*	family-style bean curd

酿豆腐	*niàng dòufu*	stuffed bean curd
蚝油芥兰	*háoyóu gàilán*	broccoli in oyster sauce
奶油白菜	*nǎiyóu báicài*	Chinese cabbage in cream sauce
炒双冬	*chǎo shuāngdōng*	sautéed black mushrooms and bamboo shoots
素什锦	*sù shíjǐn*	sautéed mixed vegetables
干煸四季豆	*gānbiān sìjìdòu*	sautéed string beans
鱼香茄子	*yúxiāng qiézi*	spicy eggplant with garlic

SOUPS

青菜豆腐汤	*qīngcài dòufu tāng*	bean curd and vegetable soup
牛肉汤	*niúròu tāng*	beef broth
玉米汤	*yùmǐ tāng*	corn chowder
蛋花汤	*dànhuā tāng*	egg-drop soup
火腿冬瓜汤	*huótuǐ dōngguā tāng*	ham and winter melon soup
醋辣汤	*suān là tāng*	hot-and-sour soup
海鲜汤	*hǎixiān tāng*	seafood soup
鱼翅汤	*yúchì tāng*	shark's fin soup

c = ts; *q* = ch; *x* = sh; *z* = dz; *zh* = j

榨菜肉丝汤	*zhàcài ròusī tāng*	shredded pork and preserved vegetable soup
汤	*tāng*	soup
馄饨汤	*húndùn tāng*	wonton soup

STARCHES

米饭	*mǐfàn*	rice
▓ 蒸饭	*zhēng fàn*	steamed rice
▓ 炒饭	*chǎo fàn*	fried rice
面包	*miànbāo*	bread
馒头	*mántóu*	steamed bread
牛肉饺	*niúròu jiǎo*	beef dumplings
猪肉饺	*zhūròu jiǎo*	pork dumplings
▓ 水饺	*shuíjiǎo*	boiled pork dumplings
▓ 锅贴	*guōtiē*	fried pork dumplings
▓ 蒸饺	*zhēngjiǎo*	steamed pork dumplings
三鲜饺	*sānxiān jiǎo*	"three delights" dumplings (usually shrimp, chicken, and pork or beef)
素菜饺	*sùcài jiǎo*	vegetarian dumplings
面条	*miàntiáo*	noodles

___炒面	___ *chǎo miàn*	fried noodles
牛肉	*niúròu*	with beef
猪肉	*zhūròu*	with pork
鸡肉	*jīròu*	with chicken
虾仁	*xiārén*	with shrimp
素菜	*sùcài*	with vegetables
汤面	*tāng miàn*	noodles in broth
担担面	*dàndan miàn*	spicy sesame noodles
薄饼	*báobǐng*	Mandarin pancakes
花卷	*huājuǎn*	steamed rolls (flower-shaped)
包子	*bāozi*	steamed stuffed pork buns
番薯	*fānshǔ*	sweet potato
馄饨	*húndùn*	wontons

ORDERING

I (don't) like to eat fish.	*Wǒ (bù) xǐhuān chī yú.* 我（不）喜欢吃鱼。
I love to eat shrimp.	*Wǒ ài chī xiā.* 我爱吃虾。
Is the fish fresh?	*Yú xīnxiān ma?* 鱼新鲜吗？
I'd like to eat meat.	*Wǒ hén xiǎng chī ròu.* 我很想吃肉。

s; *q* = ch; *x* = sh; *z* = dz; *zh* = j

I don't eat meat.	*Wǒ bù chī ròu.* 我不吃肉。	
I don't like pork.	*Wǒ bù xǐhuān chī zhūròu.* 我不喜欢吃猪肉。	
I like to eat chicken.	*Wó xǐhuān chī jīròu.* 我喜欢吃鸡肉。	
I don't want to try pigeon.	*Wǒ bú yuànyì chī gēzi.* 我不愿意吃鸽子。	
I'd like to eat a lot of vegetables.	*Wó xiǎng duō chī sùcài.* 我想多吃素菜。	
I hate vegetables.	*Wó tǎoyàn chī sùcài.* 我讨厌吃素菜。	
What kind of soup do you have?	*Nǐmén yǒu shénme tāng?* 你们有什么汤？	
I want a bowl of ____.	*Wǒ yào yì wǎn ____.* 我要一碗____。	

FRUITS AND DESSERTS

Dessert doesn't play the central role in Chinese cuisine that it does in the West. It often doesn't figure at all in the daily fare of the Chinese, who generally enjoy tea after a meal, occasionally complemented by fresh fruit. In a banquet situation, something sweet is usually served at the end of the meal, either fruit or some sort of steamed pastry.

杏仁豆腐	*xìngrén dòufu*	almond gelatin
苹果	*píngguǒ*	apple
拔丝苹果	*básī píngguǒ*	hot candied apples
香蕉	*xiāngjiāo*	banana

拔丝香蕉	*básī xiāngjiāo*	hot candied bananas
豆沙包	*dòushā bāo*	sweet bean buns
豆腐花	*dòufǔhuā*	sweet bean curd pudding
蛋糕	*dàn gāo*	cake
樱桃	*yīngtáo*	cherry
椰子	*yēzi*	coconut
新鲜水果	*xīnxiān shuíguǒ*	fresh fruit
葡萄	*pútáo*	grape
绿豆汤	*lǜdòu tāng*	green bean soup
冰淇淋	*bīngqílín*	ice cream
柠檬	*níngméng*	lemon
荔枝	*lìzhī*	lichee
芒果	*mángguǒ*	mango
哈密瓜	*hāmìguā*	muskmelon
橘子	*júzi*	orange
木瓜	*mùguā*	papaya
桃子	*táozi*	peach
梨子	*lízi*	pear
柿子	*shìzi*	persimmon
菠萝；凤梨	*bōluó; fènglí*	pineapple
李子	*lǐzi*	plum
红豆汤	*hóngdòu tāng*	red bean soup

; *q* = ch; *x* = sh; *z* = dz; *zh* = j

八宝饭	*bābǎo fàn*	eight-treasures glutinous rice pudding
西米露	*xīmǐlù*	tapioca cream
西瓜	*xīguā*	watermelon
千层糕	*qiāncéng gāo*	steamed layer cake

BEVERAGES

Formal Chinese banquets generally involve drinking and toasting. Usually the host is the first to offer a toast to his or her guests, and the principal guest is expected to reciprocate with another toast in response. While this is generally done with an alcoholic beverage, it need not be; you may toast with a soft drink if you prefer. Here are the names of beverages—some unique to China.

Do you have any ____?	*Nǐmén yǒu ____ ma?* 你们有____吗？	
I want a glass (cup) of ____.	*Wǒ yào yì bēi ____.* 我要一杯____。	
▥ milk	*niúnǎi*	牛奶
▥ juice	*guǒzhī*	果汁
▥ tea	*chá*	茶
▥ coffee	*kāfēi*	咖啡
▥ hot chocolate	*rè kěkě*	热可可
Please give me a bottle of ____.	*Qǐng géi wǒ yì píng ____.* 请给我一瓶____。	
▥ beer	*píjiǔ*	啤酒
▥ brandy	*báilándì*	白兰地
▥ Champagne	*xiāngbīnjiǔ*	香槟酒

▪ cognac	*shàngděng báilándì*	上等白兰地
▪ mineral water	*kuàngquán shuǐ*	矿泉水
▪ wine	*pútáo jiǔ*	葡萄酒
▪ rice wine	*míjiǔ*	米酒
▪ yellow rice wine	*huángjiǔ*	黄酒
▪ soda (pop)	*qìshuǐ*	汽水
▪ soda water	*sūdá shuǐ*	苏打水
▪ whiskey	*wēishìjì*	威士忌
白酒	*báijiǔ*	spirits (general term for liquor distilled from wheat, sorghum, or corn)
高粱酒	*gāoliángjiǔ*	kaoliang (also a sorghum-based spirit)
茅台酒	*Máotái jiǔ*	Maotai (distilled sorghum liquor made in Guizhou Province)
绍兴酒	*Shàoxīng jiǔ*	Shaoxing rice wine (fermented wine made in Zhejiang Province)
五粮液	*Wǔliángyè*	Five-grains liquor (made in Sichuan Province)

q = ch; *x* = sh; *z* = dz; *zh* = j

汾酒	*Fénjiŭ*	Fenjiu (a sorghum spirit made in Shanxi Province)

WESTERN FOOD

Where is the closest Western restaurant?	*Zuìjìn de Xīcānguăn zài nálĭ?*	最近的西餐馆在哪里？
Where is a fast-food restaurant?	*Nálĭ yŏu kuàicān diàn?*	哪里有快餐店？
I would like to order ____.	*Wó xiáng diăn ____.*	我想点____。
▓ a cheeseburger	*năilào hànbăo bāo*	奶酪汉堡包
▓ french fried potatoes	*zhá shŭtiáo*	炸薯条
▓ fried chicken	*zhá jī*	炸鸡
▓ a hamburger	*hànbăo bāo*	汉堡包
▓ a hot dog	*rè gŏu*	热狗
▓ onion rings	*zhá yángcōng quān*	炸洋葱圈
▓ a pizza	*bĭsà bĭng*	比萨饼
Do you have any ____?	*Nĭmén yŏu méiyŏu ____?*	你们有没有____？
▓ baked potato	*káo tŭdòu*	烤土豆
▓ mashed potatoes	*tŭdòuní*	土豆泥
▓ spaghetti	*Yìdàlì shì miàntiáo*	意大利式面条
▓ steak	*niúpái*	牛排

I would like my meat cooked ____.	*Wǒde kǎoròu yào ____.* 我的烤肉要____。	
▪ rare	*nèn yìdiǎn*	嫩一点
▪ medium	*bú nèn bù lǎo*	不嫩不老
▪ well-done	*lǎo yìdiǎn*	老一点

I would like ____ chops.	*Wó xiǎngyào ____ pái.* 我想要____排。	
▪ lamb	*yáng*	羊
▪ pork	*zhū*	猪

Please bring me a (an) ____ sandwich.	*Qǐng géi wǒ ____ sānmíngzhì.* 请给我____三明治。	
▪ bacon	*xūnròu*	熏肉
▪ bacon, lettuce, and tomato	*xūnròu shēngcài xīhóngshì*	熏肉、生菜、西红柿
▪ cheese	*nǎilào*	奶酪
▪ chicken	*jīròu*	鸡肉
▪ club	*zǒnghuì*	总会
▪ egg	*jīdàn*	鸡蛋
▪ fish	*yúròu*	鱼肉

Do you have a salad bar?	*Nǐmén yǒu méiyǒu shālā zìzhùguì?* 你们有没有沙拉自助柜？	
What kind of salad do you have?	*Nǐmén yǒu shénme yàng de shālā?* 你们有什么样的沙拉？	
▪ Caesar salad	*Kǎisā shālā*	凯萨沙拉
▪ chicken salad	*jīròu shālā*	鸡肉沙拉

▥ egg salad	*jīdàn shālā*	鸡蛋沙拉
▥ green salad	*shūcài shālā*	蔬菜沙拉
▥ spinach salad	*bōcài shālā*	菠菜沙拉
▥ tuna salad	*jīnqiāng yú shālā*	金枪鱼沙拉

I would like ____ dressing on my salad.	*Wó xiǎngyào ____ shālā jiàng.*	我想要____沙拉酱。
▥ bleu cheese	*lán nǎilào*	蓝奶酪
▥ French	*Fǎguó*	法国
▥ Italian	*Yìdàlì*	意大利
▥ oil and vinegar	*yóu cù*	油醋
▥ Russian	*Éluósī*	俄罗斯
▥ thousand island	*qiān dǎo*	千岛

Do you have any ____?	*Nǐmén yǒu méiyǒu ____?*	你们有没有____？
▥ cheese	*nǎilào*	奶酪
▥ chili sauce	*làjiāo jiàng*	辣椒酱
▥ horseradish	*làgēn jiàng*	辣根酱
▥ ketchup	*fānqié jiàng*	番茄酱
▥ mayonnaise	*dànhuáng jiàng*	蛋黄酱
▥ mustard	*jièmò*	芥末
▥ pepper	*hújiāo*	胡椒
▥ salt	*yán*	盐
▥ sour cream	*suān nǎiyóu*	酸奶油
▥ steak sauce	*niúpái jiàng*	牛排酱

What kind of soup do you have?	*Nǐmén yǒu shénme yàng de tāng?*	你们有什么样的____汤？
▥ beef	*niúròu*	牛肉
▥ chicken	*jī*	鸡

■ French onion	*Fǎshì yángcōng*	法式洋葱
■ potato	*tǔdòu*	土豆
■ vegetable	*shūcài*	蔬菜

Please let me see the dessert menu.	*Qǐng géi wǒ kàn tiándiǎn dān.* 请给我看甜点单。	
■ cookies	*bǐnggān*	饼干
■ fruit	*shuíguǒ*	水果
■ ice cream	*bīngqīlín*	冰淇淋
■ pie	*pài*	排
■ pudding	*bùdīng*	布丁

What kind of cake do you have?	*Nǐmén yǒu shénme yàng de dàngāo?* 你们有什么样的蛋糕？	
■ cheese	*nǎilào*	奶酪
■ chocolate	*qiǎokèlì*	巧克力
■ sponge	*sōnggāo*	松糕

SPECIAL CIRCUMSTANCES

Many travelers have special dietary requirements, so here are a few phrases that might help you get what you need or avoid what you don't want or can't eat. There are also some phrases you might need to voice your complaints.

I don't want anything ____.	*Wǒ bú yào ____ cài.* 我不要____菜。	
■ fried	*chǎo de*	炒的
■ sweet	*tián de*	甜的
■ spicy	*là de*	辣的
I cannot eat anything ~~made~~ with ____.	*Wǒ bù néng chī yǒu ____ de cài.* 我不能吃有____的菜。	

q = ch; x = sh; z = dz; zh = j

▥ monosodium glutamate	*wèijīng*	味精
▥ salt	*yán*	盐
▥ sugar	*táng*	糖
I don't want any dishes with meat.	*Wǒ bú yào yǒu ròu de cài.*	我不要有肉的菜。
I'm a vegetarian.	*Wǒ chī sù.*	我吃素。
I don't eat ____.	*Wǒ bù chī ____.*	我不吃___。
▥ eggs	*dàn*	蛋
▥ pork	*zhūròu*	猪肉
▥ shellfish	*yǒu ké de yú xiā*	有壳的鱼虾
This food is undercooked.	*Zhèige tài shēngle.*	这个太生了。
The table isn't clean.	*Zhuōzi bù gānjìng.*	桌子不干净。
Please wipe off the table.	*Qǐng cā zhuōzi.*	请擦桌子。
This is dirty.	*Zhèige zāng le.*	这个脏了。
I am missing ____.	*Wǒ chà ____.*	我差___。
▥ one chopstick	*yì zhī kuàizi*	一只筷子
▥ a napkin	*yì zhāng cānjīn*	一张餐巾
▥ a glass	*yíge bēizi*	一个杯子
The food is ____.	*Cài ____.*	菜___。
▥ cold	*lěng le*	冷了
▥ not hot enough	*bú gòu rè*	不够热
There is too much fat.	*Féiròu tài duō.*	肥肉太多。
This is too ____.	*Zhèige tài ____.*	这个太___。
▥ salty	*xián*	咸
▥ sour	*suān*	酸

▥ bitter	*kǔ*	苦
▥ dry	*gān*	干
▥ oily	*yóunì*	油腻

This isn't fresh.

Zhèige bù xīnxiān.
这个不新鲜。

We have been waiting a long time.

Wǒmén děng le hén jiǔ le.
我们等了很久了。

Please bring our drinks.

Qǐng bá yǐnliào sòng lái.
请把饮料送来。

SETTLING UP

The check, please.

Qǐng jié zhàng. 请结帐。

Separate checks, please.

Qǐng fēnkāi suàn. 请分开算。

I didn't order this.

Wǒ méi jiào zhèige.
我没叫这个。

I don't think the bill is correct.

Wó xiǎng zhàngdān yǒu cuò.
我想帐单有错。

Where should we pay?

Dào nálǐ fù zhàng?
在哪里付帐？

May I use a credit card?

Wǒ kéyǐ yòng xìnyòng kǎ ma?
我可以用信用卡吗？

Is a service charge included?

Bāokuò fúwùfèi ma?
包括服务费吗？

How much is the service charge?

Fúwùfèi duōshǎo?
服务费多少？

May I have a receipt?

Qǐng kāi shōujù.
请开收据。

q = ch; *x* = sh; *z* = dz; *zh* = j

REGIONAL CHINESE SPECIALTIES

Just as the Chinese spoken language varies from province to province, so does Chinese cuisine. Each province has its own specialties, its own styles of cooking, and its own local ingredients. Be sure to ask for local specialties in each place you visit in China; you won't be disappointed.

The four major schools of Chinese cooking correspond to the four major geographic areas of this vast country—north, south, east, and west. Below is a general description of their special features.

Northern Chinese cuisine, also referred to as Mandarin cuisine, is the cooking of the provinces north of the Yangzi (Yangtse) River, including Hebei (which surrounds Beijing), Henan, Shandong, Shanxi, and Liaoning. Northerners eat a lot of beef, lamb, and duck and use garlic and scallions in abundance. Their grain intake is largely in wheat products, and they prefer relatively bland cooking, eschewing seasonings that are overly salty, sweet, or spicy.

Western Chinese cuisine is best known as the cooking of Sichuan and Hunan Provinces. The climate of this area is hot and humid a good deal of the year, and the hot peppers that grow in abundance are used liberally in cooking, giving the cuisine a well-deserved, fiery reputation. The people in this area also tend to use more salt in their cooking than do people in other regions.

Eastern Chinese cuisine, the cooking of the Shanghai, Jiangsu, and Zhejiang area, takes maximum advantage of the region's proximity to the sea and its large number of lakes—it is known for many varieties of seafood. Eastern cuisine features a cornucopia of fresh vegetables, including many types of bamboo, as well as the liberal use of soy sauce and sugar.

Southern Chinese cuisine features the cooking of Guangdong Province as well as that of Fujian and Taiwan. Like Eastern cooking, it relies heavily on seafood, fresh fruit, and vegetables. To preserve the natural flavors of the food, the cooks in this area prefer not to use strong seasonings.

Due to this region's traditional contact with the outside world, foreign ingredients have slowly crept in, so that cream sauces and baked pastries are not unknown. Barbecued meats are popular, and soups are prominently featured.

Cantonese cuisine is also known for a subspecialty called **dim sum**, which is described in the next section.

DIM SUM

Dim sum, pronounced **diǎn xīn** in Mandarin, merits a separate section because of its popularity and its special nature. It is native to southern China; however, it is widely available in Hong Kong, Southeast Asia, North America, and pretty much anywhere where there are large numbers of Cantonese people.

Dim sum consists of very small portions of snack foods, served with tea from late morning until early afternoon. In the most traditional restaurants the food is pushed along on carts, and you simply signal the waiter or waitress when you want a dish of whatever is on the cart. The whole idea of dim sum is to nibble on many different types of delicacies in a single sitting. Chinese also use dim sum brunches as an opportunity to catch up with friends, since the whole meal can last for hours.

Here are some of the most popular types of dim sum, plus some useful vocabulary for ordering it.

Where can I go to eat dim sum?	*Dào nǎli qù chī Guǎngdōng diǎnxīn?* 到哪里去吃广东点心？
Please write down the address of the restaurant.	*Qǐng bǎ fànguǎn dìzhí xiě xiàlái.* 请把饭馆地址写下来。

; q = ch; x = sh; z = dz; zh = j

We are a party of six.	*Wǒmén yǒu liù wèi.* 我们有六位。	
Please bring us a pot of ____ tea.	*Qǐng gěi wǒmén ____ chá.* 请给我们____茶。	
▦ 红	*hóng*	black
▦ 菊花	*júhuā*	chrysan-themum
▦ 清	*qīng*	green
▦ 茉莉花；香片	*mòlìhuā;* *xiāngpiàn*	jasmine
▦ 乌龙	*wūlóng*	oolong
请来一碟____。	*Qǐng lái yì* *dié ____.*	Please give me a plate of ____.
▦ 牛肉丸	*niúròu wán*	beef balls
▦ 牛肚	*niúdǔ*	beef tripe
▦ 椰塔	*yētǎ*	coconut tarts
▦ 芋角	*yùjiǎo*	deep-fried taro root
▦ 蛋塔	*dàntǎ*	egg tarts
▦ 锅贴	*guōtiē*	fried pork dumplings
▦ 烧卖	*shāomài*	open-topped steamed pork dumplings
▦ 虾丸	*xiā wán*	shrimp balls
▦ 虾饺	*xiā jiǎo*	shrimp dumplings
▦ 小笼包	*xiǎolóng bāo*	small steamed pork buns

■ 排骨	*páigǔ*	spareribs
■ 春卷	*chūnjuǎn*	spring rolls (egg rolls)
■ 肠粉	*cháng fěn*	steamed stuffed rice crêpes
■ 马拉糕	*mǎlā gāo*	steamed sponge cake
■ 叉烧包	*chāshāo bāo*	steamed roast pork buns
■ 酿豆腐	*niàng dòufu*	stuffed bean curd
■ 鸭掌	*yāzhǎng*	stuffed duck feet
■ 酿青椒	*niàng qīngjiāo*	stuffed peppers
■ 豆沙包	*dòushā bāo*	sweet bean buns
■ 糯米鸡	*nuòmǐ jī*	sweet rice with meat stuffed in lotus leaves
■ 萝卜糕	*luóbo gāo*	turnip cake
■ 馄饨	*húndùn*	wontons

c = ts; *q* = ch; *x* = sh; *z* = dz; *zh* = j

GETTING TO KNOW PEOPLE

MEETING PEOPLE

The Chinese much prefer formal introductions to striking up casual conversations as a means to making new friends. When a mutual friend introduces you to someone, you are automatically someone worthy of friendship and respect. Also, many Chinese are shy by nature and find it difficult to make the first move in uncertain social situations. If there is no one to make the introduction for you, it is all right to present yourself. As a rule, you will find the Chinese people to be extremely friendly to foreigners, and it's not at all uncommon for a Chinese to approach a foreigner on the street and begin to practice a little English.

If you want to engage someone in conversation, a smile and a **Ní hǎo?** (Hello) is often all that is necessary to begin. Areas of easy conversation include your nationality, the length of your intended stay in China, cities you hope to visit, your profession, and your family.

Cultural differences are many and are fun to discover. A basic one is Chinese group-consciousness, a marked contrast to the individual-centeredness common to many Western societies. Chinese are encouraged to conform, to accept authority, and to subordinate their individual wills and desires to those of the greater group to which they belong—whether their family, class at school, or work unit. Chinese often expect their foreign guests to behave in similar ways, and difficulties can occur, for example, when many members of a tour group begin to give different signals to the guide about what they want to do or where they want to go. The Chinese expect groups to have designated leaders and to speak with one voice, and they are sometimes disoriented when this is not the case.

Another cultural difference—not so surprising, perhaps, given the overcrowding and overpopulation in China—occurs over the notion of privacy. There is no good translation for the word *privacy* in Chinese, and your affairs are not necessarily presumed to be your own. Chinese people may innocently ask you questions you consider to be embarrassing—such as how much money you make or how much you paid for something—or occasionally a hotel service person may come bounding into your room without the courtesy of knocking first.

The concept of "face" is also central to any understanding of the differences between East and West. This is a subtle, intangible commodity related to one's dignity and prestige. To cause a person to "lose face" is a major affront. Be careful of criticizing a Chinese person in front of other people, or of insulting or making fun of someone. And understand that sometimes when you fail to get a direct answer to a question you pose to a Chinese, the reason may not be that he or she is being evasive, but that he or she is trying to spare you the loss of face that saying no to you would bring on.

No discussion of why the Chinese act as they do would be complete without mention of what the Chinese call **guānxi**. This term literally means "relationship," but is actually far better translated as "connections." Guanxi is sort of a tit-for-tat, "you-scratch-my-back, I'll-scratch-yours" arrangement, whereby favors are done and rules are bent and sometimes even broken for friends. It is a reciprocal obligation, and someone with whom you have established gūanxi may well expect your aid in solving a problem.

Sometimes foreigners are approached to do things that are illegal, such as changing money; presumptuous, such as sponsoring someone they hardly know for study abroad; or impossible, such as securing a foreign visa for someone. It's important to communicate as best you can that something is out of your control or very difficult for you to do in situations such as this; if your Chinese friend believes that you are simply unwilling to help, he or she will think that you have failed to discharge an obligation.

c = ts; *q* = ch; *x* = sh; *z* = dz; *zh* = j

As a general rule, Chinese are less likely to express emotions publicly than their Western counterparts. Negative feelings, in particular, such as jealousy, anger, disappointment, or unhappiness, are considered private matters, and letting such emotions run free is regarded as ill-mannered. When you come up against a frustrating situation in China—and it's likely that you will—try at all costs to keep your cool. You can of course convey anger or dissatisfaction with a particular set of circumstances, but try to do so without appearing visibly agitated. To do so will earn you more respect and will increase the likelihood of achieving your goal.

This section includes some basic vocabulary for breaking the ice with people you have not met before.

Hello. How do you do?	*Nǐ hǎo?*	你好？
My name is ____.	*Wǒ jiào ____.*	我叫____。
What is your name?	*Nǐ jiào shénme míngzì?*	你叫什么名字？
I'm an American.	*Wǒ shì Měiguó rén.*	我是美国人。
Do you live here?	*Nǐ zhù zhèli ma?*	你住这里吗？
I am from ____.	*Wǒ cóng ____ lái de.*	我从____来的。
■ the United States	*Měiguó*	美国
■ the U.K.	*Yīngguó*	英国
■ Canada	*Jiānádà*	加拿大
■ Australia	*Àozhōu*	澳洲
■ New Zealand	*Xīnxīlán*	新西兰
I like China very much.	*Wǒ hén xǐhuān Zhōngguó.* 我很喜欢中国。	

I would like to go there.	*Wǒ hén xiǎng dào nàli qù.*	我很想到那里去。
How long will you be staying?	*Nǐ yào dāi duōjiǔ?*	你要呆多久？
I'll stay for ____.	*Wǒ yào dāi ____.*	我要呆____。
■ a few days	*jǐ tiān*	几天
■ a week	*yì xīngqī*	一个星期
Where are you living now?	*Nǐ xiànzài zhù náli?*	你现在住哪里？
What hotel are you staying at?	*Nǐ zhù něige fàndiàn?*	你住哪个饭店？
I am staying at the ____ Hotel.	*Wǒ zhù ____ Fàndiàn.*	我住____饭店。
What do you think of ____?	*Nǐ duì ____ juéde zěnmeyàng?*	你对____觉得怎么样？
I don't like it very much.	*Wǒ bú tài xǐhuān.*	我不太喜欢。
I think it's very ____.	*Wǒ juéde hěn ____.*	我觉得很____。
■ interesting	*yǒu yìsi*	有意思
■ beautiful	*měi*	美
■ wonderful	*bàng*	棒

GREETINGS AND INTRODUCTIONS

May I please introduce my ____.	*Qǐng ràng wǒ jièshào wǒ de ____.*	请让我介绍我的____。
■ boss	*láobǎn*	老板

c = ts; *q* = ch; *x* = sh; *z* = dz; *zh* = j

▥ boyfriend	*nán péngyǒu*	男朋友
▥ classmate	*tóngxué*	同学
▥ colleague	*tóngshì*	同事
▥ elder brother	*gēge*	哥哥
▥ elder sister	*jiějie*	姐姐
▥ father	*bàba*	爸爸
▥ friend	*péngyǒu*	朋友
▥ girlfriend	*nǚ péngyǒu*	女朋友
▥ husband	*zhàngfu*	丈夫
▥ mother	*māma*	妈妈
▥ staff member	*gōngzuò rényuán*	工作人员
▥ student	*xuéshēng*	学生
▥ teacher	*lǎoshī*	老师
▥ wife	*tàitai*	太太
▥ younger brother	*dìdi*	弟弟
▥ younger sister	*mèimei*	妹妹

Glad to meet you.	*Hěn gāoxìng jiàndào nǐ.* 很高兴见到你。	
I'm honored.	*Wó hěn róngxìng.* 我很荣幸。	
Please allow me to introduce myself.	*Qǐng ràng wǒ jièshào wǒ zìjǐ.* 请让我介绍我自己。	
My name is ____. And yours?	*Wǒ jiào ____.* *Nǐ ne?*	我叫____。 你呢？
I am a (an) ____.	*Wǒ shì ____.*	我是____。
▥ accountant	*kuàijì shī*	会计师
▥ artist	*yìshù jiā*	艺术家
▥ athlete	*yùndòng yuán*	运动员

▦ banker	*yínháng jiā*	银行家
▦ businessperson	*shāngrén*	商人
▦ college professor	*dàxué jiàoshòu*	大学教授
▦ computer scientist	*jìsuànjī zhuānjiā*	计算机专家
▦ dancer	*wúdǎo jiā*	舞蹈家
▦ dentist	*yáyī*	牙医
▦ designer	*shèjì jiā*	设计家
▦ doctor	*yīshēng*	医生
▦ editor	*biānjì*	编辑
▦ engineer	*gōngchéng shī*	工程师
▦ farmer	*nóngmín*	农民
▦ government official	*zhèngfǔ guānyuán*	政府官员
▦ insurance salesman	*báoxiǎn yèzhě*	保险业者
▦ lawyer	*lǜshī*	律师
▦ musician	*yīnyuè jiā*	音乐家
▦ reporter	*jìzhě*	记者
▦ retired person	*tuìxiū rényuán*	退休人员
▦ scientist	*kēxué jiā*	科学家
▦ soldier	*jūnrén*	军人
▦ student	*xuéshēng*	学生
▦ teacher	*jiàoshī*	教师
▦ technician	*jìshù rényuán*	技术人员
▦ writer	*zuòjiā*	作家

c = ts; *q* = ch; *x* = sh; *z* = dz; *zh* = j

SOCIALIZING

You will find most Chinese people very curious about people from other countries, and quite open to making friends with foreigners. Most of the time, all it takes to start a friendship is some small talk to break the ice.

Where are you from?	*Nǐ cóng nǎli lái?* 你从哪里来？
Where is your original home?	*Nǐ de lǎojiā zài nǎli?* 你的老家在哪里？
How long have you lived here?	*Nǐ zài zhèli zhùle duōjiǔ?* 你在这里住了多久？
How many people are in your family?	*Nǐ de jiā yóu jǐge rén?* 你的家有几个人？
Are you married?	*Nǐ jiéhūn le ma?* 你结婚了吗？
Do you have any children?	*Nǐ yóu xiǎohái ma?* 你有小孩吗？
What are their ages?	*Tāmen duō dà?* 他们多大？
We have children the same age.	*Wǒmèn de xiǎohái yíyàng dà.* 我们的小孩一样大。
What is your work unit?	*Nǐ zài něige dānwèi gōngzuò?* 你在哪个单位工作？
Have you ever traveled abroad?	*Nǐ dào guò guówài ma?* 你到过国外吗？
To which countries?	*Dàoguò něixiē guójiā?* 到过哪些国家？

Can you give me your telephone number?	*Nǐ néng gàosu wó nǐ de diànhuà hàomǎ ma?* 你能告诉我你的电话号码吗？
What is your telephone number?	*Nǐ de diànhuà hàomǎ duōshǎo?* 你的电话号码多少？
What is your address?	*Nǐ de dìzhǐ shì shénme?* 你的地址是什么？
Do you have a fax number?	*Nǐ yǒu chuánzhēnjī hàomǎ ma?* 你有传真机号码吗？
What is your e-mail address?	*Nǐde diànzǐ yóujiàn xìnxiāng shìshénme?* 你的电子邮件信箱是什么？
Here's my address.	*Zhè shì wǒ de dìzhǐ.* 这是我的地址。
Here's my telephone number.	*Zhè shì wǒ de diànhuà hàomǎ.* 这是我的电话号码。
May I write to you?	*Wǒ kéyǐ géi ní xiě xìn ma?* 我可以给你写信吗？
Will you write back?	*Nǐ huì huí xìn ma?* 你会回信吗？
May I take a picture of you?	*Wǒ géi nǐ zhàoxiàng hǎo ma?* 我给你照相好吗？
Please stand here.	*Qǐng zhàn zài zhèli.* 请站在这里。
Don't move.	*Bié dòng le.*　　别动了。
Smile!	*Xiào!*　　笑！

c = ts; *q* = ch; *x* = sh; *z* = dz; *zh*σj

Will you take a picture of me (us)?

Qǐng bāng wǒ (wǒmén) zhào ge xiàng hǎo ma?

请帮我（我们）照个相好吗？

Are you doing anything tomorrow?

Nǐ míngtiān yǒu shì ma?

你明天有事吗？

Are you free this evening?

Nǐ jīnwǎn yǒu kòng ma?

你今晚有空吗？

Would you like to go together?

Ní xiǎng yìqǐ qù ma?

你想一起去吗？

I'll wait for you in front of the hotel.

Wǒ zài fàndiàn ménkǒu děng nǐ.

我在饭店门口等你。

I'll pick you up at ____.

Wǒ zài ____ jiē nǐ.

我在___接你。

SAYING GOOD-BYE

I'm happy to have met you.

Hěn gāoxìng rènshi nǐ.

很高兴认识你。

I hope to see you again sometime.

Xīwàng yǐhòu zài jiàndào nǐ.

希望以后再见到你。

I wish you a safe trip.

Zhù nǐ yí lù píng ān.

祝你一路平安。

Please send my regards to ____.

Qǐng wènhòu ____.

请问候___。

This was a very nice evening.

Jīnwǎn hěn yúkuài.

今晚很愉快。

You must come to visit us.

Nǐ yídìng yào lái kàn wǒmén.

你一定要来看我们。

Good-bye.

Zàijiàn.　　再见。

GESTURES

Some of your most natural gestures may not evoke the same responses from a Chinese that they would from another Westerner. A shoulder shrug signifying "I don't know" or an erect index finger signaling "just one moment," for example, aren't readily understood in China. Some gestures, on the other hand, are very easily interpreted and occasionally even shared by the Chinese. Giving the "thumbs up" sign, for example, is read in both cultures to be a positive evaluation of something; nodding and shaking one's head for yes or no are also understood. And, unlike the Japanese, shaking hands as a form of greeting is quite normal to the Chinese. You may notice a slight nodding of the head together with the handshake—but you'll never see a Chinese bow at the waist in Japanese fashion.

You may also experience some gestures that are peculiarly Chinese. "Come here" is communicated with a palm-down hand outstretched toward the listener, waving up and down—the Chinese don't use their fingers to motion toward themselves. And the numbers from one to ten all are signified by special hand motions.

Be aware that the Chinese find some postures and movements offensive. It isn't polite, for example, to show someone the bottoms of your feet. It's also not appropriate to give an enthusiastic bear hug or a slap on the back to a Chinese you don't know well. Above all, be careful not to come into physical contact with a Chinese of the opposite sex you do not know extremely well. This could easily be misconstrued.

The Chinese, for their part, may surprise or even offend you with some of their habits. Belching, expelling mucus, and even passing gas in public are common, and little is thought of spitting on the street, though the government has been trying to discourage this habit. Chinese smokers are indiscriminate as to location; there is little recognition that smoke may be considered offensive by a nonsmoker. And pointing to people—even staring at them—is not considered a breach of etiquette.

The concept of personal distance also differs among cultures, and in China someone may jar you a bit by standing or sitting at a distance you consider to be too close. You may also be surprised if a Chinese of the same sex is quite physical around you. It's common in China for someone of the same sex to put his arm around a friend, or lean on him, or gently nudge him through a doorway, or even hold hands. You should be aware that there are generally no sexual overtones to same-sex touching in China.

SHOPPING

GOING SHOPPING

There are many wonderful things to buy in China, and many types of places that sell them. Whether you visit a small specialty store, a large department store, an outdoor market, or a street vendor, shopping can be a lot of fun. The Chinese themselves love to shop, and for this reason markets are often extremely crowded.

Large, state-run stores are usually fixed-price establishments, but bargaining is the rule elsewhere. When goods are not marked, the price quoted to a foreign visitor may sometimes be quite a bit inflated over that charged to local residents. You can usually get a merchant to shave 5 to 10 percent off any quoted price; hard bargaining can often result in even larger discounts.

Specialty shops exist side by side with large department stores in China. There are bookstores, clothing stores, shoe stores, hat shops, jewelry stores, souvenir stores, camera and photographic stores, antique stores, stationery stores, arts and crafts shops, music and electronics stores, toy stores, opticians, barber and beauty shops, newsstands, and pharmacies. For certain merchandise such as electrical appliances, housewares, and toiletries, your best bet may be the local department stores, where the selection is often quite good. Food can be purchased at supermarkets as well as open-air fruit and vegetable markets.

I'd like to go shopping today.	*Wǒ jīntiān xiǎng qù mǎi dōngxi.* 我今天想去买东西。
Where is there a(n) ____?	*Nǎli yǒu ____?* 哪里有____?

c = ts; *q* = ch; *x* = sh; *z* = dz; *zh* = j

▥ antique shop	*gúdǒng diàn*	古董店
▥ appliance store	*jiāyòng diànqì háng*	家用电器行
▥ bakery	*gāobǐng diàn*	糕饼店
▥ barbershop	*lǐfà guǎn*	理发馆
▥ beauty parlor	*měiróng yuàn*	美容院
▥ bookstore	*shūdiàn*	书店
▥ camera shop	*zhàoxiàng qìcái háng*	照相器材行
▥ candy store	*tángguǒ diàn*	糖果店
▥ coffee shop	*kāfēi diàn*	咖啡店
▥ clothing store	*fúzhuāng diàn*	服装店
▥ department store	*bǎihuò shāngdiàn*	百货商店
▥ drugstore	*yàofáng*	药房
▥ fabric store	*bù diàn*	布店
▥ florist	*huā diàn*	花店
▥ furrier	*píhuò diàn*	皮货店
▥ food market	*cài shìchǎng*	菜市场
▥ gift shop	*lǐpǐn diàn*	礼品店
▥ hardware store	*wǔjīn háng*	五金行
▥ hat shop	*màozi diàn*	帽子店
▥ Internet café	*Yīngtèwǎng kāfēitīng*	英特网咖啡厅
▥ jewelry store	*zhūbǎo diàn*	珠宝店
▥ laundry	*xǐyī diàn*	洗衣店
▥ leather goods store	*píhuò diàn*	皮货店
▥ liquor store	*mài jiǔ de diàn*	卖酒的店

▩ newsstand	*bàotān*	报摊
▩ optician	*yǎnjìng háng*	眼镜行
▩ pawnshop	*dàng pù*	当铺
▩ photographer	*zhàoxiàng guǎn*	照相馆
▩ record store	*chàngpiàn háng*	唱片行
▩ second-hand store	*jiùhuò diàn*	旧货店
▩ shoe repair shop	*xiū xié diàn*	修鞋店
▩ shoe store	*xiédiàn*	鞋店
▩ snack shop	*xiǎochī diàn*	小吃店
▩ stationery store	*wénjù diàn*	文具店
▩ supermarket	*cháojī shìchǎng*	超级市场
▩ tailor (for Western-style clothing)	*xīzhuāng diàn*	西装店
▩ tobacco shop	*yāncǎo diàn*	烟草店
▩ toy store	*wánjù diàn*	玩具店
▩ variety store	*záhuò diàn*	杂货店
▩ watch repair shop	*xiū biǎo diàn*	修表店
Sir!	*Shīfu!*	师傅！
Miss!	*Xiáojiě!*	小姐！
Young man! (service person)	*Fúwùyuán!*	服务员！
Can you help me?	*Nǐ néng bāng wǒ ma?*	你能帮我吗？

c = ts; *q* = ch; *x* = sh; *z* = dz; *zh* = j

How much is this?	*Zhèige duōshǎo qián?* 这个多少钱？
I would like three of them.	*Wó xiǎngyào sāngè.* 我想要三个。
Is the price negotiable?	*Kéyí jiǎng jià mā?* 可以讲价吗？
Can you give me a discount?	*Qǐng dá yíge zhékòu.* 请打一个折扣。
How much of a discount can you give me?	*Nǐ néng géi wǒ duōdà de zhékòu?* 你能给我多大的折扣？
I would like to return this.	*Wǒ yào tuì huò.* 我要退货。
It doesn't fit me.	*Bù héshēn.* 不合身。
It was broken when I bought it.	*Mǎilái jiù huàile.* 买来就坏了。
I don't like it.	*Wǒ bù xǐhuān.* 我不喜欢。
It's the wrong color.	*Yánsè búduì.* 颜色不对。
It's the wrong size.	*Dàxiǎo búduì.* 大小不对。
The quality is poor.	*Zhìliàng tài chà.* 质量太差。
I want my money back.	*Wǒ yāoqiú tuìkuǎn.* 我要求退款。
I want you to credit my credit card account.	*Wǒ xīwàng ní bǎ qián jìrù wǒde xìnyòng kǎ.* 我希望你把钱记入我的信用卡。

I want to see the general manager.	*Wó xiǎng jiàn zǒngjīnglǐ.* 我想见总经理。

BOOKS

Where is the biggest bookstore here?	*Zuì dà de shūdiàn zài nǎli?* 最大的书店在哪里？
I'm looking for a copy of ____.	*Wǒ yào zhǎo yì běn ____.* 我要找一本____。
The title of the book is ____.	*Shū míng shì ____.* 书名是____。
The author of the book is ____.	*Zuòzhé shì ____.* 作者是____。
I'm looking for a book about ____.	*Wó zhǎo yì běn yǒu guān ____ de shū.* 我找一本有关____的书。
I'm just looking.	*Wó zhǐ kànkan.* 我只看看。
Do you have any books (novels) in English?	*Ní yǒu Yīngwén de shū (xiǎoshuō) ma?* 你有英文的书（小说）吗？
I would like ____.	*Wó xiǎngyào* 我想要____。
■ a Chinese-English dictionary	*yì běn Hàn-Yīng zìdiǎn* 一本汉英字典
■ an English-Chinese dictionary	*yì běn Yīng-Hàn zìdiǎn* 一本英汉字典

c = ts; *q* = ch; *x* = sh; *z* = dz; *zh* = j

■ a guidebook	*yì běn lǚyóu xiǎocè*	一本旅游小册
■ a tourist map	*yì zhāng lǚyóu tú*	一张旅游图
Where can I find ____?	*Nǎli yǒu ____?*	哪里有____？
■ art books (Chinese paintings)	*huàcè (Zhōngguó huà)*	画册（中国画）
■ calligraphy books	*zìtiē*	字帖
■ books about China	*jièshào Zhōngguó de shū*	介绍中国的书
■ Chinese language texts	*xué Zhōngwén de shū*	学中文的书
■ children's books	*xiǎohái de shū*	小孩的书
■ fiction	*xiǎoshuō*	小说
■ history books	*lìshǐ shū*	历史书
I'd like these books.	*Wǒ yào mǎi zhèixiē shū.* 我要买这些书。	
Will you wrap them, please?	*Qǐng bāo qǐlái hǎo ma?* 请包起来好吗？	

CLOTHING

Would you please show me ____.	*Qǐng géi wǒ kànkan ____.* 请给我看看____。	

■ a belt	*pídài*	皮带
■ a blouse	*nǚ chènshān*	女衬衫
■ a dress	*yí tào yīfu*	一套衣服
■ a Chinese (Mao) jacket	*zhōngshān fú*	中山服
■ a chipao (cheongsam; traditional Chinese women's formal wear)	*qípáo*	旗袍
■ leather (suede) gloves	*pí (yángpí) shǒutào*	皮（羊皮）手套
■ handkerchiefs	*shǒujuàn*	手绢
■ a hat	*màozi*	帽子
■ a jacket	*wàitào*	外套
■ an overcoat	*dàyī*	大衣
■ a pair of pajamas	*shuìyī*	睡衣
■ pants	*kùzi*	裤子
■ a raincoat	*yǔyī*	雨衣
■ a robe	*páozi*	袍子
■ a scarf	*wéijīn*	围巾
■ a shirt	*chènshān*	衬衫
■ a pair of shoes	*yì shuāng xié*	一双鞋
■ short pants	*duǎn kù*	短裤
■ a skirt	*qúnzi*	裙子
■ slippers	*tuōxié*	拖鞋

c = ts; *q* = ch; *x* = sh; *z* = dz; *zh* = j

socks	*wàzi*	袜子
a suit (Western-style)	*xīzhuāng*	西装
a sweater	*máoyī*	毛衣
a sweatshirt	*yùndòng shān*	运动衫
a sweatsuit	*yùndòng yī*	运动衣
a tie	*lǐngdài*	领带
a pair of underpants	*nèikù*	内裤
an undershirt	*nèiyī*	内衣

I'd like it with ____ sleeves.	*Wǒ yào ____ xiù de.* 我要___袖的。	
short	*duǎn*	短
long	*cháng*	长
no	*méi*	没

Do you have anything ____?	*Yǒu méi yǒu ____ de?* 有没有___的？	
better	*hǎo yìdiǎn*	好一点
cheaper	*piányi yìdiǎn*	便宜一点
else	*qítā*	其他
larger	*dà yìdiǎn*	大一点
longer	*cháng yìdiǎn*	长一点
shorter	*duǎn yìdiǎn*	短一点
smaller	*xiǎo yìdiǎn*	小一点

COLORS

I don't like the color.	*Wǒ bù xǐhuān zhèige yánsè.*
	我不喜欢这个颜色。

Do you have anything in ____?	*Ní yǒu méi yǒu ____ sè de?*
	你有没有____色的？

■ black	*hēi*	黑
■ blue	*lán*	蓝
■ brown	*kāfēi*	咖啡
■ green	*lǜ*	绿
■ gray	*huī*	灰
■ orange	*júhóng*	橘红
■ pink	*fěnhóng*	粉红
■ purple	*zǐ*	紫

c = ts; *q* = ch; *x* = sh; *z* = dz; *zh* = j

red	*hóng*	红
white	*bái*	白
yellow	*huáng*	黄

| Do you have a lighter (darker) shade? | *Yǒu méi yǒu dàn (shēn) yìdiǎn de?* |
| | 有没有淡（深）一点的？ |

MATERIALS

cashmere	*kāishìmǐ*	开士米
cotton	*miánbù*	棉布
denim	*xiéwén chū miánbù*	斜纹粗棉布
lace	*huābiān*	花边
leather	*pígé zhìpǐn*	皮革制品
nylon	*nílóng*	尼龙
polyester	*huàxiān*	化纤
satin	*duànzi*	缎子
silk	*sīchóu*	丝绸
wool	*yángmáo*	羊毛

FIT, ALTERATIONS

| It doesn't fit me. | *Duì wǒ bù héshēn.* |
| | 对我不合身。 |

| It fits very well. | *Héshēn jíle.* |
| | 合身极了。 |

Please take my measurements.	*Qǐng liáng wǒ de chǐcùn.* 请量我的尺寸。
My size is ____.	*Wǒ de chǐcùn shì ____.* 我的尺寸是____。
May I try it on?	*Wǒ kéyǐ shì yí shì ma?* 我可以试一试吗？
Can you alter it?	*Nǐ néng gǎi yì gǎi ma?* 你能改一改吗？
Can you let it out?	*Nǐ néng fàng dà yìdiǎn ma?* 你能放大一点吗？
May I return this?	*Zhèige néng bù néng tuì?* 这个能不能退？
Do you have something handmade?	*Yóu shǒugōng zuò de ma?* 有手工做的吗？
The zipper is broken.	*Lāliàn huài le.* 拉链坏了。
I'll buy this one.	*Wó mǎi zhèi jiàn.* 我买这件。
Please wrap it up.	*Qǐng bāo qǐlái.* 请包起来。

SHOES

I'd like to see a pair of shoes (boots).	*Wó xiǎng kànkan yì shuāng xié (xuē).* 我想看看一双鞋（靴）。
I'd like to try the pair in the window.	*Wó xiǎng shì chúchuāng lǐ de nèi shuāng.* 我想试橱窗里的那双。

c = ts; q = ch; x = sh; z = dz; zh = j

I take size ____.	*Wǒ de chǐcùn shì ____.*	我的尺寸是____。
This pair is ____.	*Zhèi shuāng ____.*	这双____。
▦ exactly right	*gāng hǎo*	刚好
▦ too loose	*tài sōng*	太松
▦ too narrow	*tài zhǎi*	太窄
▦ too tight	*tài jǐn*	太紧
▦ too wide	*tài kuān*	太宽
I also need ____.	*Wǒ hái yào ____.*	我还要____。
▦ shoelaces	*xiédài*	鞋带
▦ shoe polish	*xiéyóu*	鞋油

AT THE SUPERMARKET

Where is (are) ____?	*____ zài nálǐ?*	____在那里？
▦ beverages	*yǐnliào*	饮料
▦ canned goods	*guàntou shípǐn*	罐头食品
▦ dairy foods	*nǎizhì pǐn*	奶制品
▦ frozen foods	*lěngdòng shípǐn*	冷冻食品
▦ fruits	*shuǐguǒ*	水果
▦ grains	*liángshí lèi*	粮食类
▦ hardware	*xiáo wǔjīn*	小五金
▦ meat	*ròu*	肉
▦ oils	*yóu lèi*	油类
▦ snacks	*xiǎochī lèi*	小吃类
▦ soaps and detergents	*féizào yú qīngjié jì*	肥皂与清洁剂
▦ spices	*tiáowèi liào*	调味料

■ vegetables   *shūcài*   蔬菜

■ wines and liquors   *jiǔ lèi*   酒类

Where can I find a shopping cart?   *Nálí yóu shǒu tuī chē?* 哪里有手推车？

May I have another shopping bag?   *Qǐng zài géi wǒ yíge gòuwù dài?* 请再给我一个购物袋？

JEWELRY

I'd like to see ____.   *Wó xiǎng kànkan*   我想看看____。

■ a bracelet   *shǒuzhuó*   手镯

■ a brooch   *xiōngzhēn*   胸针

■ a chain   *liànzi*   链子

■ a charm   *xiǎo shīwù*   小饰物

■ some earrings   *ěrhuán*   耳环

■ a necklace   *xiàngliàn*   项链

■ a pin   *biézhēn*   别针

■ a ring   *jièzhi*   戒指

■ a watch   *shóubiǎo*   手表

Is this ____?   *Zhè shì ____ de ma?*   这是____的吗？

■ cloisonné   *jǐngtàilán*   景泰蓝

■ gold   *jīn*   金

■ platinum   *báijīn*   白金

■ silver   *yín*   银

■ stainless steel   *búxiùgāng*   不锈钢

c = ts; *q* = ch; *x* = sh; *z* = dz; *zh* = j

Is it solid gold or gold-plated?	*Shì chúnjīn de háishì dùjīn de?* 是纯金的还是镀金的？	
How many carats is it?	*Yǒu duōshǎo kèlā?* 有多少克拉？	
What is that stone?	*Nà shì shénme bǎoshí?* 那是什么宝石？	
I would like ____.	*Wó xiǎngyào ____.* 我想要____。	
an amethyst	*zǐjīn*	紫晶
an aquamarine	*hǎilán bǎoshí*	海蓝宝石
a diamond	*zhuànshí*	钻石
an emerald	*lǜ bǎoshí*	绿宝石
ivory	*xiàngyá*	象牙
jade	*yù*	玉
pearls	*zhēnzhū*	珍珠
a ruby	*hóng bǎoshí*	红宝石
a sapphire	*lán bǎoshí*	蓝宝石
turquoise	*lǜsōng shí*	绿松石
I like this ring.	*Wó xǐhuān zhèige jièzhi.* 我喜欢这个戒指。	
How much is it?	*Duōshǎo qián?* 多少钱？	

MUSIC AND ELECTRONICS

Do you sell ____?	*Nǐmén mài ____ ma?* 你们卖____吗？	
cassettes	*héshì lùyīndài*	盒式录音带
CDs	*guāngpán*	光盘

▥ VCRs	*shìpín gāomì guāng pán*	视频高密光盘
▥ videocassettes	*lùxiàng dài*	录像带
▥ records	*chàngpiàn*	唱片
I want to buy ____.	*Wó xiáng mǎi ____.*	我想买____。
▥ a computer	*jìsuànjī*	计算机
▥ computer hardware	*yìngjiàn*	硬件
▥ computer software	*ruǎnjiàn*	软件
▥ a video game	*diànzi yóuxì*	电子游戏
I need a ____.	*Wǒ xūyào yígè ____.*	我需要一个____。
▥ CD-ROM	*guāng qū*	光驱
▥ cord	*diànxiàn*	电线
▥ disk holder	*cípán jià*	磁盘架
▥ floppy disk	*ruǎn cípán*	软磁盘
▥ hard disk	*yìngpán*	硬盘
▥ modem	*tiáozhì jiětiáo qì*	调制解调器
▥ monitor (CRT)	*diànnǎo xiǎnxiàng píng*	电脑显像屏
▥ mouse	*shǔbiāo*	鼠标
▥ printer	*dǎyìn jī*	打印机
Where can I find ____ software?	*Nálí yǒu ____ ruǎnjiàn?* 哪里有____软件？	
▥ business	*shāngyòng*	商用
▥ Chinese word processing	*Zhōngwén wénzì chùlǐ*	中文文字处理

c = ts; *q* = ch; *x* = sh; *z* = dz; *zh* = j

■ English word processing	*Yīngwén wénzì chùlǐ*	英文文字处理
■ game	*yóuxì*	游戏
■ graphic design	*tú xiàng shèjì*	图像设计
■ spreadsheet	*kōngbái biǎogé chéngxù*	空白表格程序
■ system	*xìtǒng*	系统
■ telecommunications	*diànxùn*	电讯

NEWSSTAND

Do you carry ____ in English?	*Nǐmén yǒu Yīngwén ____ ma?*	你们有英文____吗？
■ newspapers	*bàozhǐ*	报纸
■ magazines	*zázhì*	杂志
■ books	*shū*	书
I'd like to buy some postcards.	*Wó xiáng mǎi míngxìnpiàn.*	我想买明信片。
Do you have stamps?	*Yǒu yóupiào ma?*	有邮票吗？
How much is it?	*Duōshǎo qián?*	多少钱？

PHOTOGRAPHIC SUPPLIES

Where can I have some film developed?	*Nálǐ kéyǐ xǐ zhàopiàn?*	哪里可以洗照片？

How much does it cost to develop a roll of ____?	*Xǐ yì juǎn ____ yào duōshǎo?* 洗一卷____要多少？	
■ prints	*xiàngpiàn*	相片
■ slides	*huàndēng piàn*	幻灯片

I want ____.	*Wǒ yào ____.*	我要____。
■ an enlargement	*fàng dà*	放大
■ a glossy finish	*guāngmiàn de*	光面的
■ a matte finish	*bù guānghuá de*	不光滑的
■ a print of each	*měi yígè dǐpiàn yì zhāng*	每一个底片一张
■ two prints of each	*měi yígè dǐpiàn liǎng zhāng*	每一个底片两张

Can you develop my pictures on a disk?	*Nǐ néng bǎ zhàopiàn fàng zài pánshàng ma?* 你能把照片放在盘上吗？	
Can you print digital pictures?	*Nǐ néng dǎyìn shùmǎ zhàopiàn ma?* 你能打印数码照片吗？	

I want a roll of 24 (36) exposures of ____.	*Wǒ yào yì juǎn èrshí sì (sānshíliù) zhāng de ____.* 我要一卷二十四（三十六）张的____。	
■ color film	*cǎisè jiāo juǎn*	彩色胶卷
■ black-and-white film	*hēibái jiāo juǎn*	黑白胶卷

I would like ____ film.	*Wǒ yào ____ jiāo juǎn.* 我要____胶卷。	
■ Chinese	*Zhōngguó*	中国
■ American	*Měiguó*	美国
■ Japanese	*Rìběn*	日本

c = ts; *q* = ch; *x* = sh; *z* = dz; *zh* = j

What is the film speed?

Jiāojuǎn de sùdù shì duōshǎo?
胶卷的速度是多少？

When can I pick up the pictures?

Shénme shíhòu qǔ zhàopiàn?
什么时候取照片？

Do you sell cameras?

Nǐmén mài zhàoxiàng jī ma?
你们卖照相机吗？

I want a digital camera.

Wǒ yào yíge shùmǎ zhàoxiàng jī.
我要一个数码照相机。

I want an inexpensive one.

Wǒ yào yíge piányi de.
我要一个便宜的。

I want a better one.

Wǒ yào hǎo yìdiǎn de.
我要好一点的。

I want a completely automatic one.

Wǒ yào quán zìdòng de.
我要全自动的。

Do you sell disposable cameras?

Nǐmén mài yí cì xìng de zhàoxiàngjī ma?
你们卖一次性的照相机吗？

I need a special kind of battery.

Wǒ yào tèzhǒng diànchí.
我要特种电池。

Do you have this kind?

Nǐmén yǒu zhèizhǒng de ma?
你们有这种的吗？

Where can I find a battery to fit this camera?

Zài nálí mǎidedào pèi zhèige zhàoxiàngjī de diànchí?
在哪里买得到配这个照相机的电池？

Do you fix cameras?

Nǐmén xiū zhàoxiàng jī ma?
你们修照相机吗？

Mine is broken.

Wǒ de huàile.
我的坏了。

SOUVENIRS

China offers a vast array of handicrafts that are often welcome gifts to your friends at home and that serve as excellent souvenirs of the country. Among the most popular items are cloisonné ware, porcelain ware, jewelry, lacquer ware, pottery, fabrics, embroidery, bamboo and cane products, paper cuts, furniture, rugs, and wooden articles. One can also purchase Chinese scrolls, calligraphy, seals, brushes and inks, and other art supplies.

Would you please show me some ____?	*Qǐng géi wǒ kànkan* ____. 请给我看看____。	
▩ calligraphy	*shūfǎ*	书法
▩ carpets	*dìtǎn*	地毯
▩ carved objects	*diāokè pǐn*	雕刻品
▩ cloisonné	*jǐngtàilán*	景泰蓝
▩ dolls	*wáwa*	娃娃
▩ embroidery	*xiùhuā zhìpǐn*	绣花制品
▩ fabrics	*bùliào*	布料
▩ fans	*shànzi*	扇子
▩ furs	*pímáo*	皮毛
▩ furniture	*jiājù*	家具
▩ glass	*bōlí zhìpǐn*	玻璃制品
▩ jewelry	*zhūbǎo; shǒushī*	珠宝；首饰
▩ lace	*huābiān*	花边
▩ lacquer ware	*qīqì*	漆器
▩ leather goods	*pígé zhìpǐn*	皮革制品
▩ musical instruments	*yuèqì*	乐器

c = ts; *q* = ch; *x* = sh; *z* = dz; *zh* = j

◼ paintings	*huà*	画
◼ paper cuts	*jiánzhǐ*	剪纸
◼ porcelain	*cíqì*	瓷器
◼ pottery	*táoqì*	陶器
◼ silks	*sīzhī pǐn*	丝织品
◼ snuff bottles	*bí yān hú*	鼻烟壶
◼ stone rubbings	*mó tuōběn*	摹拓本

I don't want to spend more than ___ yuan.	*Wǒ xiǎng zuì duō huā ___ yuán.* 我想最多花___元。

ANTIQUES

There are fabulous antiques to be had in China. Vintage clocks, metalware, porcelains, silks, paintings, calligraphy, wood and lacquer ware, and furniture are sold everywhere. Some are quite beautiful, rare, and valuable.

You should be aware, however, that some Chinese antiques are subject to export restrictions. In general, objects of art such as porcelains may not be exported if they are more than about 200 years old. In the case of wood products, it is the type of wood from which an object is made rather than its age that governs whether its export is restricted. Products made from three different types of rare wood may not currently leave the country.

Antiques, whether obtained from state-run stores or from private dealers, must bear a red wax seal in order to be legally removed from China. Chinese Customs is empowered to seize any suspect goods that do not have it. The seal must be applied by the local cultural artifacts bureau, whose experts are charged with determining the age and composition of the items. Reputable dealers can often arrange for the seal to be applied to goods you wish to purchase.

You won't find bargain basement prices on rare cultural treasures, but prices on Chinese antiques in China do tend to be better than they are elsewhere in the world. Bear in mind that haggling is quite acceptable when buying antiques.

What's the price of ____ ?	____ yào duōshǎo qián?	____要多少钱？
■ this box	Zhèige hézi	这个盒子
■ this calligraphy	Zhèi fù zì	这幅字
■ this clock	Zhèige zhōng	这个钟
■ this painting	Zhèi fù huà	这幅画
■ this piece of jewelry	Zhei jiàn shǒushī	这件首饰
■ this rug	Zhèi zhāng dìtǎn	这张地毯
■ this vase	Zhèige huāpíng	这个花瓶

How old is it?	Zhèige duōshǎo nián? 这个多少年？

Does it still work?	Zhèige hái néng yòng ma? 这个还能用吗？

Which dynasty does it come from?	Něige cháodài de? 哪个朝代的？

Where is your antique furniture?	Nǐde gúdǒng jiājù zài nálǐ? 你的古董家具在哪里？

■ altar table	jìbài yòng de zhuōzi	祭拜用的桌子
■ bed	chuáng	床
■ Buddha	Fóxiàng	佛像
■ carpet	dìtǎn	地毯
■ chair	yǐzi	椅子
■ chest	guìzi	柜子

c = ts; q = ch; x = sh; z = dz; zh = j

■ idol	*shénxiàng*	神像
■ lantern	*dēnglóng*	灯笼
■ picture	*huàxiàng*	画像
■ portrait	*rénwù xiàng*	人物像
■ screen	*píngfēng*	屏风
■ statue	*diāoxiàng*	雕像
■ stool	*dèngzi*	凳子
■ table	*zhuōzi*	桌子
■ window	*chuāng*	窗

May I take it out of
China?
Néng dài chūguó ma?
能带出国吗？

Can you have the export
seal put on for me?
*Nǐ néng jiā zhǔnxǔ chūguó de
huǒqī yìn ma?*
你能加准许出国的火漆印吗？

Can you make it a little
cheaper?
Nǐ néng suàn piányi yìdiǎn ma?
你能算便宜一点吗？

TOBACCO SHOP

Please give me
a pack of ____
cigarettes.
*Qǐng gěi wǒ yì bāo ____ de
xiāngyān.*
请给我一包____的香烟。

| ■ filtered | *yǒu guò lǜzuǐ* | 有过滤嘴 |
| ■ unfiltered | *bù jiā lǜzuǐ* | 不加滤嘴 |

Do you have American
cigarettes?
Yóu Měiguó yān ma?
有美国烟吗？

I would like a carton.
Wó xiǎngyào yì tiáo.
我想要一条。

Do you have any
matches?
Yóu huǒchái ma?
有火柴吗？

TOILETRIES

Do you have ____ ?	Yǒu méi yǒu ____ ?	有没有____ ?
■ adhesive bandage	bēngdài	绷带
■ a brush	shuāzi	刷子
■ cologne	xiāngshuǐ	香水
■ a comb	shūzi	梳子
■ cotton balls	miánhuā qiú	棉花球
■ cotton swabs	miánhuā qiān	棉花签
■ deodorant	chúchòu jì	除臭剂
■ hairpins	fàjiā	发夹
■ mouthwash	shùkóu shuǐ	漱口水
■ makeup	huàzhuāng pǐn	化妆品
■ a mirror	jìngzi	镜子
■ nail clippers	jiǎn zhǐjiā dāo	剪指甲刀
■ nail polish	zhǐjiā yóu	指甲油
■ a prophylactic (condom)	bìyùntào	避孕套
■ a razor	guāhú dāo	刮胡刀
■ razor blades	dāopiàn	刀片
■ sanitary napkins	yuè jīng dài	月经带
■ scissors	jiǎndāo	剪刀
■ shampoo	xǐfà jì	洗发剂
■ soap	féizào	肥皂
■ a soap dish	féizào dié	肥皂碟

c = ts; q = ch; x = sh; z = dz; zh = j

▥ tampons	*yuèjīng yòng miánsai*	月经用棉塞
▥ tissues	*huàzhuāng yòng zhǐ*	化妆用纸
▥ toilet paper	*wèishēng zhǐ*	卫生纸
▥ a toothbrush	*yáshuā*	牙刷
▥ toothpaste	*yágāo*	牙膏

ELECTRICAL APPLIANCES/AUDIOVISUAL EQUIPMENT

I need a ____.	*Wǒ xūyào yígè ____.* 我需要一个____。	
▥ adaptor	*zhuǎnjiē qì*	转接器
▥ air conditioner	*kōngtiáo jī*	空调机
▥ alarm clock	*nàozhōng*	闹钟
▥ answering machine	*liúyán jī*	留言机
▥ blender	*jiǎo bàn qì*	搅拌器
▥ calculator	*jìsuàn qì*	计算器
▥ camcorder	*shèxiàng jī*	摄像机
▥ camera	*zhàoxiàng jī*	照相机
▥ can opener	*kāi guàn qì*	开罐器
▥ CD player	*jíguāng chàngjī*	激光唱机
▥ coffeemaker	*zìdòng kāfēi jī*	自动咖啡机
▥ computer	*jìsuàn jī*	计算机
▥ dehumidifier	*jiǎnshī qì*	减湿器
▥ dryer	*hōnggān jī*	烘干机
▥ electric fan	*diàn fēngshàn*	电风扇

■ electric grill	*diàn kǎo jià*	电烤架
■ electric knife	*diàndōng càidāo*	电动菜刀
■ electric razor	*diàndōng guāhú dāo*	电动刮胡刀
■ electric steamer	*diàn zhēng guō*	电蒸锅
■ electric wok	*diàn chǎo guō*	电炒锅
■ fax machine	*chuánzhēn jī*	传真机
■ food processor	*shípǐn jiāgōngqì*	食品加工器
■ freezer	*lěngdòng jī*	冷冻机
■ hair dryer	*chuī fēng jī*	吹风机
■ heater	*nuǎnqì jī*	暖气机
■ humidifier	*zēngshī qì*	增湿器
■ iron	*yùndǒu*	熨斗
■ juicer	*dá guǒzhī jī*	打果汁机
■ karaoke machine	*kǎlāōukèi jī*	卡拉OK机
■ lamp	*dēng*	灯
■ microwave oven	*wēibō lú*	微波炉
■ modem	*tiáozhì jiětiáo qì*	调制解调器
■ outlet	*diànyuán chāzuò*	电源插座
■ plug	*chātóu*	插头
■ printer	*dǎyìn jī*	打印机
■ radio	*shōuyīn jī*	收音机
■ refrigerator	*bīngxiāng*	冰箱
■ rice cooker	*diàn fàn guō*	电饭锅
■ slide projector	*huàndēng jī*	幻灯机

c = ts; *q* = ch; *x* = sh; *z* = dz; *zh* = j

■ smoke detector	*yānwù bàojǐng qì*	烟雾报警器
■ stereo system	*zǔhé yīnxiǎng xìtǒng*	组合音响系统
■ switch	*kāiguān qì*	开关器
■ tape recorder	*lùyīn jī*	录音机
■ telephone	*diànhuà*	电话
■ television	*diànshì jī*	电视机
■ toaster	*kǎo miànbāojī*	烤面包片机
■ toaster oven	*diàn hōngxiāng*	电烘箱
■ transformer	*biànyā qì*	变压器
■ vacuum cleaner	*xīchén qì*	吸尘器
■ videocassette recorder	*lùxiàngjī*	录像机
■ videodisc player	*yǐngdié jī*	影碟机
■ washing machine	*xǐyī jī*	洗衣机
■ wire	*diàn xiàn*	电线

HOUSEWARES

■ ashtray	*yānhuī gāng*	烟灰缸
■ basket	*lánzi*	篮子
■ bowl	*wǎn*	碗
■ candy dish	*guǒpán*	果盘
■ chair	*yǐzi*	椅子
■ chopsticks	*kuàizi*	筷子
■ cooking pot	*guō*	锅

■ cup	*bēizi*	杯子
■ cutting board	*zhēn bǎn*	砧板
■ dish towel	*mā bù*	抹布
■ fork	*chāzi*	叉子
■ frying pan	*chǎocài guō*	炒菜锅
■ kettle	*kāishuǐ hú*	开水壶
■ knife	*dāozi*	刀子
■ plate; dish	*pánzi*	盘子
■ sofa	*shāfā*	沙发
■ spatula	*guāchǎn*	刮铲
■ sponge	*hǎimián*	海绵
■ spoon	*tiáogēng*	调羹
■ steamer	*zhēnglóng*	蒸笼
■ trash can	*lājī tǒng*	垃圾筒

c = ts; *q* = ch; *x* = sh; *z* = dz; *zh* = j

PERSONAL CARE AND SERVICES

AT THE BARBER

Where is there a good barbershop?	*Náli yóu hǎo de lǐfà guǎn?* 哪里有好的理发馆？
May I make an appointment?	*Wǒ kéyǐ yùyuē lǐfà ma?* 我可以预约理发吗？
Do I have to wait long?	*Yào děng hén jiǔ ma?* 要等很久吗？
I want a shave.	*Wǒ yào guā liǎn.* 我要刮脸。
I want a haircut.	*Wǒ yào lǐfà.* 我要理发。
I'd like a trim, please.	*Qíng bǎ tóufa jiǎnqí.* 请把头发剪齐。
Don't cut it too short.	*Bíe jiǎn tài duǎn.* 别剪太短。
Please cut it a little shorter.	*Qíny jiǎn duǎn yìdiǎn* 请剪短一点。
Please cut a little more ____.	*Qǐng zài ____ zài jiǎn yìdiǎn.* 请在____再剪一点。

▟ here	*zhèli*	这里
▟ in back	*hòumiàn*	后面
▟ in front	*qiánmiàn*	前面
▟ off the sides	*liǎng páng*	两旁
▟ off the top	*dǐngshàng*	顶上

That's enough.	*Gòu le.*	够了。
Please thin it out.	*Qíng dǎbáo.*	请打薄。
I (don't) want ____.	*Wǒ (bú) yào* ____	我（不）要____。
■ a shampoo	*xǐ tóu*	洗头
■ tonic	*fàyóu*	发油
Please trim my ____.	*Qǐng xiū wǒ de* ____	请修我的____。
■ beard	*húxū*	胡须
■ mustache	*xiǎo húzi*	小胡子
■ sideburns	*liánbìng húzi*	连鬓胡子
Can you give me a massage?	*Kéyǐ wèi wǒ ànmó ma?*	可以为我按摩吗？
Please massage my head only.	*Qíng zhǐ ànmó wǒ de tóubù.*	请只按摩我的头部。
Please massage my whole body.	*Qǐng wèi wǒ quánshēn ànmó.*	请为我全身按摩。
How much do I owe you?	*Wǒ gāi fù nǐ duōshǎo?*	我该付你多少？

AT THE BEAUTY PARLOR

| Is there a beauty parlor at the hotel? | *Fàndiàn yóu měiróng yuàn ma?* | 饭店有美容院吗？ |
| Is there one nearby? | *Fùjìn yǒu yígè ma?* | 附近有一个吗？ |

c = ts; *q* = ch; *x* = sh; *z* = dz; *zh* = j

I'd like to make an appointment for ____.	*Wó xiǎng yùdìng zài* ____. 我想预定在____。	
■ this afternoon	*jīntiān xiàwǔ*	今天下午
■ tomorrow	*míngtiān*	明天

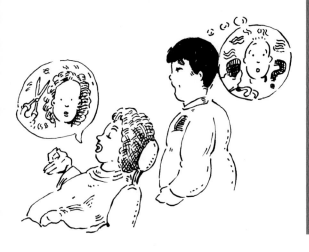

Please give me ____.	*Qǐng wèi wǒ* ____.	请为我____。
■ electrolysis	*diànshí chú máo*	电蚀除毛
■ a facial massage	*miànbù ànmó*	面部按摩
■ a haircut	*lǐfà*	理发
■ a manicure	*xiū zhǐjia*	修指甲
■ a pedicure	*xiū jiǎo zhǐjia*	修脚指甲
■ a permanent	*tàng tóufa*	烫头发

■ a shampoo · *xǐ tóu* · 洗头

■ a wash and blow dry · *xǐ hòu chuīgān.* · 洗后吹干

I need to color my hair. · *Wǒ xūyào rǎn tóufa.*
我需要染头发。

What colors do you have? · *Nǐmén yǒu nǎxiē yánsè?*
你们有哪些颜色？

Don't apply any hair spray, please. · *Qǐng búyào pēn fàjiāo.*
请不要喷发胶。

Not too much hair spray, please. · *Bú yào pēn tài duō fàjiāo.*
不要喷太多发胶。

LAUNDRY AND DRY CLEANING

Does the hotel offer laundry service? · *Fàndiàn yóu xǐyī de fúwù ma?*
饭店有洗衣的服务吗？

How about dry cleaning? · *Yǒu gānxǐ ma?*
有干洗吗？

I have a lot of clothes to be ____. · *Wó yóu xǔduō yīfu yào ____.*
我有许多衣服要____。

■ dry-cleaned · *gānxǐ* · 干洗

■ ironed · *tàng* · 烫

■ mended · *bǔ* · 补

■ washed · *xǐ* · 洗

Please don't use any starch. · *Qǐng bú yào shàng jiāng.*
请不要上浆。

c = ts; *q* = ch; *x* = sh; *z* = dz; *zh* = j

Light starch, please.	*Qǐng shàng yìdiǎn jiāng.* 请上一点浆。	
Here's the laundry list:	*Zhè shì xǐyī dān:* 这是洗衣单：	
▮ three men's shirts	*sān jiàn nán chènshān*	三件男衬衫
▮ twelve handkerchiefs	*shíèr tiáo shǒujuàn*	十二条手绢
▮ six pairs of socks	*liù shuāng wàzi*	六双袜子
▮ one blouse	*yí jiàn nǚ chènshān*	一件女衬衫
▮ four panties	*sì tiáo nǚ nèikù*	四条女内裤
▮ two pajamas	*liǎng jiàn shuìyī*	两件睡衣
▮ two suits	*liǎng tào xīzhuāng*	两套西装
▮ three ties	*sān tiáo lǐngdài*	三条领带
▮ two dresses	*liǎng jiàn yīfu*	两件衣服
▮ one sweater	*yí jiàn máoyī*	一件毛衣
▮ one pair of gloves	*yì shuāng shǒutào*	一双手套
I need them for	*Wǒ ____ jiù xūyào yòng.*	我____就需要用。
▮ tonight	*jīnwǎn*	今晚
▮ tomorrow	*míngtiān*	明天
▮ the day after tomorrow	*hòutiān*	后天
▮ next week	*xià xīngqī*	下星期
I'm leaving soon.	*Wó hěn kuài jiù yào zǒu.* 我很快就要走。	

I'm leaving tomorrow morning.	*Wǒ míngtiān zǎoshàng jiù yào zǒu.* 我明天早上就要走。	
When will you bring it back?	*Nǐ shénme shíhòu kéyǐ jiāo géi wǒ?* 你什么时候可以交给我？	
When will it be ready?	*Shénme shíhòu hǎo?* 什么时候好？	
Can you guarantee that I will have it back on time?	*Nǐ néng bǎozhèng zhǔnshí jiāo géi wǒ ma?* 你能保证准时交给我吗？	
There's a button ____.	*Yíge kòuzi ____.*	一个扣子____。

■ missing   *diū le*   丢了

■ loose   *sōng le*   松了

Please sew it back on.	*Qǐng bāng wǒ féng hǎo.* 请帮我缝好。	
This isn't my laundry.	*Zhèixiē búshì wǒ de yīfu.* 这些不是我的衣服。	

SHOE REPAIRS

Can you fix these ____?	*Nǐ néng xiū zhèi shuāng ____ ma?*	你能修这双____吗？

■ shoes   *xiézi*   鞋子

■ boots   *xuēzi*   靴子

The heel is broken.	*Hòugēn duànle.*	后跟断了。

c = ts; *q* = ch; *x* = sh; *z* = dz; *zh* = j

Please give me ____ soles.	*Qǐng wèi wǒ huàn ____ xiédǐ.* 请为我换____鞋底。	
■ full	*quán*	全
■ half	*bàn*	半

I'd like rubber heels.　　　*Wǒ yào xiàngpí hòugēn.*
　　　　　　　　　　　　我要橡皮后跟。

Please shine them.　　　*Qǐng wèi wǒ cā xié.*
　　　　　　　　　　请为我擦鞋。

When will they be ready?　*Shénme shíhòu hǎo?*
　　　　　　　　　　　什么时候好？

I need them by
Saturday without fail.　*Wǒ xīngqīliù yídìng děi yào.*
　　　　　　　　　　我星期六一定得要。

MEDICAL CARE

AT THE PHARMACY

Is there a pharmacy nearby?	*Fùjìn yǒu yàofáng ma?*	附近有药房吗？
At what time does the pharmacy open (close)?	*Yàofáng jídiǎn kāi (guān)?*	药房几点开（关）？
Do you sell Western medicine?	*Yǒu mài Xīyào ma?*	有卖西药吗？
I don't want any traditional Chinese medicine.	*Wǒ búyào Zhōngyào.*	我不要中药。
I need something for ____.	*Wǒ yào zhì ____ de yào.*	我要治____的药。
■ an allergy	*guòmǐn*	过敏
■ a cold	*shāngfēng*	伤风
■ constipation	*biànmì*	便秘
■ a cough	*késòu*	咳嗽
■ diarrhea	*xiè dùzi*	泻肚子
■ a fever	*fāshāo*	发烧
■ the flu	*liúxíngxìng gǎnmào*	流行性感冒
■ hay fever	*huāfěn rè*	花粉热
■ a headache	*tóutòng*	头痛
■ insomnia	*shīmián*	失眠
■ nausea	*zuò ǒu*	作呕

c = ts; *q* = ch; *x* = sh; *z* = dz; *zh* = j

■ sunburn	*pífū shàishāng*	皮肤晒伤
■ a toothache	*yá tòng*	牙痛
■ an upset stomach	*dùzi tòng*	肚子痛
It's an emergency.	*Zhè shì jízhěn.*	这是急诊。
How long will it take?	*Yào duōjiǔ?*	要多久？
When can I pick it up?	*Shénme shíhòu qǔ yào?*	什么时候取药？
I would like ____.	*Wó xiǎngyào ____.*	我想要____。
■ adhesive tape	*jiāobù*	胶布
■ alcohol	*jiǔjīng*	酒精
■ an antacid	*kàngsuān yào*	抗酸药
■ an antiseptic	*xiāodú jì*	消毒剂
■ aspirin	*āsīpǐlín*	阿司匹林
■ bandages	*bēngdài*	绷带
■ corn plasters	*jīyǎn gāoyào*	鸡眼膏药
■ absorbent cotton	*miánhuā*	棉花
■ cough drops	*késòu yào*	咳嗽药
■ cough syrup	*késòu tángjiāng*	咳嗽糖浆
■ eardrops	*ěr yàoshuǐ*	耳药水
■ eyedrops	*yǎn yàoshuǐ*	眼药水
■ a (mild) laxative	*(qīng de) xièyào*	（轻的）泻药
■ milk of magnesia	*yǎnghuàměi rǔyè*	氧化镁乳液
■ suppositories	*zuòyào*	坐药
■ a thermometer	*wēndù jì*	温度计
■ tincture of iodine	*diánjiǔ*	碘酒

■ tranquilizers	*zhènjìng jì*	镇静剂
■ vitamins	*wéishēng sù*	维生素

DOCTORS

You never know when you might need a doctor while you are on vacation. In China you are likely to run into physicians with a wide range of skills and training. Many are schooled in traditional Chinese remedies as well as Western medicine.

Larger Chinese cities usually have one or more state-run hospitals designated for the care of foreigners where English is spoken, and some now have private hospitals that offer first-rate care. These may sometimes have equipment that is quite modern.

Medical evacuation can be arranged in emergency situations through foreign embassies and international health organizations.

If your doctor does not speak English, the following phrases and expressions will help you communicate.

I don't feel well.	*Wǒ bú tài shūfu.* 我不太舒服。
I'm sick.	*Wǒ bìng le.* 我病了。
I want to see a doctor.	*Wǒ yào kàn yīshēng.* 我要看医生。
Is there a doctor who speaks English?	*Yǒu néng shuō Yīngwén de yīshēng ma?* 有能说英文的医生吗？
Where is his office?	*Tā de zhěnsuǒ zài nálǐ?* 他的诊所在哪里？

c = ts; *q* = ch; *x* = sh; *z* = dz; *zh* = j

I'm dizzy.	*Wǒ tóuyūn.*	我头晕。
I feel weak.	*Wó gǎndào shuāiruò wúlì.*	我感到衰弱无力。
I want to sit down for a while.	*Wó xiǎng zuò xiàlái.*	我想坐下来。
My temperature is normal (37°C).	*Wǒ de tǐwēn zhèngcháng (Shèshì sānshíqī dù).*	我的体温正常（摄氏三十七度）。

PARTS OF THE BODY

abdomen	*dùzi*	肚子
ankle	*jiǎohuái*	脚踝
appendix	*lánwěi*	阑尾
arm	*shǒubèi*	手臂
back	*bèi*	背
breast	*rǔfáng*	乳房
chest	*xiōngqiāng*	胸腔
chin	*xiàba*	下巴
clitoris	*yīndì*	阴蒂
ear	*ěrduō*	耳朵
elbow	*shóuzhǒu*	手肘
eye	*yǎnjīng*	眼睛
face	*liǎn*	脸
finger	*shóuzhǐ*	手指
foot	*jiǎo*	脚
forehead	*é tóu*	额头
groin	*shǔxībù*	鼠蹊部
gums	*yáyín*	牙龈
hand	*shǒu*	手

head	*tóu*	头
heart	*xīnzàng*	心脏
heel	*jiǎo hòugēn*	脚后跟
hip	*túnbù*	臀部
knee	*xī*	膝
leg	*tuǐ*	腿
lips	*chún*	唇
mouth	*zuǐba*	嘴巴
neck	*bózi*	脖子
nipple	*rǔtóu*	乳头
nose	*bízi*	鼻子
penis	*yīnjīng*	阴茎
shoulder	*jiānbǎng*	肩膀
skin	*pífū*	皮肤
testicle	*gǎowán*	睾丸
throat	*hóulóng*	喉咙
toe	*jiáozhǐ*	脚趾
tonsils	*biǎntáo xiàn*	扁桃腺
tooth	*yáchǐ*	牙齿
vagina	*yīndào*	阴道
waist	*yāo*	腰
wrist	*shóuwǎnzi*	手腕子

TELLING THE DOCTOR

I have ____.	*Wǒ ____.*	我____。
■ an abscess	*yǒu nóngzhǒng*	有脓肿
■ a broken bone	*gǔtóu duànle*	骨头断了

c = ts; *q* = ch; *x* = sh; *z* = dz; *zh* = j

▪ a bruise	*cāshāng le*	擦伤了
▪ a burn	*shāoshāng le*	烧伤了
▪ the chills	*fā lěng*	发冷
▪ a cold	*gǎnmào le*	感冒了
▪ cramps	*chōujīn le*	抽筋了
▪ a cut	*bèi gēshāng le*	被割伤了
▪ diarrhea	*xiè dùzi le*	泻肚子了
▪ dysentery	*yǒu lìji*	有痢疾
▪ a fever	*fāshāo le*	发烧了
▪ a fracture	*gǔtóu zhéduàn le*	骨头折断了
▪ a headache	*tóutòng*	头痛
▪ an infection	*fāyán le*	发炎了
▪ something in my eye	*yán lǐtóu yǒu dōngxi*	眼里头有东西
▪ a sore throat	*hóulóng tòng*	喉咙痛
▪ a stomachache	*dùzi tòng*	肚子痛
▪ a wound	*shòushāng le*	受伤了

I am constipated.	*Wó yǒu biànmì.*	我有便秘。
I have swollen glands.	*Wǒ de xiàntí zhǒng le.* 我的腺体肿了。	
It hurts me here.	*Wǒ zhèli tòng.*	我这里痛。
My whole body hurts.	*Wǒ quánshēn tòng.*	我全身痛。
My ___ hurts.	*Wǒ de ___ tòng.*	我的___痛。
▪ back	*bèi*	背
▪ buttocks	*pìgu*	屁股
▪ leg	*tuǐ*	腿
▪ shoulder	*jiānbǎng*	肩膀

| throat | *hóulóng* | 喉咙 |
| thumb | *dà múzhǐ* | 大拇指 |

| I've had this pain since yesterday. | *Wǒ cóng zuótiān jiù tòng le.* 我从昨天就痛了。 |

| There's (no) history of ____ in my family. | *Wǒ jiā (méi) yǒu ____ de bìnglì.* 我家（没）有____的病历。 |

| asthma | *qìchuǎn bìng* | 气喘病 |
| diabetes | *tángniào bìng* | 糖尿病 |

| I'm allergic to antibiotics (penicillin). | *Wǒ duì kàngshēng sù (pánníxīlín) guòmǐn.* 我对抗生素（盘尼西林）过敏。 |

| I have a pain in my chest. | *Wó gǎndào xiōngqiāng tòng.* 我感到胸腔痛。 |

| I had a heart attack ____ years ago. | *Wǒ ____ nián qián fāguò xīnzàng bìng.* 我____年前发过心脏病。 |

| I have never been vaccinated against ____. | *Wǒ hái méiyóu dǎ ____ yùfángzhēn.* 我还没有打____预防针。 |

cholera	*huòluàn*	霍乱
diphtheria	*báihóu*	白喉
hepatitis A	*jiǎxíng gānyán*	甲型肝炎
hepatitis B	*yǐxíng gānyán*	乙型肝炎
hepatitis C	*bǐngxíng gānyán*	丙型肝炎
polio	*xiǎoér mábìzhèng*	小儿麻痹症
smallpox	*tiānhuā*	天花
tetanus	*pò shāngfēng*	破伤风

c = ts; *q* = ch; *x* = sh; *z* = dz; *zh* = j

■ typhoid fever	*shānghán*	伤寒
■ yellow fever	*huángrè bìng*	黄热病

My blood type is ____. — *Wǒde xiěxíng shì ____.* — 我的血型是____。

I have never had ____. — *Wǒ cónglái méiyǒu déguò ____.* — 我从来没有得过____。

■ chicken pox	*shuǐdòu*	水痘
■ German measles	*Déguó mázhěn*	德国麻疹
■ measles	*mázhěn*	麻疹
■ mumps	*liúxíngxìng sāixiànyán*	流行性腮腺炎

I'm currently taking this medicine. — *Wǒ xiànzài yòng zhèige yào.* — 我现在用这个药。

I'm pregnant. — *Wǒ huáiyùn le.* — 我怀孕了。

I feel all right now. — *Wǒ xiànzài hǎoxiē le.* — 我现在好些了。

I feel a lot better. — *Wó hǎo duō le.* — 我好多了。

I feel worse. — *Wó gǎndào gèng bù shūfu.* — 我感到更不舒服。

Do I have ____? — *Wó yǒu ____ ma?* — 我有____吗？

■ appendicitis	*lánwěi yán*	阑尾炎
■ the flu	*liúxíngxìng gǎnmào*	流行性感冒
■ tonsilitis	*biǎntáoxiàn yán*	扁桃腺炎
■ AIDS	*àizībìng*	艾滋病
■ diabetes	*tángniào bìng*	糖尿病
■ a fever	*fāshāo*	发烧

- gonorrhea | *línbìng* | 淋病
- hemorrhoids | *zhìchuāng* | 痔疮
- high blood pressure | *gāo xuěyā* | 高血压
- low blood pressure | *dī xuěyā* | 低血压
- syphillis | *méidú* | 梅毒
- tuberculosis | *fèibìng* | 肺病
- an ulcer | *kuìyáng* | 溃疡
- venereal disease | *xìngbìng* | 性病

Is it serious? | *Yánzhòng ma?* | 严重吗？

Is it contagious? | *Chuánrǎn ma?*
传染吗？

Do I have to go to the hospital? | *Wǒ xūyào shàng yīyuàn ma?*
我需要上医院吗？

When can I continue my trip? | *Wǒ shénme shíhòu kéyǐ jìxù lǚxíng?*
我什么时候可以继续旅行？

DOCTOR'S INSTRUCTIONS

Please open your mouth. | *Qíng bá zuǐ zhāngkāi.*
请把嘴张开。

Please stick out your tongue. | *Qíng bǎ shétóu shēn chūlái.*
请把舌头伸出来。

Cough. | *Késòu.*
咳嗽。

Breathe deeply. | *Shēn hūxī.*
深呼吸。

c = ts; *q* = ch; *x* = sh; *z* = dz; *zh* = j

Please take off your clothing.	*Qíng bǎ yīfu tuōdiào.*	请把衣服脱掉。
Lie down.	*Tǎng xià.*	躺下。
Stand up.	*Zhàn qǐlái.*	站起来。
Please get dressed.	*Qǐng chuān yī.*	请穿衣。

PATIENT

Are you going to give me a prescription?	*Nǐ yào géi wǒ kāi yàofāng ma?* 你要给我开药方吗？
What's the dosage for this medicine?	*Zhèige yào zěnme yòng?* 这个药怎么用？
How long do I have to stay in bed?	*Wǒ zài chuángshàng yào tǎng duōjiǔ?* 我在床上要躺多久？
I don't wish to take Chinese traditional medicine.	*Wǒ bú yào chī Zhōngyào.* 我不要吃中药。
Can you prescribe some Western medicine, please?	*Nǐ néng géi wǒ kāi Xīyào ma?* 你能给我开西药吗？
I don't wish to undergo acupuncture.	*Wǒ bù xiǎng yòng zhēnjiǔ zhì.* 我不想用针灸治。
Thank you very much.	*Fēicháng xièxie nǐ.* 非常谢谢你。
What is the fee?	*Fèiyòng duōshǎo?* 费用多少？
I wish to be evacuated to Hong Kong.	*Wǒ xīwàng bèi sòng dào Xiānggǎng qù.* 我希望被送到香港去。

Please inform the U.S. Embassy (Consulate) to make arrangements.

Qǐng tōngzhī Měiguó Dàshíguǎn (Lǐngshìguǎn) zuòchū ānpái.

请通知美国大使馆（领事馆）作出安排。

IN THE HOSPITAL (ACCIDENTS)

Help!

Jiùmìng!

救命！

Call a doctor, quickly!

Gǎnkuài jiào yīshēng!

赶快叫医生！

Call an ambulance, quickly!

Gǎnkuài jiào jiùhù chē!

赶快叫救护车！

Take me (him, her) to the hopsital.

Sòng wǒ (tā) dào yīyuàn qù.

送我（他）到医院去。

I need first aid.

Wǒ xūyào jíjiù.

我需要急救。

c = ts; q = ch; x = sh; z = dz; zh = j

I've fallen.	*Wǒ diējiāo le.*	我跌交了。
I was ____ by a car.	*Wǒ bèi qìchē ____.*	我被汽车____。
▦ knocked down	*chuàngdǎo le*	撞倒了
▦ run over	*niǎnguò le*	碾过了
I've had a heart attack.	*Wǒ xīnzàng bìng fāle.*	我心脏病发了。
I ____ myself.	*Wǒ bèi ____ le.*	我被____了。
▦ burned	*shāoshāng*	烧伤
▦ cut	*gēshāng*	割伤
I'm bleeding.	*Wǒ zài liú xiě.*	我在流血。
I think the bone is ____.	*Wó xiáng gǔtóu ____ le.*	我想骨头____了。
▦ broken	*duàn*	断
▦ dislocated	*tuōjiù*	脱臼
▦ fractured	*zhéduàn*	折断
My leg is swollen.	*Wǒ de tuǐ fāzhǒng.*	我的腿发肿。
My ankle (wrist) is sprained.	*Wǒ de jiǎohuái (shóuwǎnzi) niǔle.*	我的脚踝（手腕子）扭了。
I can't move my elbow (knee).	*Wǒ de shóuzhǒu (xīgài) bù néng dòng.*	我的手肘（膝盖）不能动。

AT THE DENTIST

Chinese dentistry is somewhat behind that of the West. Few foreign residents of China go to local dentists for other than emergency care; for extensive dental work most prefer to see a dentist outside of China.

I have to go to the dentist.	*Wǒ yào qù kàn yáyī.* 我要去看牙医。
Can you recommend a dentist?	*Nǐ jièshào yígè yáyī hǎo ma?* 你介绍一个牙医好吗？
My tooth hurts a great deal.	*Wǒ de yáchǐ hěn tòng.* 我的牙齿很痛。
I've lost a filling.	*Wǒ de yáchōngtián diūle.* 我的牙充填丢了。
I've broken a tooth.	*Wǒ de yáchǐ duànle.* 我的牙齿断了。
I can't chew.	*Wǒ bù néng yǎo.* 我不能咬。
My gums hurt me.	*Wǒ de yáyín tòng.* 我的牙龈痛。
Is there an infection?	*Yǒu méi yǒu fāyán?* 有没有发炎？
Can the tooth still be repaired?	*Yá hái néng bǔ ma?* 牙还能补吗？
Must you extract the tooth?	*Yídìng yào bǎ yá bádiào ma?* 一定要把牙拔掉吗？
I won't have it pulled.	*Wǒ bú yuànyì bádiào.* 我不愿意拔掉。

c = ts; *q* = ch; *x* = sh; *z* = dz; *zh* = j

I will wait and ask my dentist at home.	*Wǒ yào huíjiā wèn wǒ de yáyī.*	我要回家问我的牙医。
Can you fill it ____?	*Nǐ néng ____ tián ma?*	你能____填吗？
■ with amalgam	*yòng gǒnghéjīn*	用汞合金
■ with gold	*yòng jīn*	用金
■ with silver	*yòng yín*	用银
■ temporarily	*zhànshí de*	暂时的
Can you fix ____?	*Nǐ néng bǔ zhèige ____ ma?*	你能补这个____吗？
■ this bridge	*chǐqiáo*	齿桥
■ this crown	*chǐguàn*	齿冠
■ this denture	*jiǎyá*	假牙
When should I come back?	*Shénme shíhòu zài lái?*	什么时候再来？
What is your fee?	*Fèiyòng duōshǎo?*	费用多少？

AT THE EYE DOCTOR/OPTICIAN

My eye ____.	*Wǒde yǎn ____.*	我的眼____。
■ hurts	*tòng*	痛
■ is red	*fā hóng*	发红
■ is swollen	*fā zhǒng*	发肿
■ itches	*fā yǎng*	发痒
My vision is blurred.	*Wǒ de yǎn móhu.*	我的眼模糊。
I lost my glasses.	*Wǒde yǎnjìng diūle.*	我的眼镜丢了。

I need a pair of glasses.	*Wǒ yào pèi yífù yǎnjìng.* 我需要配一副眼镜。
I need a pair of contact lenses.	*Wǒ yào pèi yǐngxíng yǎnjìng.* 我需要配隐形眼镜。
I don't have my prescription.	*Wǒ méiyǒu chǔfāng.* 我没有处方。
Would you examine me, please?	*Qǐng géi wó jiǎnchá yíxià.* 请给我检查一下。
I would like a pair of bifocals.	*Wǒ yào yífù shuāngguāng yǎnjìng.* 我要一副双光眼镜。
How long will it take?	*Yào děng duōjiǔ?* 要等多久？

COMMUNICATIONS

POST OFFICE

You probably won't have to visit the post office while you are in China, since the majority of major hotels have postal counters that offer most services. Here are some useful phrases.

I want to mail a letter.	*Wǒ yào jì yì fēng xìn.*	
	我要寄一封信。	
Where's the post office?	*Yóujú zài nálí?*	
	邮局在哪里？	
Where's a mailbox?	*Yóutǒng zài nálí?*	
	邮筒在哪里？	
What is the postage for ____ to the United States?	*Jì ____ dào Měiguó yào duōshǎo qián?*	
	寄____到美国要多少钱？	

▥	this aerogram	*zhèi zhāng yóujiǎn*	这张邮简
▥	this airmail letter	*zhèi fēng hángkōng xìn*	这封航空信
▥	this express letter	*zhèi fēng kuài xìn*	这封快信
▥	this insured letter	*zhèi fēng bǎojià xìn*	这封保价信
▥	this letter	*zhèi fēng xìn*	这封信
▥	this registered letter	*zhèi fēng guàhào xìn*	这封挂号信
▥	this special delivery letter	*zhèi fēng xiànshí zhuānsòng xìn*	这封限时专送信

■ this package	*zhèige bāoguǒ*	这个包裹
■ this postcard	*zhèi zhāng míngxìnpiàn*	这张明信片

When will it arrive?	*Shénme shíhòu jìdào?* 什么时候寄到？	
Where can I purchase stamps?	*Nǎli kéyǐ mǎidào yóupiào?* 哪里可以买到邮票？	
Are there any letters for me?	*Yǒu méi yóu wǒ de xìn?* 有没有我的信？	
My name is ____.	*Wǒ jiào ____.*	我叫____。
I'd like ____.	*Wó xiǎngyào ____.*	我想要____。
■ five airmail stamps	*wǔ zhāng hángkōng yóupiào*	五张航空邮票
■ four aerogram	*sì zhāng yóujiǎn*	四张邮简
Need I fill out a customs declaration?	*Wǒ yào tián bàoguān dān ma?* 我要填报关单吗？	
Must I open this for inspection?	*Xūyào dǎkāi jiǎnchá ma?* 需要打开检查吗？	
I didn't bring my passport.	*Wǒ méi dài hùzhào.* 我没带护照。	
I collect stamps.	*Wǒ shōují yóupiào.* 我收集邮票。	
Do you have any pretty stamps?	*Ní yǒu méi yóu hěn piàoliàng de yóupiào?* 你有没有很漂亮的邮票？	

c = ts; *q* = ch; *x* = sh; *z* = dz; *zh* = j

TELECOMMUNICATIONS

    The Chinese government has been moving very quickly in recent years to install new telephone lines. Bad connections, busy signals, and busy circuits are increasingly becoming things of the past.

    You can't make an international or even a domestic long-distance call from just any phone in China; the line must be specially designated for international direct dialing (IDD) or domestic direct dialing (DDD) service. For international calls, it is sometimes cheaper when the billing is done outside of China, so calling home collect may save you some money. Note, however, that "call-back" services—through which you place a call and automatically receive a call back from another country—are illegal in China.

    An increasing number of public telephones in China accept domestic calling cards which are widely sold. But not all phones accept all kinds of cards.

    While most Chinese families still do not own computers, this has not stopped the Internet from making extensive inroads into China. Helping this process along is a proliferation of Internet cafés where you can rent a computer and an Internet connection by the hour. This is also useful for travelers who are far from home but still wish to receive e-mail. At the end of this section you will find basic vocabulary for logging in.

Where is a public telephone?	*Nǎli yǒu gōngyòng diànhuà?* 哪里有公用电话？	
May I use your phone?	*Wǒ kéyǐ yòng nǐ de diànhuà ma?* 我可以用你的电话吗？	
I want to make a(n) ____.	*Wǒ yào dǎ yíge ____ diànhuà.* 我要打一个____电话。	
▓ international call	*guójì chángtú*	国际长途
▓ local call	*běndì*	本地

■ long-distance call   *chángtú*   长途

■ person-to-person call   *jiàorén de chángtú*   叫人的长途

Can I dial direct?   *Néng zhíjiē bō ma?*
能直接拨吗？

Does this phone have _____?   *Zhèige diànhuà yǒu _____ ma?*
这个电话有_____吗？

■ domestic direct dialing (DDD)   *guónèi zhíjiē chángtú bōhào*
国内直接长途拨号

■ international direct dialing (IDD)   *guójì zhíjiē chángtú bōhào*
国际直接长途拨号

How do I get the operator?   *Zǒngjī zěnme dǎ?*
总机怎么打？

Operator, please connect me with number 6500-2231.   *Zǒngjī, qǐng jiē liùwǔ línglíng èrèr sānyī hào.*
总机，请接六五零零二二三一号。

My telephone number is _____.   *Wǒ de diànhuà hàomǎ shì _____.*
我的电话号码是_____。

Hello?   *Wèi!*   喂！

Please _____.   *Qǐng _____.*   请_____。

■ connect me with extension 46   *jiē sìliù hào fēnjī*
接四六号分机

■ connect me with Mr. Wang   *zhuǎn Wáng Xiānsheng*
转王先生

c = ts; *q* = ch; *x* = sh; *z* = dz; *zh* = j

I'd like to speak with ____.	*Wó zhǎo ____.*	我找____。
Is ____ in?	*____ zài ma?*	____在吗？
When will he be back?	*Tā shénme shíhòu huílái?* 他什么时候回来？	
It is I.	*Wǒ jiù shì.*	我就是。
Who is calling?	*Qǐng wèn něiwèi?*	请问哪位？
I can't hear.	*Wǒ tīng bù qīng.*	我听不清。
Please speak louder.	*Qǐng dà shēng yìdiǎn.*	请大声一点。
Don't hang up.	*Bié guàdiào.*	别挂掉。
This is ____.	*Wǒ shì ____.*	我是____。
Operator, there is no answer.	*Zǒngjī, méi rén jiē.*	总机，没人接。

The line is busy.	*Zhàn xiàn.* 占线。
The number you gave me was wrong.	*Nǐ géi wǒ de hàomǎ cuòle.* 你给我的号码错了。
I was cut off.	*Duànle.* 断了。
I want to leave a message for ____.	*Wó xiǎng liúhuà géi ____.* 我想留话给____。
Where can I go to send a fax?	*Dào nálǐ qù fā chuánzhēn?* 到哪里去发传真？
My surname is ____.	*Wǒ xìng ____.*　我姓____。
My telephone number is ____.	*Wǒ de diànhuà shì ____.* 我的电话是____。
My extension is ____.	*Wǒ de fēnjī hàomǎ shì ____.* 我的分机号码是____。
Please tell him (her) to call me back.	*Qǐng jiào tā huí wǒ diànhuà.* 请叫他回我电话。
Please tell him (her) to wait for my call.	*Qǐng jiào tā déng wǒde diànhuà.* 请叫他等我的电话。
Where can I rent a cell phone?	*Zài nálǐ kéyǐ zūdào shǒujī?* 在哪里可以租到手机？
How much does it cost?	*Yào duōshǎo qián?* 要多少钱？
Do you charge by the minute?	*Nǐ shì àn shíjiān suàn ma?* 你是按时间算吗？

c = ts; *q* = ch; *x* = sh; *z* = dz; *zh* = j

When must I return it?	*Shénme shíhòu huán?* 什么时候还？
Where can I get on the Internet?	*Dào nǎlǐ qù shàng yīngtèwǎng?* 到哪里去上英特网？
Where is an Internet café?	*Nǎlǐ yǒu yīngtèwǎng kāfēi diàn?* 哪里有英特网咖啡店？
May I use a computer?	*Wǒ kéyǐ yòng diànǎo ma?* 我可以用电脑吗？
How much for an hour?	*Yígè xiǎoshí duōshǎo qián?* 一个小时多少钱？
How do I get on-line?	*Zěnmeyàng shàng wǎng?* 怎么样上网？
I would like to check my e-mail.	*Wó xiǎng chá wǒ de diànzi yóujiàn.* 我想查我的电子邮件。
I would like to search the Internet.	*Wó xiǎng chá Yīngtèwǎng.* 我想查英特网。
How can I find that homepage?	*Zěnmeyàng cái zhǎodédào nèige wǎngyè?* 怎么样才找得到那个网页？
Is this web page blocked?	*Zhèige wǎngyè bèi fēngle ma?* 这个网页被封了吗？
How fast is this modem?	*Zhèige tiáozhì jiětiáoqì de sùdù shì duōshǎo?* 这个调制解调器的速度是多少？
This computer is broken.	*Zhèige diànǎo huàile.* 这个电脑坏了。
I lost my connection.	*Wǒde xiàn duànle.* 我的线断了。

How can I reconnect?	*Zěnmeyàng zài jiēshàng?* 怎么样再接上？
Where can I print?	*Nǎlǐ kéyǐ dǎyìn?* 哪里可以打印？

GENERAL INFORMATION

TELLING TIME

When the Chinese tell time, they generally state the period of the day before the exact hour. The period between midnight and dawn is the early morning, or **qīngzǎo**. From about 6:00 A.M. to noon is the morning, **zǎoshàng**. Noon to 6:00 P.M. is **xiàwǔ**, the afternoon. And from 6:00 P.M. until midnight is **wǎnshàng**. So 7:00 P.M. is expressed as **wǎnshàng qīdiǎn**, and 11:30 A.M. is **zǎoshàng shíyīdiǎn bàn**. Only when the time of day isn't specified does one say, simply, **liùdiǎn bàn** (6:30).

Official time is sometimes expressed according to the 24-hour clock. You will find that trains and planes are often scheduled using these terms. The 24-hour clock is never used in normal conversation, however, so a plane departing at 15:00 is still said to leave at **xiàwǔ sāndiǎn**, or "three in the afternoon."

Remember that all of China is officially in one time zone. There are not different zones for different regions as there are elsewhere in the world, so when it is six in the morning in Beijing, it is six in Sichuan Province, even though it may be quite dark there.

What time is it?	*Jídiǎn zhōng?*	几点钟？
■ hour	*xiǎoshí; zhōngtóu*	小时；钟头
■ half an hour	*bàn xiǎoshí*	半小时
■ an hour and a half	*yì xiǎoshí bàn*	一小时半
■ quarter (15 minutes)	*kè*	刻
■ minute	*fēn*	分
■ second	*miǎo*	秒
It is now ____.	*Xiànzài shì____.*	现在是____。
■ noon	*zhōngwǔ*	中午
■ 1:05	*yìdiǎn língwǔ fēn*	一点零五分
■ 2:10	*liángdiǎn shí fēn*	两点十分
■ 3:15	*sāndiǎn shíwǔ fēn; sāndiǎn yíkè*	三点十五分；三点一刻
■ 4:20	*sìdiǎn èrshí fēn*	四点二十分
■ 5:25	*wǔdiǎn èrshíwǔ fēn*	五点二十五分
■ 6:30	*liùdiǎn sānshí fēn; liùdiǎn bàn*	六点三十分；六点半
■ 7:35	*qīdiǎn sānshíwǔ fēn*	七点三十五分
■ 8:40	*bādiǎn sìshí fēn*	八点四十分

c = ts; *q* = ch; *x* = sh; *z* = dz; *zh* = j

■ 9:45	*jiúdiǎn sìshíwǔ fēn; jiúdiǎn sānkè*	九点四十五分；九点三刻
■ 10:50	*shídiǎn wǔshí fēn*	十点五十分
■ 11:55	*shíyīdiǎn wǔshíwǔ fēn*	十一点五十五分
■ 8:00	*bādiǎn zhōng*	八点钟
■ midnight	*wǔyè*	午夜

EXPRESSIONS OF TIME

When?	*Shénme shíhòu?*	什么时候？
At what time?	*Jídiǎn?*	几点？
■ at _____ o'clock	*zài _____ diǎn zhōng*	在_____点钟
■ at noon	*zài zhōngwǔ*	在中午
■ at 4:00 P.M. sharp	*zài xiàwǔ sìdián zhěng* 在下午四点正	
■ an hour from now	*zài yígè zhōngtóu* 再一个钟头	
■ not before 2:00 A.M.	*bú yào zài zǎoshàng liángdiǎn yǐqián* 不要在早上两点以前	
■ after 3:00 P.M.	*xiàwǔ sāndián yǐhòu* 下午三点以后	
■ at about 9:00 P.M.	*dàyuē wǎnshàng jiúdiǎn* 大约晚上九点	
■ between six and seven o'clock	*zài liùdiǎn hé qīdiǎn zhījiān* 在六点和七点之间	

■ until five o'clock	*yìzhí dào wúdiǎn* 一直到五点	

Since what time ____?	*Cóng jídiǎn kāishǐ ____?* 从几点开始____?	
per hour	*měi xiǎoshí*	每小时
three hours ago	*sānge xiǎoshí yǐqián* 三个小时以前	
early	*zǎo*	早
late	*wǎn*	晚
late in arriving	*chídào le*	迟到了
on time	*zhǔnshí*	准时
in the morning	*zài zǎoshàng*	在早上
in the afternoon	*zài xiàwǔ*	在下午
in the evening	*zài wǎnshàng*	在晚上

DAYS OF THE WEEK

What day is today?	*Jīntiān xīngqī jǐ?*	今天星期几？
Today is ____.	*Jīntiān shì ____.*	今天是____。
▨ Monday	*Xīngqīyī*	星期一
▨ Tuesday	*Xīngqīèr*	星期二
▨ Wednesday	*Xīngqīsān*	星期三
▨ Thursday	*Xīngqīsì*	星期四
▨ Friday	*Xīngqīwǔ*	星期五
▨ Saturday	*Xīngqīliù*	星期六
▨ Sunday	*Xīngqītiān*	星期天
last Monday	*shàngge Xīngqīyī*	上个星期一
this Wednesday	*zhèige Xīngqīsān*	这个星期三
next Tuesday	*xiàge Xīngqīèr*	下个星期二

NOTE: Use the above expressions and similar ones carefully. The Chinese use **zhèige** to describe days within the current week, beginning this past Monday and ending this coming Sunday. Any day before this past Monday is considered part of last week, and is described with **shàngge**. And similarly, a day after this coming Sunday is not part of this week and can't be described with the expression "zhèige"; as part of next week it is properly spoken of as **xiàge**.

birthday	*shēngrì*	生日
the day after tomorrow	*hòutiān*	后天
the day before	*qián yì tiān*	前一天
the day before yesterday	*qiántiān*	前天

during the day	*zài báitiān*	在白天
during the evening	*zài wǎnshàng*	在晚上
during the week	*zài zhōunèi*	在周内
every day	*měitiān*	每天
in five days	*wǔtiān yǐhòu*	五天以后
from this day on	*cóng jīntiān qǐ*	从今天起
holiday	*jiérì*	节日
last week	*shàngge xīngqī*	上个星期
the next day	*dìèr tiān*	第二天
next week	*xiàge xīngqī*	下个星期
six days ago	*liùtiān yǐqián*	六天以前
this week	*zhèige xīngqī*	这个星期
today	*jīntiān*	今天
tomorrow	*míngtiān*	明天
two days ago	*dà qiántiān;* *liǎng tiān qián*	大前天；两天前
two days from now	*dà hòutiān*	大后天
vacation day	*jiàrì*	假日
within five days	*wǔtiān yǐnèi*	五天以内
yesterday	*zuótiān*	昨天
the week after next	*xiàxiàge xīngqī*	下下个星期
the weekend	*zhōumò*	周末
a week from today	*xià xīngqī de tóng yī tiān*	下星期的同一天

c = ts; *q* = ch; *x* = sh; *z* = dz; *zh* = j

MONTHS OF THE YEAR

January	*Yīyuè*	一月
February	*Èryuè*	二月
March	*Sānyuè*	三月
April	*Sìyuè*	四月
May	*Wǔyuè*	五月
June	*Liùyuè*	六月
July	*Qīyuè*	七月
August	*Bāyuè*	八月
September	*Jiǔyuè*	九月
October	*Shíyuè*	十月
November	*Shíyīyuè*	十一月
December	*Shíèryuè*	十二月
last month	*shàngge yuè*	上个月
next month	*xiàge yuè*	下个月
this month	*zhèige yuè*	这个月
two months ago	*liǎngge yuè yǐqián*	两个月以前
in two months	*liǎngge yuè yǐhòu*	两个月以后
the month after next	*xiàxiage yuè*	下下个月
the month before last	*qiánge yuè*	前个月
during the month of ____	*zài ____ yuè yǐnèi*	在____月以内

since the month of ____	*cóng* ____ *yuè kāishǐ*	从____月开始
every month	*měige yuè*	每个月
What is today's date?	*Jīntiān jǐhào?*	今天几号？
Today is ____.	*Jīntiān shì* ____	今天是____。
▪ Monday, May 11	*Wǔyuè shíyī rì, Xīngqīyī* 五月十一日，星期一	
▪ Tuesday, June 1	*Liùyuè yī rì, Xīngqīèr* 六月一日，星期二	

NOTE: When weekdays and dates are given together, as in the two examples above, the date precedes the day of the week. It is expressed just the opposite of the way it is in English.

all year	*quánnián*	全年
during the year	*zài yìnián yǐnèi*	在一年以内
last year	*qù nián*	去年
next year	*míngnián*	明年
per year; every year	*měinián*	每年
the year after next	*hòunián*	后年
the year before last	*qiánnián*	前年

THE FOUR SEASONS

| spring | *chūnjì* | 春季 |
| summer | *xiàjì* | 夏季 |

c = ts; *q* = ch; *x* = sh; *z* = dz; *zh* = j

fall	*qiūjì*	秋季
winter	*dōngjì*	冬季
in the springtime	*zài chūntiān*	在春天
in the summertime	*zài xiàtiān*	在夏天
before the fall	*qiūjì yǐqián*	秋季以前
after the winter	*dōngjì yǐhòu*	冬季以后

WEATHER

What is the weather like?	*Tiānqì zěnmeyàng?*	天气怎么样？
It is bad.	*Bùhǎo.*	不好。
It is beautiful.	*Hǎo jíle.*	好极了。
It is cold.	*Mán lěng de.*	蛮冷的。
It is very cold.	*Hén lěng.*	很冷。
It is comfortable.	*Hěn shūfu.*	很舒服。
It is cool.	*Hěn liángkuài.*	很凉快。
It is foggy.	*Yǒu wù.*	有雾。
It is hot.	*Mán rè de.*	蛮热的。
It is very hot.	*Hěn rè.*	很热。
It is raining.	*Xià yǔ le.*	下雨了。
It is snowing.	*Xià xuě le.*	下雪了。
It is sunny.	*Yǒu tàiyáng.*	有太阳。
It is windy.	*Fēng dà.*	风大。

It's too hot to go out.	*Tài rè le, bù chūqù ba.*	太热了，不出去吧。
Is it going to rain today?	*Jīntiān huì xià yǔ ma?*	今天会下雨吗？
It's very dry.	*Hěn gānzào.*	很干燥。
It's very humid.	*Hěn mēnrè.*	很焖热。
Today's temperature is ____.	*Jīntiān de wēndù shì ____.*	今天的温度是____。

■ 75 degrees Fahrenheit   *qīshíwǔ Huáshì dù*
七十五华氏度

■ 20 degrees Centigrade   *èrshí Shèshì dù*
二十摄氏度

TEMPERATURE CONVERSIONS

To change Fahrenheit to **Centigrade**: subtract 32 and multiply by $\frac{5}{9}$.

To change **Centigrade** to Fahrenheit: multiply by $\frac{9}{5}$ and add 32.

DIRECTIONS

above	*zài shàngmiàn de*	在上面的
back	*hòumiàn*	后面
below	*zài xiàmiàn de*	在下面的
down	*xiàmiàn*	下面
east	*dōngfāng*	东方
front	*qiánmiàn*	前面

c = ts; *q* = ch; *x* = sh; *z* = dz; *zh* = j

left	*zuǒbiān*	左边
middle	*zhōngjiān*	中间
north	*běifāng*	北方
right	*yòubiān*	右边
south	*nánfāng*	南方
up	*shàngmiàn*	上面
west	*xīfāng*	西方

IMPORTANT SIGNS

小心	*xiǎoxīn*	be careful
非营业时间	*fēi yíngyè shíjiān*	closed for business
危险	*wéixiǎn*	danger
不许进入	*bùxǔ jìnrù*	do not enter
紧急出口	*jǐnjí chūkǒu*	emergency exit
闲人免入	*xiánrén miǎnrù*	employees only
入口	*rùkǒu*	entrance
出口	*chūkǒu*	exit
医院	*yīyuàn*	hospital
询问处	*xúnwèn chù*	information desk
女厕所	*nǚ cèsuǒ*	ladies' room
男厕所	*nán cèsuǒ*	men's room
不许停车	*bùxǔ tíng chē*	no parking
请勿吸烟	*qǐng wù xīyān*	no smoking

请勿吐痰	*qǐng wù tǔtán*	no spitting
非饮用水	*fēi yǐnyòng shuǐ*	nonpotable water
开	*kāi*	open
月台	*yuètái*	platform
请勿动手	*qǐng wù dòngshǒu*	please don't touch
拉	*lā*	pull
推	*tuī*	push
停止	*tíngzhǐ*	stop
厕所	*cèsuǒ*	toilets
休息室	*xiūxi shì*	waiting room

STANDARD MEASUREMENTS

centimeter	*límǐ; gōngfēn*	厘米；公分
foot	*yīngchǐ*	英尺
inch	*yīngcùn*	英寸
kilometer	*gōnglǐ*	公里
meter	*mǐ; gōngchǐ*	米；公尺
mile	*yīnglǐ*	英里
millimeter	*háomǐ*	毫米
yard	*mǎ*	码

NOTE: Linear measurements are easily converted into square or cubic measurements in Chinese. For square

c = ts; *q* = ch; *x* = sh; *z* = dz; *zh* = j

measurements, simply attach the prefix **píngfāng** (平方), as in **píngfāng mǐ**, square meters. For cubic measurements, the prefix is **lìfāng** (立方).

acre	*yīngmǒu*	英亩
gallon	*jiālún*	加仑
gram	*gōngkè*	公克
hectare	*gōngqǐng*	公顷
kilogram	*gōngjīn*	公斤
liter	*shēng*	升
metric ton	*gōngdùn*	公吨
milligram	*háokè*	毫克
milliliter	*háoshēng*	毫升
ounce	*àngsī*	盎斯
pint	*pǐntuō*	品脱
pound	*bàng*	磅
quart	*kuātuō*	夸脱
ton	*dùn*	吨

CENTIMETERS/INCHES

The Chinese use the metric system for measurement, and they probably won't understand you if you talk in feet and inches. For many situations you'll probably want to use the following conversion tables.

CONVERSION TABLES

Inches		Millimeters	Cu. Feet		Cu. Meters
0.039	1	25.40	35.315	1	0.028
0.079	2	50.80	70.629	2	0.057
0.118	3	76.20	105.943	3	0.085
0.157	4	101.60	141.258	4	0.113
0.197	5	127.00	176.572	5	0.142

Feet		Meters	Cu. Yards		Cu. Meters
3.281	1	0.305	1.308	1	0.765
6.562	2	0.610	2.616	2	1.529
9.843	3	0.914	3.924	3	2.294
13.123	4	1.219	5.232	4	3.058
16.404	5	1.524	6.540	5	3.823

Yards		Meters	Pints		Liters
1.094	1	0.914	1.761	1	0.568
2.187	2	1.829	3.521	2	1.136
3.281	3	2.743	5.282	3	1.704
4.375	4	3.658	7.043	4	2.272
5.468	5	4.572	8.804	5	2.840

Miles		Kilometers	Gallons		Liters
0.621	1	1.609	0.220	1	4.546
1.243	2	3.219	0.440	2	9.092
1.864	3	4.828	0.660	3	13.638
2.485	4	6.437	0.880	4	18.184
3.107	5	8.047	1.101	5	22.730

Sq. Feet		Sq. Meters	Ounces		Grams
10.764	1	0.093	0.035	1	28.350
21.528	2	0.186	0.071	2	56.699
32.292	3	0.279	0.106	3	85.049
43.056	4	0.372	0.141	4	113.398
53.819	5	0.465	0.176	5	141.748

c = ts; q = ch; x = sh; z = dz; zh = j

Sq. Yards		Sq. Meters	Pounds		Kilograms
1.196	1	0.836	2.205	1	0.454
2.392	2	1.672	4.409	2	0.907
3.588	3	2.508	6.614	3	1.361
4.784	4	3.345	8.819	4	1.814
5.980	5	4.181	11.023	5	2.268

To use this table, refer to the 1–5 numbers in the center columns. For example, 1 in the feet-meters section means that 1 foot equals 0.305 meter and that 1 meter equals 3.281 feet.

To convert centimeters to inches, multiply by .39. To convert inches to centimeters, multiply by 2.54.

Centimeters

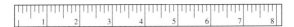

Inches

LIQUID MEASUREMENTS

1 liter = 1.06 quarts
4 liters = 1.06 gallons

For quick, approximate conversions, multiply the number of gallons by 4 to get liters. Divide the number of liters by 4 to get gallons.

TEMPERATURE

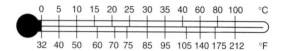

SPEED

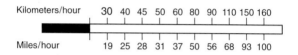

TIRE PRESSURES

lb/sq in	20	22	24	26	28	30	32	34
kg/sq cm	1.41	1.55	1.69	1.83	1.97	2.11	2.25	2.39

CHINESE TRADITIONAL MEASUREMENTS

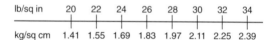

Though China officially uses the metric system, some traditional measurements survive and you may come across them. Here are the most commonly used ones with their equivalents.

c = ts; q = ch; x = sh; z = dz; zh = j

UNIT	PRONUN-CIATION	CHINESE CHARACTER	EQUIVALENTS
Chinese inch	*cùn*	寸	3.33 centimeters 1.31 inches
Chinese foot	*chǐ*	尺	.33 meter 1.09 feet
10 Chinese feet	*zhàng*	丈	3.33 meters 3.65 yards
Chinese mile	*lǐ*	里	.5 kilometers .31 mile
Chinese ounce	*liǎng*	两	.05 kilogram 1.76 ounces
catty	*jīn*	斤	.5 kilogram 1.1 pounds
picul	*dàn*	担	50 kilograms
Chinese quart	*shēng*	升	1.76 pints .22 gallon
Chinese peck	*dǒu*	斗	10 liters
Chinese acre	*mǔ*	亩	.067 hectare .16 acre
Chinese hectare	*qǐng*	顷	6.67 hectares

PUBLIC HOLIDAYS AND TRADITIONAL CELEBRATIONS

Three "Golden Week" holidays are celebrated in China—one full week off for Spring Festival, the traditional Lunar New Year celebration; a week around May 1 (Labor Day), and a third week at the beginning of October to mark the October 1 National Day Holiday. Note that people in Hong Kong and Taiwan and other overseas Chinese do not necessarily celebrate all of these holidays.

PUBLIC HOLIDAYS

January 1	New Year's Day, or **Yuándàn** (元旦). Also called **Xīnnián** (新年).
January or February	Spring Festival, or **Chūnjié** (春节). A weeklong celebration marking the lunar new year. The exact dates change from year to year because the holiday is still set according to the lunar calendar.
May 1	Labor Day, **Láodòngjié** (劳动节). Also referred to as **Wǔyī** (五一), meaning the first of May. A weeklong holiday.
October 1	National Day, or **Guóqìng** (国庆). Anniversary of the founding of the People's Republic of China in 1949. Another weeklong celebration.

In addition to the public holidays, there are also some traditional Chinese festivals that are widely observed. The dates of these holidays vary from year to year because they are set by the lunar calendar. The most important ones are listed below.

CELEBRATIONS

January or February	Lantern Festival, or **Yuánxiāojié** (元宵节). This occurs on the fifteenth day of the lunar new year and marks the end of the Spring Festival. It is a colorful festival during which people, especially children, carry lanterns through the streets and marketplaces in the evening. It is also a time for eating boiled dumplings called **tāngyuán** (汤圆), which are small glutinous rice balls filled with sesame paste or red bean paste.
April	Pure Brightness Festival, or **Qīngmíngjié** (清明节). This is a spring holiday to honor ancestors. Traditional activities include the burning of mock paper money (for use by the departed in the next world) and the sweeping off of the graves of one's ancestors. The holiday is no longer widely celebrated in the PRC.

c = ts; q = ch; x = sh; z = dz; zh = j

CELEBRATIONS	
June	Dragon Boat Festival, or **Duānwǔjié** (端午节). The fifth day of the fifth lunar month. Commemorates the death of Qǔ Yúan, a patriotic poet of the Warring States Period (475–221 B.C.). Festivities include dragon boat races and the eating of **zòngzi** (粽子), glutinous rice dumplings with various fillings, steamed in lotus leaves.
September	Mid-autumn Festival, or **Zhōngqiūjié** (中秋节). Celebrated on the fifteenth day of the eighth lunar month. Commemorates an unsuccessful rebellion against the Mongolian rulers of the Yuan Dynasty (A.D. 1271–1368), but is also a kind of harvest festival. Traditional activities include family reunions and the consumption of **yuèbǐng** (月饼), or moon cakes, a round lotus-seed pastry.

TIMELINE OF CHINESE HISTORY

B.C.

ca. 2697	Legendary Yellow Emperor, common ancestor of the Chinese race, assumes throne. Legend credits him with the invention of the compass.
1766–1066	Shang Dynasty. The Great Bronze Age.
1066–256	Zhou Dynasty. Age of the Great Philosophers.
ca. sixth or seventh century	Laozi (Lao Tzu), founder of Taoism, describes the harmonious relationship between human individuals and the universal order, and advocates pacifism.
551–479	Kongzi (Confucius), the great thinker and teacher, expounds theories of ethics and statecraft.
479–438	Mozi (Mo Tzu) puts forth theory of religious piety and universal love.

fourth to third century	Extensive well building and construction of canals and irrigation systems.
399–295	Zhuangzi (Chuang Tzu) describes theory of infinity and advocates intellectual and artistic freedom.
371–289	Mengzi (Mencius), the most famous disciple of Confucius, authors theory of the goodness of human nature.
360–290	Sunzi (Sun Tzu) writes of *The Art of War*.
221	Qin Shihuang unites China and becomes its first emperor. He unifies the measuring system and written language and builds a transportation network.
214	The Great Wall is completed.
ca. 90	Sima Qian (Ssu-ma Ch'ien) compiles *Grand Historical Records*, 130 volumes of Chinese history.

A.D.

65	Buddhism is introduced into northern China.
105	Paper is invented by Cai Lun.
600	Block printing is invented by Bi Sheng.
405–972	The Golden Age of Buddhist Philosophy in China.
610	Canal system, including the Grand Canal linking Beijing to Yangzhou on the Changjiang (Yangtse River), is completed.
eighth century	Li Bai (Li Po, 701–761) and Du Fu (Tu Fu, 712–770), famous Tang Dynasty poets.
ca. tenth century	Gunpowder is invented.
960–1644	Revival of Confucianism.
1215	Beijing falls to Genghis Khan.
1271	Kublai Khan declares himself Emperor of China and establishes the Yuan (Mongol) Dynasty.

c = ts; *q* = ch; *x* = sh; *z* = dz; *zh* = j

1275	Marco Polo visits China.
1601	Jesuit Matteo Ricci arrives in Beijing.
1644	Manchus conquer China and establish the Qing Dynasty.
1745	*The Dream of the Red Chamber* is written by Cao Xueqin.
1839–1842	The Opium (Anglo-Chinese) War.
1842	Treaty of Nanking opens five Chinese ports, including Hong Kong, to the British.
1850–1864	The Taiping Rebellion, a peasant uprising.
1866	Sun Yat-sen, founder of modern China, is born.
1887	Chiang Kai-shek is born.
1893	Mao Zedong (Mao Tse-tung) is born.
1894–1895	First Sino-Japanese War.
1899	U.S. Secretary of State John Hay issues "Open Door Notes" seeking equal access to Chinese markets for American traders.
1900	The Boxer Rebellion, violent popular resistance against the foreign presence in China.
1905	Sun Yat-sen establishes the "Three Principles of the People" (Nationalism, Democracy, and Socialism).
1908	Death of Ci Xi (Tzu Hsi), the Empress Dowager, who dominated Chinese politics for nearly half a century.
1911	The Qing Dynasty is overthrown; the Republic of China is proclaimed.
1916	General Yuan Shikai fails in an attempt to reestablish the monarchy.
1919	The May Fourth Movement, a movement by Chinese intellectuals espousing a number of cultural and political reforms.
1921	The Communist Party is established.
1925	Sun Yat-sen dies.
1926	Nationalist Party (KMT, or Guomindang) begins Northern Expedition to fight

	powerful local warlords in an attempt to unify China.
1934–1935	Communist Party undertakes the Long March to flee the Nationalists' extermination campaign, then establishes party headquarters at Yan'an, Shaanxi Province.
1936	Xi'an Incident. Chiang Kai-shek is kidnapped and Nationalists and Communists form a United Front against the Japanese.
1937–1945	Second Sino-Japanese War.
1949	Nationalists withdraw to Taiwan; the People's Republic of China is founded.
1957	The Hundred Flowers Movement, in which intellectuals are encouraged to voice political opinions, followed by the Anti-Rightist Campaign in which dissenters are purged.
1958	The Great Leap Forward, an unsuccessful effort to accelerate industrial and agricultural development, and the establishment of people's communes, a move to collectivize agriculture.
1966–1976	The Great Proletarian Cultural Revolution, a ten-year mass campaign of repudiation of traditional values and reactionaries and radicalization of the party, the military, and the government.
1971	U.S. Secretary of State Henry Kissinger visits China. Nationalist regime is expelled from China's seat in the United Nations in favor of the Communist government.
1972	U.S. President Richard Nixon visits China and signs the Shanghai Joint Communiqué, setting the groundwork for normalization of bilateral relations.

c = ts; q = ch; x = sh; z = dz; zh = j

1975	Chiang Kai-shek dies.
1976	Mao Zedong dies; the Gang of Four falls.
1978	Deng Xiaoping ascends to power. The Four Modernizations program—modernizing agriculture, industry, national defense, and science and technology—and the new Open Door Policy, which opens China to the outside world, are implemented.
1979	Normalization of relations between China and the United States. Deng Xiaoping visits the United States.
1980	The trial of the Gang of Four.
1984	British Prime Minister Margaret Thatcher and Chinese Premier Zhao Ziyang sign a landmark agreement providing for the return of the British crown colony of Hong Kong to Chinese sovereignty in 1997.
1985	President Li Xiannian visits the United States, becoming the first PRC head of state ever to do so.
1988	Taiwan President Chiang Ching-kuo, son of Chiang Kai-shek, dies. Lee Teng-hui assumes presidency.
1989	Protesters are killed by People's Liberation Army troops in Tian'anmen Square following months of peaceful demonstrations.
1992	Jiang Zemin assumes the post of Communist Party secretary and the following year becomes president of the PRC.
1995	The U.S. government grants a visa to Taiwan President Lee Teng-hui to visit his alma mater, Cornell University. This provokes threatening military exercises in the Taiwan Strait early the following year by the People's Liberation Army.

1996	Lee Teng-hui is again chosen president of Taiwan in the first popular election for a senior leader in Chinese history.
1997	The colony of Hong Kong is returned to Chinese sovereignty after more than 150 years of British rule. President Jiang Zemin pays a state visit to the United States and President Bill Clinton reciprocates the following year. Deng Xiaoping dies.
1999	The Portuguese government returns the colony of Macao to Chinese sovereignty after ruling it for nearly 450 years.

THE CHINESE DYNASTIES

PINYIN	TRADITIONAL DESCRIPTION	CHINESE CHARACTER	YEARS
Xià	Hsia	夏	2205–1765 B.C.
Shāng	Shang	商	1766–1066 B.C.
Zhōu	Chou	周	1066–256 B.C.
Xī Zhōu	Western Chou	西周	1066–771 B.C.
Dōng Zhōu	Eastern Chou	东周	770–256 B.C.
Chūn Qiū	Spring and Autumn	春秋	770–476 B.C.
Zhàn Guó	Warring States	战国	475–221 B.C.
Qín	Ch'in	秦	221–207 B.C.
Hàn	Han	汉	206 B.C.–220 A.D.
Xī Hàn	Western Han	西汉	206 B.C.–24 A.D.
Dōng Hàn	Eastern Han	东汉	25–220 A.D.
Sān Guó	Three Kingdoms	三国	220–280 A.D.
Wèi	Wei	魏	220–265 A.D.
Shǔ Hàn	Shu Han	蜀汉	221–263 A.D.
Wú	Wu	吴	222–280 A.D.

c = ts; *q* = ch; *x* = sh; *z* = dz; *zh* = j

PINYIN	TRADITIONAL DESCRIPTION	CHINESE CHARACTER	YEARS
Jìn	Chin	晋	265–420 A.D.
Xī Jìn	Western Chin	西晋	265–316 A.D.
Dōng Jìn	Eastern Chin	东晋	317–420 A.D.
Liù Cháo	Six Dynasties	六朝	420–589 A.D.
Suí	Sui	隋	581–618 A.D.
Táng	T'ang	唐	618–907 A.D.
Wǔ Dài	Five Dynasties	五代	907–960 A.D.
Shí Guó	Ten Kingdoms	十国	902–979 A.D.
Sòng	Sung	宋	960–1279 A.D.
Běi Sòng	Northern Sung	北宋	960–1127 A.D.
Nán Sòng	Southern Sung	南宋	1127–1279 A.D.
Jīn	Kin	金	1115–1234 A.D.
Yuán	Yuan	元	1271–1368 A.D.
Míng	Ming	明	1368–1644 A.D.
Hóng Wǔ	Hung Wu	洪武	1368–1398 A.D.
Jiàn Wén	Chien Wen	建文	1399–1402 A.D.
Yǒng Lè	Yung Lo	永乐	1403–1424 A.D.
Hóng Xī	Hung Hsi	洪熙	1425 A.D.
Xuān Dé	Hsuan Te	宣德	1426–1435 A.D.
Zhèng Tǒng	Cheng T'ung	正统	1436–1449 A.D.
Jǐng Tài	Ching T'ai	景泰	1450–1456 A.D.
Tiān Shùn	T'ien Shun	天顺	1457–1464 A.D.
Chéng Huà	Ch'eng Hua	成化	1465–1487 A.D.
Hóng Zhì	Hung Chih	弘治	1488–1505 A.D.
Zhèng Dé	Cheng Te	正德	1506–1521 A.D.
Jiā Jìng	Chia Ching	嘉靖	1522–1566 A.D.
Lóng Qìng	Lung Ch'ing	隆庆	1567–1572 A.D.
Wàn Lì	Wan Li	万历	1573–1619 A.D.
Tài Chāng	T'ai Ch'ang	泰昌	1620 A.D.
Tiān Qǐ	T'ien Ch'i	天启	1621–1627 A.D.
Chóng Zhēn	Ch'ung Chen	崇祯	1628–1644 A.D.
Qīng	Ching	清	1644–1911 A.D.
Shùn Zhì	Shun Chih	顺治	1644–1661 A.D.
Kāng Xī	Kang Hsi	康熙	1662–1722 A.D.
Yōng Zhèng	Yung Cheng	雍正	1723–1735 A.D.
Qián Lóng	Chien Lung	乾隆	1736–1796 A.D.
Jiā Qìng	Chia Ch'ing	嘉庆	1796–1820 A.D.
Dào Guāng	Tao Kuang	道光	1821–1850 A.D.
Xián Fēng	Hsien Feng	咸丰	1851–1862 A.D.
Tóng Zhì	T'ung Chih	同治	1862–1874 A.D.
Guāng Xù	Kuang Hsu	光绪	1875–1908 A.D.
Xuān Tǒng	Hsuan T'ung	宣统	1908–1911 A.D.

MINI-DICTIONARY FOR THE BUSINESS TRAVELER

advisor	*gùwèn*	顾问
air freight	*kōng yùn*	空运
amount	*jīn é*	金额
appraise	*gūjià*	估价
arbiter	*zhòngcáizhe*	仲裁者
arbitration	*zhòngcái*	仲裁
assistant manager	*zhùlǐ jīnglǐ*	助理经理
authorize	*shòuquán*	授权
bank	*yínháng*	银行
bankrupt	*pòchǎn*	破产
bargain (v.)	*tǎojià*	讨价
barter	*yǐhuò yìhuò*	以货易货
bill (noun)	*piàoju*	票据
bill (verb)	*kāi zhàngdān*	开帐单
bill of lading	*tíhuò dān*	提货单
board of directors	*dǒngshì huì*	董事会
bond	*zhài quàn*	债券
borrow	*jiè*	借
bribery	*huìluò*	贿赂
business hours	*yíngyè shíjiān*	营业时间
buy	*mǎi*	买

c = ts; *q* = ch; *x* = sh; *z* = dz; *zh* = j

cash (noun)	*xiànkuǎn*	现款
cash a check	*duìxiàn*	兑现
certified check	*bǎofù zhīpiào*	保付支票
chairman	*dǒngshìzhǎng*	董事长
C.I.F.	*dào àn jiàgé*	到岸价格
claim	*suōpéi*	索赔
company; corporation	*gōngsī*	公司
compensation for damage	*sǔnshī péicháng*	损失赔偿
compensation trade	*bǔcháng màoyì*	补偿贸易
competition	*jìngzhēng*	竞争
competitive price	*jù yǒu jìngzhēnglì de jiàgé*	具有竞争力的价格
conflict of interest	*lìyì chōngtù*	利益冲突
consulting company	*zīxún gōngsī*	咨询公司
contract	*hétóng*	合同
contractual obligations	*hétóng de yìwù*	合同的义务
co-owner	*gòngtóng yōngyóuzhě*	共同拥有者
coproduction	*hézuò shēngchǎn*	合作生产
corporate law	*gōngsī fǎ*	公司法

corruption	*fǔbài*	腐败
cost	*chéngběn*	成本
countertrade	*fǎnxiāo màoyì*	反销贸易
court	*fǎyuàn*	法院
credit	*xìndài*	信贷
currency	*huòbì*	货币
Customs	*Hǎiguān*	海关
director	*dǒngshì*	董事
discount	*zhékòu*	折扣
distributor	*xiāoshòuzhě*	销售者
distribution center	*xiāoshòu zhōngxīn*	销售中心
due	*dàoqī*	到期
duty free	*miǎnshuì*	免税
enforcement	*zhífǎ*	执法
enterprise	*qǐyè*	企业
exchange rate	*duìhuàn lǜ*	兑换率
expedite delivery	*xùnsù jiāohuò*	迅速交货
expenses	*fèiyòng*	费用
export	*chūkǒu*	出口
F.O.B.	*chuánshàng jiāohuò*	船上交货
foreign exchange	*wàihuì*	外汇
general manager	*zǒngjīnglǐ*	总经理
goods	*huòwù*	货物

c = ts; *q* = ch; *x* = sh; *z* = dz; *zh* = j

import	*jìnkǒu*	进口
income	*shōurù*	收入
income tax	*suǒdé shuì*	所得税
installment	*fēnqī fù kuǎn*	分期付款
insurance	*báoxiǎn*	保险
interest	*lìxī*	利息
interest rate	*lìlǜ*	利率
international law	*guójì fǎ*	国际法
investment	*tóuzī*	投资
joint venture	*hézī qǐyè*	合资企业
lawsuit	*sùsòng*	诉讼
lawyer	*lǜshī*	律师
lend	*jiè gěi*	借给
letter of credit	*xìnyòng zhèng*	信用证
letter of intent	*yìxiàng shū*	意向书
liability	*zhàiwù*	债务
license	*xúkě zhèng*	许可证
loan	*dàikuǎn*	贷款
loss	*kuī sǔn*	亏损
manager	*jīnglǐ*	经理
market price	*shìchǎng jiàgé*	市场价格
marketing	*shìchǎng yíngxiāo*	市场营销
memorandum of understanding	*liàngjié bèiwànglù*	谅解备忘录

mortgage	*dǐyā*	抵押
ownership	*yōngyǒuquán*	拥有权
partial payment	*bùfèn fù kuǎn*	部分付款
partner	*héhuǒ rén*	合伙人
patent	*zhuānlì*	专利
payment	*fù kuǎn*	付款
president	*zǒngcái*	总裁
price	*jiàgé*	价格
pricing	*biāojià*	标价
processing	*jiāgōng*	加工
product	*chánpǐn*	产品
profit	*lìrùn*	利润
property	*cáichǎn*	财产
purchasing agent	*dàigòu rén*	代购人
representative	*dàilǐrén*	代理人
retail	*língshòu*	零售
sale	*xiāoshòu*	销售
salesperson	*shòuhuòyuán*	售货员
sales tax	*yíngyè shuì*	营业税
sea freight	*hǎi yùn*	海运
security	*zhèng quàn*	证券
sell	*shòumài*	售卖
send	*yùnsòng*	运送
send back	*sònghuí*	送回

c = ts; *q* = ch; *x* = sh; *z* = dz; *zh* = j

send C.O.D.	*huòdào fù kuǎn*	货到付款
share	*gǔfèn*	股份
shipment	*zhuāngyùn*	装运
shipping	*yùnsòng*	运送
store	*shāngdiàn*	商店
stock	*gǔpiào*	股票
tariff	*guānshuì*	关税
tax	*shuì*	税
tax rate	*shuì lǜ*	税率
technology transfer	*jìshù zhuǎnràng*	技术转让
trade	*màoyì*	贸易
transaction	*jiāoyì*	交易
transportation charges	*yùnshū fèiyòng*	运输费用
vice president	*fù zǒngcái*	副总裁
wages	*gōngzī*	工资
wholesale	*pīfā*	批发
wholly foreign-owned venture	*quánzī yōngyǒu de wàiqǐ*	全资拥有的外企

QUICK GRAMMAR GUIDE

Compared to that of many other languages, including most European languages, Chinese grammar is not particularly difficult to master. More often than not, word order in Chinese is intuitive to English speakers. And in many instances Chinese is quite a bit simpler—for example, you don't have to conjugate verbs or learn verb tenses.

The synopsis of Chinese grammar that follows is by necessity oversimplified. Rather than employ the complicated terminology of the linguist, we have attempted to analyze Chinese grammar using parts of speech familiar to English speakers.

NOUNS AND PRONOUNS

Like most Chinese words, nouns can be one or more characters in length. No distinction is made between singular and plural nouns—there is no equivalent of adding *s* as is done in English. When it is necessary to distinguish plurals, this is done through the use of auxiliary measure words. There is also no distinction between subjects and objects; the same word can serve both purposes. And unlike nouns in the Romance languages, Chinese nouns are not assigned genders.

Examples of nouns:

树	*shù*	tree
东西	*dōngxi*	thing
电视	*diànshì*	television
桌子	*zhuōzi*	table

c = ts; *q* = ch; *x* = sh; *z* = dz; *zh* = j

Pronouns stand in for nouns, just as they do in English. They also do not change whether used as subjects or objects.

Simple pronouns:

我	*Wǒ*	I; me
你	*nǐ*	you (singular)
他；她；它	*tā*	he; she; it (the written characters change for each of these three meanings, but their pronunciation is the same)
我们	*wǒmén*	we
你们	*nǐmén*	you (plural)
他们	*tāmén*	they

NOTE: The **mén** (们) character that is added to **wǒ**, **nǐ**, and **tā** to render them in the plural form (as above) may *not* be used to make plural nouns or pronouns representing inanimate objects.

POSSESSIVES AND MEASURE WORDS

To make a possessive out of a noun or pronoun, simply add the particle **de** (的). Thus "my" or "mine" is **wǒ de** in Chinese; "their" or "theirs" is **tāmén de**. Similarly,

老师的	*lǎoshī de*	the teacher's
车子的	*chēzi de*	of the car; the car's

Chinese nouns are counted by using measure words. We do this to some extent in English when we say "a ream of paper" or "a school of fish." But while in English we have the option of simply saying "a book" or "three tables," in Chinese you *must* use a measure word in order to specify number. So in Chinese "a book" is not "yì shū," ("one" + "book"), it is **yìběn shū** (一本书), or one volume of books. Similarly, three tables is **sān zhāng zhuōzi** (三张桌子).

There isn't one unique measure word for each noun; measure words describe classes of objects with similar characteristics. Thus the word **zhāng** (张) in the example above can be used to describe wide, flat objects of many types—not only tables, but also pieces of paper and sheets. **Tiáo** (条), another measure word, is used for counting long, thin objects like sticks and poles.

The general-use measure word is **gè** (个). It is present throughout this volume in such combinations as **zhèige** and **nèige**. You can generally get away with using **gè** when you're not sure what the measure word of choice is for a particular noun. It may not be the exact word, but it will certainly be understood.

一棵树	*yì kē shù*	a tree
四支笔	*sì zhī bǐ*	four pens
一所房子	*yī suǒ fángzi*	a house
几个人	*jǐge rén*	some people

VERBS

Verbs are simple affairs in Chinese. They, too, may be one or more characters in length. Chinese verbs are not conjugated, but keep one simple form regardless of the subject and regardless of the tense. Thus the verb **qù** (去), meaning "to go," is the same whether the subject is I, you, he,

c = ts; *q* = ch; *x* = sh; *z* = dz; *zh* = j

we, or they, and whether the action took place yesterday or will happen three weeks from now. There are, of course, ways to indicate tense in Chinese sentences (see below), but auxiliaries do this job; the verb is never inflected.

Examples of verbs:

买	*mǎi*	to buy; also buy, buys, will buy, buying, bought, etc.
看	*kàn*	to see
来	*lái*	to come
学习	*xuéxí*	to study

VERB TENSES

Since the verb form in Chinese doesn't change to reflect the time that an action takes place, helping words do the trick. To suggest that an action took place in the past, the particles **le** (了) and/or **guò** (过) are employed, usually either directly after the verb or else at the end of the sentence. **Le** tends to imply that an action has recently been completed, whereas **guò** can apply to one that took place either far in the past or at some unspecified time in the past.

我吃了。	*Wǒ chī le.*	I've eaten.
他买了书。 (他买书了。)	*Tā mǎi le shū.* (*Tā mǎi shū le.*)	He bought (a) book.
猫走了。	*Māo zǒu le.*	The cat has gone.
我看过。	*Wǒ kàn guò.*	I've already seen (it).
我去过了。	*Wǒ qù guò le.*	I've gone (there) before.

Future tense is generally expressed using the helping words **yào** (要) or **huì** (会). Since **yào** also means "to want," it can imply intention as well.

我要离开。	*Wǒ yào líkāi.*	I will (want to) leave.
东西会破。	*Dōngxi huì pò.*	The thing is going to break.

Specific time words can naturally add precision when it is called for. If you use the word **zuótiān**, meaning "yesterday," for example, you make it clear exactly when the action took place. Unlike English, time words generally follow the subject and precede the verb, as in the examples below.

她昨天走了。	*Tā zuótiān zǒu le.*	She left yesterday.
我明年要买。	*Wǒ míngnián yào mǎi.*	I'm going to buy (something) next year.
你们后天会看到。	*Nǐmén hòutiān huì kàndào.*	You'll see (it) the day after tomorrow.

ADJECTIVES

Adjectives in Chinese don't need to agree in gender or number with the nouns they modify, as they do in many languages. The adjective **hǎo** (好), which means "good," can be used with I, you, he, she, it, we, and they without changing its form. Adjectives also don't require the verb "to be" in the sentence; **Tā lèi**, which means "he is tired," is in fact literally

c = ts; *q* = ch; *x* = sh; *z* = dz; *zh* = j

just "he tired." Adding the verb "to be" to form "Tā shì lèi" would be incorrect in Chinese.

When adjectives modify nouns in phrases they generally precede the noun, often using the auxiliary **de** in between.

Some examples of adjectives and adjectival phrases:

红	*hóng*	red
聪明	*cōngmíng*	smart; intelligent
你聪明。	*Nǐ cōngmíng.*	You are smart.
我们矮。	*Wǒmén ǎi.*	We are short.
蓝的书	*lán de shū*	blue book
大的人	*dà de rén*	big person

ADVERBS

Adverbs modify verbs or adjectives. Examples are **yě** (也), meaning "also"; **hěn** (很), meaning "very"; and **zǒng** (总), meaning "always." They precede the verb or the adjective they modify.

弟弟也去。	*Dìdi yě qù.*	Younger brother is also going.
中国很大。	*Zhōngguó hěn dà.*	China is very large.
天总下雨。	*Tiān zǒng xià yǔ.*	It always rains.

NEGATIVES

The insertion of a single word will generally turn a Chinese declarative sentence into its negative. The most common negative is the word **bù** (不), and it is placed just before the verb in the sentence. (**Bù**, by the way, is normally said in the fourth tone; when it precedes another fourth tone, however, it is pronounced in the second tone, as **bú**).

王先生不来。	*Wáng Xiānsheng bù lái.*	Mr. Wang isn't coming.
桌子不平。	*Zhuōzi bù píng.*	The table isn't flat.
他们不累。	*Tāmén bú lèi.*	They aren't tired.

The word **méi** (没) may also be used to indicate negation. It *must* be used to negate the verb **yǒu**, "to have"—"bù" isn't acceptable here. **Méi** is used widely as well to indicate an action which has not been completed.

你没有书。	*Nǐ méi yǒu shū.*	You don't have a book.
她没去。	*Tā méi qù.*	She hasn't gone. or She didn't go.

One final note: there isn't one single way to say "not" in Chinese. To communicate disagreement or unwillingness, one simply negates whatever verb has just been used. So if someone asks a question with the verb "to be," for example, **Nǐ shì Měiguórén ma?** ("Are you American?"), the way to say no is **bú shì**. Similarly, questions with **yǒu méi yǒu** ("do you have any" or "did you") are negated with **méiyǒu**, and **Nǐ qù bú qù?** ("Are you going?") would be answered in the negative as **bú qù**.

INTERROGATIVES

There are three basic ways to form questions in Chinese. The simplest and most common way is to add the particle **ma**

c = ts; *q* = ch; *x* = sh; *z* = dz; *zh* = j

(吗), pronounced in the neutral tone, to the very end of a declarative sentence.

她累吗？	*Tā lèi ma?*	Is she tired?
李先生饿吗？	*Lǐ Xiānsheng è ma?*	Is Mr. Li hungry?

The second way to ask a question is to use the choice method. This presents the listener with two opposite alternatives and allows him or her to select one. For example, **zǒu** (走) means "to leave" and, of course, **bù zǒu** means "to not leave." So "Are you leaving?" which could be expressed as **Ní zǒu ma** (see above), can also be asked as **Ní zǒu bù zǒu?**

人高不高？	*Rén gāo bù gāo?*	Is the person tall?
你去不去北京？	*Nǐ qù bú qù Běijīng?*	Are you going to Beijing?
他有没有书？	*Tā yǒu méi yǒu shū?*	Does he have any books?

The third method is by employing an interrogative pronoun. Examples are **shéi** (谁) or "who," **zěnme** (怎么) or "how," **shénme** (什么) or "what," **wèishénme** (为什么) or "why," and **náli** (哪里) or "where." Thus **Nǐ shì shéi?**, literally "You are who?" is understood to be the question "Who are you?"

这是什么？	*Zhè shì shénme?*	What is this?
你为什么不来？	*Nǐ wèishénme bù lái?*	Why won't you come?
车站在哪里？	*Chēzhàn zài náli?*	Where is the station?

NOTE: In answering a question in Chinese, follow the grammar of the question. The answer to **Zhè shì shénme**, above, might be **Zhè shì yǐzi** ("This is a chair"). You just substitute the noun for the interrogative pronoun. Similarly, the answer to **Tā yǒu méi yǒu shū** should be either **Tā yǒu**

shū ("He has books") or else **Tā méi yǒu shū**, ("He doesn't have any books") and the answer to **Tā lèi ma?** is **Tā lèi** ("She is tired") or **Tā bú lèi** ("She isn't tired"). Just stick to the word order of the original question and you won't go too far wrong.

c = ts; q = ch; x = sh; z = dz; zh = j

ENGLISH-CHINESE DICTIONARY

A

a; an *yī; yígè* 一；一个

able *néng* 能

above *shàngmiàn* 上面

abroad *guówài* 国外

according to *ànzhào* 按照

accountant *kuàijì shī* 会计师

ache *tòng* 痛

  headache *tóu tòng* 头痛

  stomachache *dùzi tòng* 肚子痛

  toothache *yá tòng* 牙痛

actor *yǎnyuán* 演员

acupuncture *zhēnjiǔ* 针灸

adaptor (electrical) *zhuǎnjiē qì* 转接器

add *jiā* 加

address *dìzhǐ* 地址

adult *chéngrén* 成人

advertisement *guǎnggào* 广告

advice *jiànyì* 建议

aerogram *hángkōng yóujiǎn* 航空邮简

airline *hángkōng gōngsī* 航空公司

afraid *pà* 怕

after *yǐhòu* 以后

afternoon *xiàwǔ* 下午

again *zài* 再

agree *tóngyì* 同意

ahead *qiántóu* 前头

air conditioning *kōngtiáo* 空调

airmail letter *hángkōng xìn* 航空信

airplane *fēijī* 飞机

airport *fēijī chǎng* 飞机场

à la carte *língdiǎn* 零点

alcohol (ethyl) *jiǔjīng* 酒精

all *quán; dōu* 全；都

  all day *quán tiān* 全天

  all over (ended) *quánbù jiéshù* 全部结束

  all together (in all) *zǒnggòng* 总共

allergy *guòmǐn* 过敏

almost *jīhū* 几乎

alone *dāndú* 单独

already *yǐjīng* 已经

also *yě* 也

always *zǒngshì* 总是

ambulance *jiùhù chē* 救护车

America *Měiguó* 美国

American (n) *Měiguórén* 美国人

American (adj) *Měiguó de* 美国的

among *zài . . . zhōng* 在…中

and *hé* 和

answer *huídá* 回答

antique *gǔdǒng* 古董

any *rènhé* 任何

anybody *rènhé rén* 任何人

anyplace *rènhé dìfāng*
  任何地方
anything *rènhé dōngxi*
  任何东西
anytime *rènhé shíjiān*
  任何时间
appendicitis *lánwěi yán*
  阑尾炎
appetizer *kāiwèi xiǎocài*
  开胃小菜
apple *píngguǒ* 苹果
appliance *jiāyòng diànqì*
  家用电器
appointment *yuēhuì* 约会
approximately *dàyuē* 大约
argument *zhēnglùn* 争论
arm *shǒubèi* 手臂
arrive *dàodá* 到达
artist *yìshù jiā* 艺术家
ask (a question) *wèn* 问
asthma *qìchuǎn bìng* 气喘病
at *zài* 在
athlete *yùndòng yuán* 运动员
auditorium *lǐtáng* 礼堂
August *Bāyuè* 八月
Australia *Àodàlìyà* 澳大利亚
author *zuòzhě* 作者
automatic teller machine
  (ATM) *tíkuǎn jī* 提款机
automobile *qìchē* 汽车
avoid *bìmiǎn* 避免
awaken *xǐng* 醒

B

back (body) *bèi* 背
back (location) *hòumiàn*
  后面

backward *luòhòu* 落后
bacon *xūnròu* 薰肉
bad *huài* 坏
baggage *xínglǐ* 行李
bake *kǎo* 烤
bakery *gāobǐng diàn* 糕饼店
bamboo shoot *zhúsǔn* 竹笋
banana *xiāngjiāo* 香蕉
bandage *bēngdài* 绷带
bank *yínháng* 银行
bar *jiǔbā* 酒吧
barber *lǐfà shī* 理发师
barbershop *lǐfà guǎn* 理发馆
bargain (v) *jiǎngjià* 讲价
bargain (v) *tǎojià* 讨价
baseball *bàngqiú* 棒球
basket *lánzi* 篮子
basketball *lánqiú* 篮球
bathe *xǐzǎo* 洗澡
bathing suit *yóuyǒng yī*
  游泳衣
bathroom (for bathing) *xǐzǎo
  jiān* 洗澡间
bathroom (lavatory) *cèsuǒ*
  厕所
bathtub *zǎopén* 澡盆
battery *diànchí* 电池
be *shì* 是
beach *hǎitān* 海滩
bean curd *dòufu* 豆腐
beautiful *měilì* 美丽
beauty parlor *měiróng yuàn*
  美容院
because *yīnwèi* 因为
become *chéngwéi* 成为
bed *chuáng* 床
bedroom *wòfáng* 卧房
beef *niúròu* 牛肉

beer *píjiǔ* 啤酒

before *yǐqián* 以前

begin *kāishǐ* 开始

behind *zài hòumiàn* 在后面

believe *xiāngxìn* 相信

below *zài dǐxià* 在底下

belt *pídài* 皮带

beside *zài pángbiān* 在旁边

better *gèng hǎo* 更好

between *zài . . . zhījiān*
在…之间

beverage *yǐnliào* 饮料

bicycle *zìxíng chē* 自行车

big *dà* 大

bill (currency note) *chāopiào*
钞票

bill (invoice) *zhàngdān* 帐单

　settle a bill *jié zhàng*
　结帐

birthday *shēngrì* 生日

bitter *kǔ* 苦

black *hēi* 黑

blanket *tǎnzi* 毯子

bleed *liú xiě* 流血

blood *xiě* 血

　blood type *xiěxíng* 血型

blouse *nǚ chèn shān* 女衬衫

blue *lán* 蓝

boat *chuán* 船

body *shēntǐ* 身体

bone *gǔ* 骨

book (n) *shū* 书

bookstore *shūdiàn* 书店

boot *xuē* 靴

borrow *jiè* 借

boss (n) *lǎobǎn* 老板

bottle *píngzi* 瓶子

bowl *wǎn* 碗

box (n) *hézi* 盒子

boy *nán háizi* 男孩子

boyfriend *nán péngyou*
男朋友

bracelet *shǒuzhuó* 手镯

brandy *báilándì* 白兰地

bread *miànbāo* 面包

break (v) *dǎpò* 打破

breakfast *zǎocān* 早餐

bright *liàng* 亮

bring *dàilái* 带来

broccoli *xīlánhuā* 西蓝花

brother *xiōngdì* 兄弟

　elder brother *gēge* 哥哥

　younger brother *dìdi* 弟弟

brown *kāfēi sè* 咖啡色

brush *shuāzi* 刷子

　toothbrush *yáshuā* 牙刷

Buddha *Fó* 佛

building (n) *dàlóu* 大楼

bulb *dēngpào* 灯泡

burn (injury) *shāoshāng* 烧伤

bus *gōnggòng qìchē* 公共汽车

bus stop *chē zhàn* 车站

business class *gōngwù cāng*
公务舱

businessman *shāngrén* 商人

busy *máng* 忙

but *dànshì* 但是

butter *huángyóu* 黄油

button (n) *kòuzi* 扣子

buy *mǎi* 买

C

cake *dàngāo* 蛋糕

calculator *jìsuàn qì* 计算器

call (v) *jiào* 叫

camcorder *shèxiàng jī*
摄像机

camera *zhàoxiàng jī* 照相机

can (be able to) *néng* 能

can (tin of food) *guàntóu* 罐头

Canada *Jiānádà* 加拿大

cancel *qǔxiāo* 取消

candy *tángguǒ* 糖果

can opener *kāi guàn qì* 开罐器

Cantonese dialect *Guǎngdōnghuà* 广东话

car *qìchē* 汽车

card *kǎpiàn* 卡片

care for *zhàogu* 照顾

careful *xiǎoxīn* 小心

carpet *dìtǎn* 地毯

carrot *hú luóbo* 胡萝卜

carry *dài* 带

cash (n) *xiànkuǎn* 现款

cash a check *duìxiàn* 兑现

cashew *yāoguǒ* 腰果

cashier *chūnàyuán* 出纳员

cassette *héshì lùyīndài* 盒式录音带

cat *māo* 猫

cauliflower *càihuā* 菜花

CD *guāngpán* 光盘

CD-ROM *guāngqū* 光驱

celery *qíncài* 芹菜

cell phone *shǒu jī* 手机

cemetery *mùdì* 基地

Centigrade *shèshì* 摄氏

centimeter *gōngfēn* 公分

chair *yǐzi* 椅子

Champagne *xiāngbīnjiǔ* 香槟酒

change (coins) *língqián* 零钱

change (alter, vary) *gǎibiàn* 改变

change (switch, as planes) *huàn* 换

change money *huàn qián* 换钱

charge (expense, cost) *fèiyòng* 费用

cheap *piányi* 便宜

cheat *qīpiàn* 欺骗

check (an order for money) *zhīpiào* 支票

traveler's check *lǚxíng zhīpiào* 旅行支票

check (restaurant bill) *zhàngdān* 帐单

check (examine) *chá* 查

check (consign, as baggage) *tuōyùn* 托运

cheers (toast) *gānbēi* 干杯

cheese *nǎilào* 奶酪

chicken *jī* 鸡

child *xiǎohái* 小孩

China *Zhōngguó* 中国

Chinese (person) *Zhōngguórén* 中国人

Chinese language *pǔtōnghuà; guóyǔ; hànyǔ; huáyǔ;* also *Zhōngwén* and *Zhōngguóhuà* 普通话；国语；汉语；华语；中文；中国话

chocolate *qiǎokèlì* 巧克力

choice *xuǎnzé* 选择

choose *xuǎn* 选

chopsticks *kuàizi* 筷子

church *jiàotáng* 教堂

cigarette *xiāngyān* 香烟

city *chéngshì* 城市

classmate *tóngxué* 同学

clean (adj) *gānjìng* 干净

clean (v) *nòng gānjìng* 弄干净

clock *zhōng* 钟

   alarm clock *nào zhōng* 闹钟

cloisonné *jǐngtàilán* 景泰蓝

close (v) *guān* 关

closed (store, bank, etc.) *guānle* 关了

closet *yī guì* 衣柜

cloth *bù* 布

clothing *yīfu* 衣服

coat *dà yī* 大衣

coffee *kāfēi* 咖啡

cognac *shàngděng báilándì* 上等白兰地

cold (adj) *lěng* 冷

cold (n) *shāngfēng* 伤风

collar *lǐngzi* 领子

colleague *tóngshì* 同事

color *yánsè* 颜色

comb (n) *shūzi* 梳子

come *lái* 来

comfortable *shūfu* 舒服

compact disc *guāngpán* 光盘

company (business) *gōngsī* 公司

complain *bàoyuàn* 抱怨

computer *diànnǎo* 电脑

concert *yīnyuè huì* 音乐会

conference *huìyì* 会议

confirm *quèrèn* 确认

congratulations *gōngxǐ* 恭喜

consulate *lǐngshìguǎn* 领事馆

contact lens *yǐnxíng yǎnjìng* 隐形眼镜

contagious *chuánrǎn de* 传染的

contest *bǐsài* 比赛

contract (n) *hétóng* 合同

convenient *fāngbiàn* 方便

cook (n) *chúshī* 厨师

cook (v) *zuò cài* 做菜

cookie *bǐnggān* 饼干

cool *liángkuài* 凉快

corn *yùmǐ* 玉米

cost (of production) *chéngběn* 成本

cost (price) *jiàgé* 价格

costly *guì* 贵

cotton *miánhuā* 棉花

cough *késòu* 咳嗽

count (v) *suàn* 算

country *guójiā* 国家

countryside *xiāngxià* 乡下

court of law *fǎyuàn* 法院

courtyard *yuànzi* 院子

cover *gài* 盖

cover charge *rùchǎng fèiyòng* 入场费用

crab *pángxiè* 螃蟹

cream *nǎiyóu* 奶油

credit card *xìnyòng kǎ* 信用卡

cry (v) *kū* 哭

cucumber *huángguā* 黄瓜

cup *bēizi* 杯子

curtain *chuānglián* 窗帘

custom *fēngsú* 风俗

customer *gùkè* 顾客

Customs *hǎiguān* 海关

Customs official *hǎiguān guānyuán* 海关官员

cut (v) *gē* 割

D

daily *měitiān* 每天

dance (n) *wǔhuì* 舞会

dance (v) *tiàowǔ* 跳舞

dangerous *wéixiǎn* 危险

dark *àn* 暗

date (calendar) *rìqī* 日期

date (appointment) *yuēhuì* 约会

daughter *nǚér* 女儿

day *tiān* 天

  yesterday *zuótiān* 昨天

  day after tomorrow *hòutiān* 后天

deceive *qīpiàn* 欺骗

decide *juédìng* 决定

delegation *dàibiǎotuán* 代表团

deliver *yùnsòng* 运送

deliver *sòng* 送

dentist *yáyī* 牙医

deodorant *chúchòujì* 除臭剂

depart *líkāi* 离开

department store *bǎihuò shāngdiàn* 百货商店

detergent *qīngjié jì* 清洁剂

diamond *zhuànshí* 钻石

diaper *niàobù* 尿布

diarrhea *xiè dùzi* 泻肚子

dictionary *zìdiǎn* 字典

different *bùtóng* 不同

difficult *nán* 难

difficulty *kùnnán* 困难

dine *chī* 吃

dining car *cānchē* 餐车

dining room *cāntīng* 餐厅

dinner *wǎncān* 晚餐

direct flight *zhífēi de hángbān* 直飞的航班

direction *fāngxiàng* 方向

dirty *zāng* 脏

disappointment *shīwàng* 失望

discount *zhékòu* 折扣

dish *pánzi* 盘子

distance *jùlí* 距离

district *dìqū* 地区

disturb *dárǎo* 打扰

dizzy *tóuyūn* 头晕

do *zuò* 做

doctor *yīshēng* 医生

dog *gǒu* 狗

doll *wáwa* 娃娃

dollar (U.S.) *měiyuán* 美元

door *mén* 门

doorbell *ménlíng* 门铃

down *xià* 下

  to go down *xiàqù* 下去

downstairs *lóuxià* 楼下

downtown *shì zhōngxīn* 市中心

drain (n) *páishuǐguǎn* 排水管

dress (n) *yí tào yīfu* 一套衣服

dress (v) *chuān* 穿

dress up *dǎbàn* 打扮

drink (n) *yǐnliào* 饮料

drink (v) *hē* 喝

driver *sījī* 司机

drugstore *yàofáng* 药房

drunk (adj) *zuì* 醉

dry (adj) *gān* 干

dry (v) *nòng gān* 弄干

dry-clean *gānxǐ* 干洗

duck (n) *yā* 鸭

dumpling *jiǎozi* 饺子

during *zài . . . zhōng* 在⋯中

dynasty *cháodài* 朝代

c = ts; *q* = ch; *x* = sh; *z* = dz; *zh* = j

E

each *měige* 每个

each other *hùxiāng* 互相

ear *ěrduō* 耳朵

early *zǎo* 早

earn *zhuàn* 赚

earrings *ěrhuán* 耳环

East (Orient) *Dōngfāng* 东方

easy *róngyì* 容易

eat *chī* 吃

economy class *pǔtōng cāng* 普通舱

egg *dàn* 蛋

eight *bā* 八

eighteen *shíbā* 十八

eighty *bāshí* 八十

electricity *diàn* 电

electronic game *diànzi yóuxì* 电子游戏

elevator *diàntī* 电梯

eleven *shíyī* 十一

e-mail *diànzi yóujiàn* 电子邮件

embassy *dàshí guǎn* 大使馆

embroidery *xiùhuā* 绣花

emergency *jízhěn* 急诊

empty *kōng* 空

end (v) *wán* 完

engineer *gōngchéng shī* 工程师

English (adj) *Yīngguó de* 英国的

English (language) *Yīngwén* 英文

English (person) *Yīngguó rén* 英国人

enough *gòu* 够

enter *jìnrù* 进入

entire *quánbù* 全部

entrance *jìnkǒu* 进口

envelope *xìnfēng* 信封

especially *tèbié* 特别

evening *wǎnshàng* 晚上

every *měi* 每

every day *měitiān* 每天

everybody *měige rén* 每个人

everywhere *měige dìfāng* 每个地方

examine *jiǎnchá* 检查

example *lìzi* 例子

exchange (money) *duìhuàn* 兑换

exchange rate *duìhuàn lù* 兑换率

Excuse me. (apologizing) *Duìbuqǐ.* 对不起。

Excuse me. (getting attention) *Láojià.* 劳驾。

exhibition *zhǎnlǎn* 展览

exit *chūkǒu* 出口

expensive *guì* 贵

export *chūkǒu* 出口

eye (n) *yǎnjīng* 眼睛

F

fabric *bùliào* 布料

face (n) *liǎn* 脸

factory *gōngchǎng* 工厂

Fahrenheit *Huáshì* 华氏

fall (season) *qiūjì* 秋季

fall (v) *diào* 掉

false *jiǎde* 假的

family *jiātíng* 家庭

fan (n) *shànzi* 扇子

far *yuǎn* 远

farmer *nóngmín* 农民

fast (adv) *kuài* 快

fat *pàng* 胖

father *fùqīn* 父亲

   dad *bàba* 爸爸

faucet *shuǐlóngtóu* 水龙头

fax *chuánzhēn* 传真

fax machine *chuánzhēn jī*
   传真机

February *Èryuè* 二月

fee *fèiyòng* 费用

feel *gǎndào* 感到

festival *jiérì* 节日

fever *fāshāo* 发烧

few *shǎo* 少

   a few *jǐge* 几个

fifteen *shíwǔ* 十五

fifty *wǔshí* 五十

film (rolls, for camera)
   jiāojuǎn 胶卷

film (movie) *diànyǐng* 电影

finger *shóuzhǐ* 手指

finished *wánchéng* 完成

fire (n) *huǒ* 火

first *dìyī* 第一

first aid *jíjiù* 急救

first class *tóuděng cāng*
   头等舱

fish (n) *yú* 鱼

fish (v) *diào yú* 钓鱼

five *wǔ* 五

fix *xiū* 修

flashlight *shǒudiàntǒng*
   手电筒

flat (adj) *píng* 平

flavor *wèidào* 味道

flight (airline) *hángbān* 航班

   flight attendant
   chéngwùyuán 乘务员

floor (ground) *dìmiàn* 地面

floor (story) *lóu* 楼

floppy disk *ruǎn cípán*
   软磁盘

flower *huā* 花

fly (v) *fēi* 飞

fog *wù* 雾

follow *gēnzhe* 跟着

food *shípǐn* 食品

foot (anatomy) *jiǎo* 脚

foot (measurement) *yīngchǐ*
   英尺

foreign *wàiguó de* 外国的

foreign exchange *wàihuì*
   外汇

forget *wàngjì* 忘记

fork (n) *chāzi* 叉子

former *yǐqián de* 以前的

forty *sìshí* 四十

forward *xiàng qián* 向前

four *sì* 四

fourteen *shísì* 十四

free (without cost) *miǎnfèi*
   免费

freedom *zìyóu* 自由

fresh *xīnxiān* 新鲜

freezer *lěngdòng jī* 冷冻机

Friday *Xīngqīwǔ* 星期五

friend *péngyǒu* 朋友

Friendship Store *Yǒuyì*
   Shāngdiàn 友谊商店

front *qiánmiàn* 前面

fruit *shuǐguǒ* 水果

fur *pímáo* 皮毛

furniture *jiājù* 傢具

G

garbage *lājī* 垃圾

garden *huāyuán* 花园

---

c = ts; *q* = ch; *x* = sh; *z* = dz; *zh* = j

garlic *dà suàn* 大蒜

gas station *jiāyóu zhàn* 加油站

gasoline *qìyóu* 汽油

general manager *zǒngjīnglǐ* 总经理

get up *qǐlái* 起来

gift *lǐpǐn* 礼品

ginger *jiāng* 姜

girl *nǚ háizi* 女孩子

girlfriend *nǚ péngyou* 女朋友

give *gěi* 给

glass (material) *bōli* 玻璃

glass (cup) *bēizi* 杯子

glasses (spectacles) *yǎnjìng* 眼镜

glove *shǒutào* 手套

glue *jiāoshuǐ* 胶水

go (leave) *zǒu* 走

go down *xià qù* 下去

gold *jīn* 金

good *hǎo* 好

Good-bye. *Zàijiàn.* 再见。

goose *é* 鹅

gram *kè* 克

grape *pútáo* 葡萄

gray *huī sè* 灰色

green *lǜ* 绿

ground (n) *dìmiàn* 地面

guide (lead sightseeing) *dǎoyóu* 导游

guidebook *lǚyóu shǒucè* 导游手册

H

hair *tóufa* 头发

haircut *lǐfà* 理发

half *bàn* 半

ham *huótuǐ* 火腿

hamburger *hànbǎo bāo* 汉堡包

hand *shǒu* 手

handicapped person *cánjī rén* 残疾人

handkerchief *shǒujuàn* 手绢

handsome *hǎokàn* 好看

hanger (clothes) *yījià* 衣架

happy *gāoxìng* 高兴

hat *màozi* 帽子

have *yǒu* 有

have just *gāngcái* 刚才

have to *bìxū* 必需

he *tā* 他

head *tóu* 头

healthy *jiànkāng* 健康

hear *tīngjiàn* 听见

heart *xīnzàng* 心脏

heart attack *xīnzàng bìng* 心脏病

heat (n) *nuǎnqì* 暖气

heater *nuǎnqì jī* 暖气机

height *gāodù* 高度

Hello. *Nǐ hǎo.* 你好。

help (assist) *bāng máng* 帮忙

help (for emergencies) *jiù mìng* 救命

here *zhèlǐ* 这里

high *gāo* 高

high school *gāo zhōng* 高中

highway *gōnglù* 公路

hire *gùyòng* 雇用

hit *dǎ* 打

hold *ná* 拿

holiday *jiérì* 节日

homepage *Wǎng yè* 网页

honey *fēngmì* 蜂蜜

hope *xīwàng* 希望

horse *mǎ* 马

hospital *yīyuàn* 医院
host (n) *zhǔrén* 主人
host (v) *zhāodài* 招待
hot *rè* 热
hot dog *rè gǒu* 热狗
hotel *lǚguǎn* 旅馆
  fàndiàn 饭店
hot pepper sauce *làjiāo jiàng*
  辣椒酱
hour *xiǎoshí* 小时
house (n) *fángzi* 房子
how *zěnme* 怎么
how many (for a few) *jǐgè*
  几个
how many (any number)
  duōshǎo 多少
humid *mēnrè* 焖热
hundred *bǎi* 百
  one hundred *yìbǎi* 一百
  two hundred *liángbǎi*
  两百
hungry *è* 饿
hurry (quickly) *kuài* 快
  in a hurry (pressed) *jí* 急
husband *zhàngfu* 丈夫

I

I (me) *wǒ* 我
ice *bīng* 冰
ice cream *bīngqílín* 冰淇淋
if *jiǎrú* 假如
ill (get sick) *bìngle* 病了
immediately *mǎshàng* 马上
import (trade goods) *jìnkǒu*
  进口
important *zhòngyào* 重要
impossible *bù kěnéng* 不可能

in *zài . . . lǐ* 在…里
inch *yīngcùn* 英寸
include *bāokuò* 包括
income *shōurù* 收入
infection *fāyán* 发炎
information *xìnxī* 信息
information desk *xúnwèn*
  chù 询问处
inside *zài . . . lǐmiàn*
  在…里面
instead of *dàitì* 代替
insurance *bǎoxiǎn* 保险
intelligent *cōngmíng* 聪明
interesting *yǒu yìsi* 有意思
international *guójì* 国际
Internet *Yīngtèwǎng* 英特网
interpreter *fānyì* 翻译
introduce *jièshào* 介绍
investment *tóuzī* 投资
invite *yāoqǐng* 邀请
iron (v) *tàng* 烫
iron (n) *yùndǒu* 熨斗
island *dǎo* 岛
it *tā* 它
itch *yǎng* 痒
itinerary *rìchéng* 日程

J

jacket *wàitào* 外套
jade *yù* 玉
jam *guǒjiàng* 果酱
January *Yīyuè* 一月
jewelry *zhūbǎo* 珠宝
jewelry shop *zhūbǎo diàn*
  珠宝店
joke *xiàohuà* 笑话
journey *lǚxíng* 旅行

juice (n) *guǒzhī* 果汁
July *Qīyuè* 七月
June *Liùyuè* 六月
just (very recently) *gāngcái* 刚才
just (only) *zhǐ* 只

K

karaoke *kǎlāōukèi* 卡拉OK
keep *liú* 留
ketchup *fānqié jiàng* 番茄酱
key *yàoshi* 钥匙
kilogram *gōngjīn* 公斤
kilometer *gōnglǐ* 公里
kitchen *chúfáng* 厨房
knife (n) *dāozi* 刀子
know (facts) *zhīdào* 知道
know (people) *rènshi* 认识

L

lake *hú* 湖
lamb (mutton) *yángròu* 羊肉
lamp *dēng* 灯
land (n) *dì* 地
landscape (n) *fēngjǐng* 风景
language *yǔyán* 语言
laptop computer *biànxié shì diànnǎo* 便携式电脑
large *dà* 大
last (final) *zuìhòu* 最后
late *wǎn* 晚
late in arriving *chídào* 迟到
laugh *xiào* 笑
launder (clothing) *xǐyī* 洗衣
lawyer *lǜshī* 律师
learn *xuéxí* 学习
least *zuì shǎo* 最少
  at least *zhìshǎo* 至少

leather *pígé* 皮革
leave (v) *líkāi* 离开
left (direction) *zuǒbiān* 左边
leg *tuǐ* 腿
lemon *níngméng* 柠檬
lend *jiè (gěi)* 借 (给)
less *shǎo* 少
letter (correspondence) *xìn* 信
lettuce *shēng cài* 生菜
library *túshūguǎn* 图书馆
light (weight) *qīng* 轻
  lighter *qīng diǎn* 轻点
lighter (cigarette) *dǎ huǒ jī* 打火机
like (similar to) *xiàng* 像
like (v) *xǐhuān* 喜欢
lipstick *kǒuhóng* 口红
liquor *jiǔ* 酒
list *dānzi* 单子
listen *tīng* 听
liter *shēng* 升
little (adj) *xiǎo* 小
little (adv) *shǎo* 少
live (exist) *huó* 活
live (reside) *zhù* 住
loan *dàikuǎn* 贷款
lobby *dàtīng* 大厅
lobster *lóngxiā* 龙虾
local *běndì* 本地
lock *suǒ* 锁
long *cháng* 长
long distance *chángtú* 长途
look at *kàn* 看
look for *zhǎo* 找
lose (misplace) *diū* 丢
lose (not win) *shū* 输
lose your way *mí lù* 迷路
lots (many) *hěn duō* 很多
love *ài* 爱

low (in height) *dī* 低
luck *yùnqì* 运气
luggage *xíngli* 行李
lunch (n) *wǔcān* 午餐

M

magazine *zázhì* 杂志
mail (v) *jì xìn* 寄信
mailbox *yóutǒng* 邮筒
mailman *yóuchāi* 邮差
make *zuò* 做
makeup *huàzhuāng pǐn*
  化妆品
man *nán rén* 男人
manager *jīnglǐ* 经理
  general manager
  zǒngjīnglǐ 总经理
Mandarin (dialect) *Pǔtōnghuà*
  普通话
manicure *xiū zhǐjia* 修指甲
many *hěn duō* 很多
  too many *tài duō* 太多
map *dìtú* 地图
March *Sānyuè* 三月
market *shìchǎng* 市场
marry *jiéhūn* 结婚
massage *ànmó* 按摩
matches (lighter) *huǒchái*
  火柴
material (cloth) *bùliào* 布料
matter (affair) *shìqíng* 事情
  It doesn't matter. *Méi yǒu
  guānxi.* 没有关系
  What's the matter? *Zěnme
  le?* 怎么了？
mattress *chuáng diàn* 床垫
May *Wǔyuè* 五月

maybe *kěnéng* 可能
mayonnaise *dànhuáng jiàng*
  蛋黄酱
me *wǒ* 我
meal *cān* 餐
meaning *yìsi* 意思
measure (v) *liáng* 量
meat *ròu* 肉
medicine *yào* 药
medium (cooking) *bú nèn bù
  lǎo* 不嫩不老
meet with *huìjiàn* 会见
meeting *huìyì* 会议
menu *càidān* 菜单
merchant *shāngrén* 商人
meter *gōngchǐ* 公尺
meter *biǎo* 表
microwave oven *wēibō lú*
  微波炉
middle *zhōngjiān* 中间
  in the middle of *zài . . .
  zhōngjiān* 在…中间
midnight *wǔyè* 午夜
milk *niúnǎi* 牛奶
million *bǎi wàn* 百万
minute (time) *fēn* 分
mirror (n) *jìngzi* 镜子
miss (think of, remember)
  xiǎngniàn 想念
Miss *Xiáojiě* 小姐
mistake (n) *cuòwù* 错误
misunderstanding *wùhuì*
  误会
money *qián* 钱
month *yuè* 月
morning *zǎoshàng* 早上
  good morning *zǎoshàng
  hǎo* 早上好

c = ts; *q* = ch; *x* = sh; *z* = dz; *zh* = j

mother *mǔqīn* 母亲
  mom *māma* 妈妈
mountain *shān* 山
mouth *zuǐbā* 嘴吧
movie *diànyǐng* 电影
Mr. *Xiānsheng* 先生
Mrs. *Fūren* 夫人
museum *bówùguǎn* 博物馆
mushroom *mógū* 蘑菇
music *yīnyuè* 音乐
musician *yīnyuè jiā* 音乐家
mustard *jièmò* 芥末
my *wǒde* 我的

N

name *míngzì* 名字
  surname *xìng* 姓
  My name is *wǒ jiào* 我叫
  What's your name?
    Nǐ jiào shénme míngzì
    你叫什么名字？
napkin *cānjīn* 餐巾
napkin, sanitary *yuèjīng dài*
    月经带
near (to) *lí . . . jìn* 离…近
necessary *bìxū* 必需
neck *bózi* 脖子
necklace *xiàngliàn* 项链
need *xūyào* 需要
needle *zhēn* 针
negative (film) *dǐpiàn* 底片
neighbor *línjū* 邻居
never *yǒngbù* 永不
new *xīn* 新
news *xīnwén* 新闻
newspaper *bàozhǐ* 报纸
New Zealand *Xīn Xīlán*
    新西兰
next *xià yígè* 下一个

night *wǎnshàng* 晚上
nine *jiǔ* 九
nineteen *shíjiǔ* 十九
ninety *jiǔshí* 九十
no (not true) *bú shì* 不是
noisy *chǎo* 吵
nonstop flight *zhídá de
    hángbān* 直达的航班
noodle *miàntiáo* 面条
noon *zhōngwǔ* 中午
north *běifāng* 北方
nose *bízi* 鼻子
notebook *bǐjì běn* 笔记本
novel (story) *xiǎoshuō* 小说
now *xiànzài* 现在
number (numeral) *hàomǎ*
    号码
  room number *fángjiān
    hàomǎ* 房间号码
number (quantity) *shùzì* 数字
nurse *hùshì* 护士

O

obtain *dédào* 得到
ocean *hǎiyáng* 海洋
of course *dāngrán* 当然
offer (proffer) *tígòng* 提供
office *bàngōngshì* 办公室
  box office *shòupiào chù*
    售票处
post office *yóujú* 邮局
often *jīngcháng* 经常
oil *yóu* 油
O.K. *kéyǐ* 可以
old *lǎo* 老
  How old are you? *Nǐ duō
    dà le?* 你多大了？
on (top of) *zài . . . shàng*
    在…上

one (number) *yī* 一
one (item) *yígè* 一个
onion *yángcōng* 洋葱
on-line *shàngwǎng* 上网
only (sole) *wéiyī* 惟一
only have *zhǐyǒu* 只有
open *kāi* 开
opera *gējù* 歌剧
operator (switchboard) *zǒngjī*
　　总机
opportunity *jīhuì* 机会
opposite *xiāngfǎn* 相反
or (conjunctive) *huòzhe*
　　或者
or (disjunctive) *háishì* 还是
orange (fruit) *júzi* 橘子
orange (color) *júhóng sè*
　　橘红色
orchestra *yuèduì* 乐队
other (those left out) *qítā*
　　其他
other (alternative) *lìngwài*
　　另外
outside *wàimiàn* 外面
over (finished) *wánle* 完了
over (on top of) *zài . . .*
　　shàngmiàn 在…上面
overcoat *dàyī* 大衣
overseas *hǎiwài* 海外
owe *qiàn* 欠

P

package *bāoguǒ* 包裹
pain *tòng* 痛
painting *huà* 画
pair (n) *shuāng* 双
　　duì 对

pajamas *shuìyī* 睡衣
pants *kùzi* 裤子
paper *zhǐ* 纸
　　toilet paper *wèishēng zhǐ*
　　卫生纸
　　wrapping paper *bāozhuāng*
　　zhǐ 包装纸
　　writing paper *xiězì zhǐ*
　　写字纸
park (n) *gōngyuán* 公园
passport *hùzhào* 护照
pay (v) *fù* 付
peach *táozi* 桃子
peanuts *huāshēngmǐ* 花生米
pear *lí* 梨
pen (ballpoint) *yuánzhū bǐ*
　　圆珠笔
pencil *qiānbǐ* 铅笔
pepper *hújiāo* 胡椒
perfect (adj) *wánměi* 完美
perfume *xiāngshuǐ* 香水
permit (n) *xúkězhèng* 许可证
permit (v) *ràng* 让
person *rén* 人
pharmacy *yàofáng* 药房
photograph (n) *zhàopiàn*
　　照片
photograph (v) *zhàoxiàng*
　　照相
picnic *yěcān* 野餐
picture (painting) *huà* 画
pie *pài* 排
piece *kuài; jiàn* 块；件
pigeon *gēzi* 鸽子
pillow *zhěntou* 枕头
pilot *jiàshǐ* 驾驶
pin (safety pin or brooch)
　　biézhēn 别针

c = ts; *q* = ch; *x* = sh; *z* = dz; *zh* = j

pin (straight) *dàtóu zhēn* 大头针

pineapple *bōluó* 菠萝

pink *fěnhóng sè* 粉红色

pizza *bǐsà bǐng* 比萨饼

place (n) *dìfāng* 地方

plan *jìhuà* 计划

plate *pánzi* 盘子

platform *yuètái* 月台

play (drama) *huàjù* 话剧

play (v) *wán* 玩

please *qǐng* 请

plug (electrical) *chātóu* 插头

pocketbook *qiánbāo* 钱包

police *jǐngchá* 警察

police station *jǐngchá jú* 警察局

poor (not rich) *qióng* 穷

poor (pitiful) *kělián* 可怜

porcelain *cíqì* 瓷器

pork *zhūròu* 猪肉

porter *fúwùyuán* 服务员

post office *yóujú* 邮局

postage *yóufèi* 邮费

postcard *míngxìnpiàn* 明信片

pot *guōzi* 锅子

potato *tǔdòu* 土豆

pottery *táoqì* 陶器

pound (weight) *bàng* 磅

pound sterling, British *Yīng bàng* 英磅

practice (v) *liànxí* 练习

pregnant *huáiyùn* 怀孕

prepare *zhǔnbèi* 准备

prescription *yàofāng* 药方

pretty *piàoliàng* 漂亮

price (n) *jiàgé* 价格

printer *dǎyìn jī* 打印机

private *sīrén* 私人

problem *wèntí* 问题

processing fee *shǒuxù fèi* 手续费

profession *zhíyè* 职业

profit *lìrùn* 利润

program (n) *jiémù* 节目

promise (v) *yǔnnuò* 允诺

pronounce (sound) *fāyīn* 发音

protect *bǎohù* 保护

public (adj) *gōnggòng* 公共

pudding *bùdīng* 布丁

pull *lā* 拉

purchase *mǎi* 买

purple *zǐsè* 紫色

purse *qiánbāo* 钱包

push *tuī* 推

put *fàng* 放

Q

quality *zhìliàng* 质量

quantity *shùliàng* 数量

quarter (fraction) *sì fēn zhī yī* 四分之一

 three quarters *sì fēn zhī sān* 四分之三

question (n) *wèntí* 问题

quiet *ānjìng* 安静

quick *kuài* 快

quilt *miánbèi* 棉被

R

radio (n) *shōuyīnjī* 收音机

railroad *tiělù* 铁路

railroad station *huǒchē zhàn* 火车站

rain (n) *yǔ* 雨

rain (v) *xià yǔ* 下雨

raincoat *yǔyī* 雨衣
rare (cooking) *nèn* 嫩
rate of exchange *duìhuàn lù* 兑换率
raw *shēng de* 生的
razor *dāopiàn* 刀片
read *dú* 读
ready *zhǔnbèi hǎole* 准备好了
really *zhēn de* 真的
rear *hòumiàn* 后面
reason (n) *lǐyóu* 理由
receipt *shōujù* 收据
receive *shōudào* 收到
recently *zuìjìn* 最近
recommend *tuījiàn* 推荐
record (disk) *chàngpiàn* 唱片
red *hóng* 红
refrigerator *bīngxiāng* 冰箱
refund *tuì qián* 退钱
refuse (v) *jùjué* 拒绝
regret *yíhàn* 遗憾
regular *píngcháng* 平常
regulation *guīzé* 规则
remember *jìde* 记得
remote control *yáokòng qì* 遥控器
rent (v) *zū* 租
repair *xiūlǐ* 修理
repeat *chóngfù* 重复
representative *dàibiǎo* 代表
resemble *xiàng* 像
reservation (booking) *yùdìng* 预定
responsible for *fùzé* 负责
rest (v) *xiūxi* 休息
restaurant *fànguǎn* 饭馆
retail *língshòu* 零售

return (come back) *huílái* 回来
return (give back) *guīhuán* 归还
rice *mǐfàn* 米饭
  rice cooker *diàn fàn guō* 电饭锅
right (direction) *yòubiān* 右边
right (correct) *duì* 对
ring (jewelry) *jièzhǐ* 戒指
river *hé* 河
road *lù* 路
roof *wūdǐng* 屋顶
room *fángjiān* 房间
rug *xiǎo dìtǎn* 小地毯
rule (regulation) *guīdìng* 规定
ruler (straightedge) *chǐ* 尺
run (v) *pǎo* 跑
runway *pǎodào* 跑道

S

safe (adj) *ānquán* 安全
safe (n) *bǎoxiǎn guì* 保险柜
salad *shālā* 沙拉
  salad dressing *shālā jiàng* 沙拉酱
salesman *shòuhuò yuán* 售货员
salt *yán* 盐
same *yí yàng* 一样
sample *yàngpǐn* 样品
sanitary napkin *yuèjīng dài* 月经带
satin *duànzi* 缎子
satisfied *mǎnyì* 满意

---

c = ts; *q* = ch; *x* = sh; *z* = dz; *zh* = j

Saturday *Xīngqīliù* 星期六

sausage *xiāngcháng* 香肠

say *shuō* 说

scarf *wéijīn* 围巾

schedule (timetable) *shíjiān biǎo* 时间表

school *xuéxiào* 学校

scissors *jiǎndāo* 剪刀

sea *hǎi* 海

seafood *hǎixiān* 海鲜

season (n) *jìjié* 季节

seat (n) *wèizi* 位子

seat belt *ānquán dài* 安全带

second (in a series) *dì èr* 第二

second (unit of time) *miǎo* 秒

see *kànjiàn* 看见

seem *hǎoxiàng* 好像

sell *mài* 卖

send (deliver, see off) *sòng* 送

send (assign, appoint) *pài* 派

service *fúwù* 服务

service charge *fúwù fèi* 服务费

settle a bill *jié zhàng* 结帐

seven *qī* 七

seventeen *shíqī* 十七

seventy *qīshí* 七十

several *jǐge* 几个

sew *féng* 缝

shampoo (n) *xǐfà jì* 洗发剂

shave (v) *guā hú* 刮胡

she *tā* 她

sheet (bed) *chuáng dān* 床单

shirt *chènshān* 衬衫

shoe *xiézi* 鞋子

shoelace *xiédài* 鞋带

shop (n) *shāngdiàn* 商店

shop (v) *mǎi dōngxi* 买东西

short (length) *duǎn* 短

short (height) *ǎi* 矮

shorts (briefs) *duǎn kù* 短裤

show to . . . *gěi . . . kàn* 给…看

shower *línyù* 淋浴

shrimp *xiā* 虾

sick *bìngle* 病了

side (location) *pángbiān* 旁边

sightseeing *guānguāng* 观光

sign (poster) *biāojì* 标记

sign (one's name) *qiān zì* 签字

silk *sīchóu* 丝绸

silver *yín* 银

since (until now) *zìcóng* 自从

since (because) *yīnwèi* 因为

sing *chàng* 唱

single *dān* 单

single person *dānshēn* 单身

single room *dānrén fáng* 单人房

sir *xiānsheng* 先生

sister *jiěmèi* 姐妹

elder sister *jiějie* 姐姐

younger sister *mèimei* 妹妹

sit *zuò* 坐

six *liù* 六

sixteen *shíliù* 十六

sixty *liùshí* 六十

size (n) *dàxiǎo* 大小

skin (n) *pífū* 皮肤

skirt (n) *qúnzi* 裙子

sleep (v) *shuì* 睡

to be sleepy *kùn le* 睏了

sleeve *xiùzi* 袖子

slide (photograph) *huàn dēng piàn* 幻灯片

slippers *tuō xié* 拖鞋

slow *màn* 慢

small *xiǎo* 小

smoke (n) *yān* 烟

smoke (v) *chōu yān* 抽烟

snack *xiǎochī* 小吃

snow (n) *xuě* 雪

snow (v) *xià xuě* 下雪

soap *féizào* 肥皂

socks *wàzi* 袜子

soda (pop) *qìshuǐ* 汽水

soda (water) *sūdá shuǐ* 苏打水

sofa *shāfā* 沙发

soft *ruǎn* 软

software *ruǎnjiàn* 软件

soldier *jūnrén* 军人

some *yì xiē* 一些

someone *mǒu rén* 某人

something *shénme* 什么

sometimes *yǒu shíhòu* 有时候

somewhere *shénme dìfāng* 什么地方

son *érzi* 儿子

song *gē* 歌

soon *hěn kuài* 很快

sorry *bàoqiàn* 抱歉

soup *tāng* 汤

south *nánfāng* 南方

souvenir *jìniàn pǐn* 纪念品

soy sauce *jiàngyóu* 酱油

space (place) *dìfāng* 地方

space (outer) *kōngjiān* 空间

spaghetti *Yìdàlì shì miàntiáo* 意大利式面条

speak *shuō* 说

speed *sùdù* 速度

spell (v) *pīn* 拼

spend money *huā qián* 花钱

spice *tiáowèi liào* 调味料

spicy (hot) *là* 辣

spinach *bōcài* 菠菜

spoon *tiáogēng* 调羹

spring (season) *chūnjì* 春季

square (adj) *fāng de* 方的

square (public) *guángchǎng* 广场

stadium *yùndòng chǎng* 运动场

stadium *tǐyù chǎng* 体育场

staircase *lóutī* 楼梯

staff member *gōngzuò rényuán* 工作人员

stamp (postage) *yóupiào* 邮票

state (province) *zhōu* 州

state (nation) *guójiā* 国家

stay (reside) *zhù* 住

steak *niúpái* 牛排

steal *tōu* 偷

stereo system *zǔhé yīnxiǎng xìtǒng* 组合音响系统

steward(ess) *fúwùyuán* 服务员

stock (securities) *gǔpiào* 股票

stockings *chángtǒng wàzi* 长统袜子

stomach (n) *dùzi* 肚子

stone (n) *shítóu* 石头

stop (v) *tíng* 停

stop *tíngzhǐ* 停止

store (n) *shāngdiàn* 商店

---

c = ts; *q* = ch; *x* = sh; *z* = dz; *zh* = j

story (tale) *gùshi* 故事

street *jiēdào* 街道

string (n) *xiàn* 线

strong *qiáng* 强

student *xuésheng* 学生

subtitles *zìmù* 字幕

suburb *jiāowài* 郊外

subway *dìtiě* 地铁

sugar *táng* 糖

suit (clothes) *xīzhuāng* 西装

suitcase *xíngli* 行李

summer *xiàjì* 夏季

sun (n) *tàiyáng* 太阳

Sunday *Xīngqītiān* 星期天

sunglasses *tàiyáng yǎnjìng* 太阳眼镜

supermarket *chāojí shìchǎng* 超级市场

supper *wǎnfàn* 晚饭

surname *xìng* 姓

sweater *máoyī* 毛衣

sweet *tián* 甜

swim *yóuyǒng* 游泳

swimming pool *yóuyǒng chí* 游泳池

syrup *tángjiāng* 糖浆

T

table (n) *zhuōzi* 桌子

tablecloth *zhuō bù* 桌布

tailor (n) *cáifeng* 裁缝

take *ná* 拿

take off (clothing) *tuō* 脱

tampon *yuèjīng yòng miánsāi* 月经用棉塞

tape (cellophane) *jiāodài* 胶带

tape (for recording) *lùyīndài* 录音带

tape recorder *lùyīn jī* 录音机

taste (flavor) *wèidào* 味道

taste (style) *qùwèi* 趣味

taste (v) *cháng* 尝

taxi *chūzū qìchē* 出租汽车

tea *chá* 茶

teacher *lǎoshī* 老师

team (n) *duì* 队

telecommunications *diànxùn* 电讯

telephone *diànhuà* 电话

make a phone call *dǎdiànhuà* 打电话

television *diànshì* 电视

tell *gàosu* 告诉

temperature *wēndù* 温度

temple *miào* 庙

temporary *zhànshí* 暂时

ten *shí* 十

tennis *wǎngqiú* 网球

tent *zhàngpeng* 帐篷

Thank you. *Xièxie nǐ.* 谢谢你。

that *nèige* 那个

there *nàli* 那里

there is (are) *yǒu* 有

they *tāmén* 他们

thick *hòu* 厚

thief *xiǎotōu* 小偷

thin (skinny) *shòu* 瘦

thin (not thick) *báo* 薄

thing *dōngxi* 东西

think *xiǎng* 想

third (in a series) *dì sān* 第三

third (fraction) *sān fēn zhī yī* 三分之一

thirsty *kě* 渴

thirteen *shísān* 十三

thirty *sānshí* 三十

this *zhèige* 这个

thousand *qiān* 千

   ten thousand *wàn* 万

three *sān* 三

throat *hóulóng* 喉咙

through (finished) *wán le* 完了

through (passed into) *tōng guò* 通过

Thursday *Xīngqīsì* 星期四

ticket *piào* 票

   one-way ticket *dānchéng piào* 单程票

   round-trip ticket *láihuí piào* 来回票

ticket window *shōupiào kǒu* 售票口

tie (neck) *lǐngdài* 领带

time (instance) *cì* 次

   once *yí cì* 一次

   twice *liǎng cì* 两次

time (of day) *shíjiān* 时间

   At what time? *Shénme shíhòu?* 什么时候

   on time *zhǔnshí* 准时

timetable *shíjiān biǎo* 时间表

tip (n) *xiǎo fèi* 小费

tired *lèi* 累

tissue (facial) *huàzhuāng yòng zhǐ* 化妆用纸

toast (bread) *kǎo miànbāo* 烤面包

toast (with drinks) *zhù jiǔ* 祝酒

tobacco *yāncǎo* 烟草

today *jīntiān* 今天

toe *jiǎozhǐ* 脚趾

tofu *dòufu* 豆腐

together *yìqǐ* 一起

toilet *cèsuǒ* 厕所

toilet paper *wèishēng zhǐ* 卫生纸

tomato *xīhóngshì* 西红柿

tomorrow *míngtiān* 明天

ton *dùn* 吨

tooth *yáchǐ* 牙齿

toothbrush *yáshuā* 牙刷

toothpaste *yágāo* 牙膏

toothpick *yáqiān* 牙签

touch (v) *mō* 摸

tourist *lǚyóu zhě* 旅游者

toward *xiàng* 向

towel *máojīn* 毛巾

toy *wánjù* 玩具

trade (commerce) *màoyì* 贸易

traffic (vehicular) *jiāotōng* 交通

train (railroad) *huǒchē* 火车

transformer (electrical) *biànyā qì* 变压器

translate *fānyì* 翻译

travel *lǚxíng* 旅行

travel agency *lǚxíngshè* 旅行社

traveler's check *lǚxíng zhīpiào* 旅行支票

tree *shù* 树

trip (travel) *lǚxíng* 旅行

trouble *máfan* 麻烦

truck *kǎchē* 卡车

true *zhēnde* 真的

try (v) *shì* 试

Tuesday *Xīngqī'èr* 星期二

tuna fish *jīnqiāng yú* 金枪鱼

turn (v) *zhuǎn* 转

---

c = ts; *q* = ch; *x* = sh; *z* = dz; *zh* = j

twelve *shíèr* 十二
twenty *èrshí* 二十
two (numeral) *èr* 二
two (measure) *liǎng* 两

U

ugly *nánkàn* 难看
umbrella *yǔsǎn* 雨伞
under *zài . . . dǐxià* 在…底下
underpants *nèikù* 内裤
undershirt *nèiyī* 内衣
understand *dǒng* 懂
United Kingdom *Yīngguó* 英国
university *dàxué* 大学
until *zhídào* 直到
up *shàng* 上
  get up *qǐlái* 起来
  go up *shàng qù* 上去
upstairs *lóushàng* 楼上
urgent *jǐnjí* 紧急
us *wǒmén* 我们
use *yòng* 用
used up *yòng wánle* 用完了
useful *yǒu yòng de* 有用的
useless *wú yòng de* 无用的

V

vacation *jiàqī* 假期
valid *yǒu xiào* 有效
value (n) *jiàzhí* 价值
van *miànbāo chē* 面包车
vase *huāpíng* 花瓶
VCD *shì pín gāomì guāng pán* 视频高密光盘
vegetable *shūcài* 蔬菜
vegetarian *sùshí zhě* 素食者
very *hěn* 很

vicinity *fùjìn* 附近
videodisc *yǐngdié* 影碟
video game *diànzǐ yóuxì* 电子游戏
videocassette *lùxiàng dài* 录像带
  videocassette recorder *lùxiàng jī* 录像机
village *cūnzhuāng* 村庄
vinegar *cù* 醋
visa *qiānzhèng* 签证
visit *fǎngwèn* 访问
volleyball *páiqiú* 排球
volume (sound) *yīnliàng* 音量
voltage *diànyā* 电压

W

waist *yāo* 腰
wait *děng* 等
waiter; waitress *fúwùyuán* 服务员
walk (v) *zǒu* 走
  take a walk *sàn bù* 散步
wall *qiáng* 墙
wallet *qiánbāo* 钱包
want *yào* 要
war *zhànzhēng* 战争
warm *wēnnuǎn* 温暖
wash *xǐ* 洗
washing machine *xǐyī jī* 洗衣机
washroom *xǐshǒu jiān* 洗手间
watch (wrist) *biǎo* 表
watch (v) *kànkan* 看看
watch out *xiǎoxīn* 小心
water *shuǐ* 水
watermelon *xīguā* 西瓜

way (method) *fāngfǎ* 方法

way (direction) *fāngxiàng* 方向

weak *ruò* 弱

wear (clothing) *chuān* 穿

weather *tiānqì* 天气

Wednesday *Xīngqīsān* 星期三

week *xīngqī* 星期

weekend *zhōumò* 周末

weigh *chēng* 称

weight *zhòngliàng* 重量

welcome (greeting) *huānyíng* 欢迎

well (adv) *hǎo* 好

well done (cooking) *lǎo* 老

West (Occident) *Xīfāng* 西方

Western food *Xīcān* 西餐

wet (adj) *shī* 湿

what *shénme* 什么

when *shénme shíhòu* 什么时候

where (question) *nǎli* 哪里

which (question) *něige* 哪个

white *bái* 白

who *shéi* 谁

whole *quánbù; zhěnggè* 全部；整个

wholesale *pīfā* 批发

why *wèishénme* 为什么

wife *qīzi; tàitai* 妻子；太太

willing *yuànyì* 愿意

win *yíng* 赢

wind (n) *fēng* 风

window *chuāngzi* 窗子

wine *pútáo jiǔ* 葡萄酒

winter *dōngjì* 冬季

wire *diàn xiàn* 电线

wish *xīwàng* 希望

without *méiyǒu* 没有

woman *nǚrén* 女人

won ton *húndùn* 馄饨

wood *mùtóu* 木头

wool *yángmáo* 羊毛

word *zì* 字

work *gōngzuò* 工作

 work unit *dānwèi* 单位

world *shìjiè* 世界

wrap *bāo* 包

wrapping *bāozhuāng* 包装

write *xiě* 写

wrong *cuò* 错

Y

year *nián* 年

yellow *huáng* 黄

yes *shì de* 是的

yesterday *zuótiān* 昨天

yogurt *suānnǎi* 酸奶

you *nǐ* 你

young *niánqīng* 年轻

You're welcome. *Bú kèqi.* 不客气。

Z

zero *líng* 零

zoo *dòngwùyuán* 动物园

CHINESE-ENGLISH DICTIONARY

A

ǎi short (height) 矮
ài love 爱
àn dark 暗
ānjìng quiet 安静
ànmó massage 按摩
ānquán safe; safety 安全
ānquán dài seat belt 安全带
ànzhào according to 按照
Àodàlìyà Australia 澳大利亚

B

bā eight 八
bàba dad 爸爸
bái white 白
bǎi hundred 百
bǎihuò shāngdiàn department store 百货商店
báilándì brandy 白兰地
bǎiwàn million 百万
bàn half 半
bàng pound (weight) 磅
bāng máng help (assist) 帮忙
bàngōngshì office 办公室
bàngqiú baseball 棒球
bāo wrap 包
bāoguǒ package 包裹
bǎohù protect 保护
bāokuò include 包括
bàoqiàn sorry 抱歉

báoxiǎn insurance 保险
bàoyuàn complain 抱怨
bàozhǐ newspaper 报纸
bāozhuāng wrapping 包装
bāshí eighty 八十
Bāyuè August 八月
bèi back 背
bēizi cup 杯子
běifāng north 北方
běndì local 本地
bēngdài bandage 绷带
biànxié shì diànnǎo laptop computer 便携式电脑
biànyā qì transformer (electrical) 变压器
biǎo wristwatch 錶
biǎo meter 表
biāojì sign (poster) 标记
biézhēn pin 别针
bǐjì běn notebook 笔记本
bìmiǎn avoid 避免
bīng ice 冰
bǐnggān cookie 饼干
bìngle sick; ill 病了
bīngqílín ice cream 冰淇淋
bīngxiāng refrigerator 冰箱
bǐsài contest 比赛
bǐsà bǐng pizza 比萨饼
bìxū necessary 必需
bízi nose 鼻子
bōcài spinach 菠菜
bōlí glass (material) 玻璃
bōluó pineapple 菠萝

bówùguǎn museum 博物馆

bózi neck 脖子

bùdīng pudding 布丁

bù kěnéng impossible
不可能

bú kèqi you're welcome
不客气

bùliào fabric; cloth 布料

bú nèn bù lǎo medium
(cooking) 不嫩不老

bú shì no; not true 不是

bùtóng different 不同

C

càidān menu 菜单

cáifeng tailor 裁缝

càihuā cauliflower 菜花

cān meal 餐

cānchē dining car 餐车

cānjīn napkin 餐巾

cánjí rén handicapped person
残疾人

cāntīng dining room 餐厅

cèsuǒ toilet 厕所

chá check; examine 查

chá tea 茶

cháng long 长

cháng taste 尝

chàng sing 唱

chàngpiàn record (disk) 唱片

chángtǒng wàzi stockings
长统袜子

chǎo noisy 吵

cháodài dynasty 朝代

chāojí shìchǎng supermarket
超级市场

chāopiào bill (currency note)
钞票

chātóu electrical plug 插头

chāzi fork 叉子

chēng weigh 称

chéngběn production cost
成本

chéngrén adult 成人

chéngshì city 城市

chéngwéi become 成为

chéngwùyuán flight attendant
乘务员

chènshān shirt 衬衫

chī eat 吃

chǐ straightedge ruler 尺

chóngfù repeat 重复

chōu yān smoke 抽烟

chuān wear 穿

chuán boat 船

chuáng bed 床

chuáng dān bed sheet 床单

chuáng diàn mattress 床垫

chuānglián curtain 窗帘

chuāngzi window 窗子

chuánrǎn de contagious
传染的

chuánzhēn fax 传真

chuánzhēn jī fax machine
传真机

chúchòujì deodorant 除臭剂

chúfáng kitchen 厨房

chūkǒu exit; export 出口

chūnàyuán cashier 出纳员

chūnjì spring (season) 春季

chúshī cook; chef 厨师

chūzū qìchē taxi 出租汽车

cì time (instance) 次

cíqì porcelain 瓷器

c = ts; *q* = ch; *x* = sh; *z* = dz; *zh* = j

cōngmíng intelligent 聪明
cù vinegar 醋
cūnzhuāng village 村庄
cuò wrong 错
cuòwù mistake 错误

D

dǎ hit 打
dà big; large 大
dǎ diànhuà telephone
打电话
dài carry 带
dàibiǎo representative 代表
dàibiǎotuán delegation
代表团
dàikuǎn loan 贷款
dàilái bring 带来
dàitì instead of 代替
dàlóu building 大楼
dān single 单
dàn egg 蛋
dāndú alone 单独
dàngāo cake 蛋糕
dāngrán of course 当然
dànhuáng jiàng mayonnaise
蛋黄酱
dànshì but 但是
dānwèi work unit 单位
dānzi list 单子
dǎo island 岛
dàodá arrive 到达
dāopiàn razor 刀片
dǎoyóu guide 导游
dāozi knife 刀子
dǎpò break; smash 打破
dárǎo disturb 打扰
dàshǐguǎn embassy 大使馆
dà suàn garlic 大蒜
dàtīng lobby 大厅

dàxiǎo size 大小
dàxué university 大学
dàyī overcoat 大衣
dǎyìn jī printer 打印机
dàyuē approximately 大约
dédào obtain 得到
dēng lamp 灯
děng wait 等
dēngpào light bulb 灯泡
dī low (height) 低
dì land; ground 地
diàn electricity 电
diànchí battery 电池
diàn fàn guō rice cooker
电饭锅
diànhuà telephone 电话
diànnǎo computer 电脑
diànshì television 电视
diàntī elevator 电梯
diàn xiàn wire 电线
diànxùn telecommunications
电讯
diànyā voltage 电压
diànyǐng movie 电影
diànzǐ yóujiàn e-mail
电子邮件
diànzǐ yóuxì electronic game;
video game 电子游戏
diào fall 掉
dìdi younger brother 弟弟
dìfāng place; space 地方
dìmiàn floor; ground 地面
dǐpiàn negative (film) 底片
dìqū district 地区
dìtǎn carpet 地毯
dìtiě subway 地铁
dìtú map 地图
diū lose (misplace) 丢
dìyī first 第一
dìzhǐ address 地址

dǒng understand 懂

Dōngfāng East; Orient 东方

dōngjì winter 冬季

dòngwùyuán zoo 动物图

dōngxi thing 东西

dòufu bean curd; tofu 豆腐

dú read 读

duǎn short (length) 短

duǎn kù shorts; briefs 短裤

duànzi satin 缎子

duì right (correct) 对

duì team 队

Duìbuqǐ. Excuse me. (apologizing) 对不起

duìhuàn exchange money 兑换

duìhuàn lǜ exchange rate 兑换率

dùn ton 吨

duō many 多

dùzi stomach 肚子

E

è hungry 饿

é goose 鹅

èr two 二

ěrduō ear 耳朵

ěrhuán earrings 耳环

èrshí twenty 二十

Èryuè February 二月

érzi son 儿子

F

fàng put 放

fāng de square 方的

fāngbiàn convenient 方便

fāngfǎ way; method 方法

fángjiān room 房间

fànguǎn restaurant 饭馆

fǎngwèn visit 访问

fāngxiàng direction 方向

fángzi house 房子

fānqié jiàng ketchup 番茄酱

fānyì interpreter; translate 翻译

fāshāo fever 发烧

fāyán infection 发炎

fāyīn pronunciation 发音

fǎyuàn court of law 法院

fēi fly 飞

fēijī airplane 飞机

fēijī chǎng airport 飞机场

fèiyòng fee; charge 费用

féizào soap 肥皂

fēn divide; minute; Chinese cent 分

fēng wind 风

féng sew 缝

fēngjǐng landscape; scenery 风景

fēngmì honey 蜂蜜

fēngsú custom 风俗

fěnhóng sè pink 粉红色

Fó Buddha 佛

fù pay 付

fùjìn vicinity 附近

fùqīn father 父亲

Fūren Mrs. 夫人

fúwù service 服务

fúwù fèi service charge 服务费

fúwùyuán service person 服务员

fùzé responsible for 负责

c = ts; *q* = ch; *x* = sh; *z* = dz; *zh* = j

G

gài cover 盖
gān dry 干
Gānbēi. Cheers. (toast) 干杯。
gǎndào feel 感到
gāngcái just; have just 刚才
gānjìng clean 干净
gānxǐ dry clean 干洗
gāo high 高
gāobǐng diàn bakery 糕饼店
gāo zhōng high school 高中
gāodù height 高度
gàosù tell 告诉
gāoxìng happy 高兴
gē cut 割
gē song 歌
gēge elder brother 哥哥
gěi give 给
gěi . . . kàn show to 给…看
gējù opera 歌剧
gèng hǎo better 更好
gēnzhe follow 跟着
gēzi pigeon 鸽子
gōngchǎng factory 工厂
gōngchéng shī engineer 工程师
gōngfēn centimeter 公分
gōnggòng public 公共
gōnggòng qìchē bus 公共汽车
gōngjīn kilogram 公斤
gōnglǐ kilometer 公里
gōnglù highway 公路
gōngsī company (business) 公司
gōngwù cāng business class 公务舱
gōngxǐ congratulations 恭喜
gōngyuán park 公园
gōngzuò work 工作

gōngzuò rényuán staff member 工作人员
gǒu dog 狗
gòu enough 够
guā húzi shave 刮胡子
guān close; shut 关
Guǎngdōnghuà Cantonese dialect 广东话
guǎnggào advertisement 广告
guāngpán CD 光盘
guāngqū CD-ROM 光驱
guānguāng sightseeing 观光
gǔdǒng antique 古董
guì expensive 贵
guīdìng rule; regulation 规定
guīzé regulation 规则
gùkè customer 顾客
guójì international 国际
guójiā country 国家
guǒjiàng jam 果酱
guòmǐn allergy 过敏
guówài abroad 国外
guóyǔ Chinese language 国语
guǒzhī juice 果汁
guōzi pot 锅子
gǔpiào stock (securities) 股票
gùshi story (tale) 故事
gǔtóu bone 骨头
gùyòng hire 雇用

H

hǎi sea 海
hǎiguān Customs 海关
hǎiguān guānyuán Customs official 海关官员
háishì or (disjunctive) 还是
hǎitān beach 海滩
hǎiwài overseas 海外
hǎixiān seafood 海鲜

hǎiyáng ocean 海洋

hànbǎo bāo hamburger 汉堡包

hángbān airline flight 航班

hángkōng gōngsī airline
航空公司

hángkōng xìn airmail letter
航空信

hángkōng yóujiǎn aerogram
航空邮简

hànyǔ Chinese language 汉语

hǎo good; well 好

hǎokàn handsome 好看

hàomǎ number 号码

hǎoxiàng seem 好像

hē to drink 喝

hé and 和

hé river 河

hēi black 黑

hěn very 很

hěn duō many 很多

hěn kuài soon; fast 很快

héshì lùyīndài cassette
盒式录音带

hétóng contract 合同

hézi box 盒子

hóng red 红

hòu thick 厚

hóulóng throat 喉咙

hòumiàn rear 后面

hú lake 湖

huā flower 花

huà draw; paint; picture 画

huā qián spend money 花钱

huài bad 坏

huáiyùn pregnant 怀孕

huàjù play (drama) 话剧

huàn dēng piàn slide
(photograph) 幻灯片

huáng yellow 黄

huānyíng welcome 欢迎

huángyóu butter 黄油

huāpíng vase 花瓶

huāshēngmǐ peanuts 花生米

huáshì Fahrenheit 华氏

huáyǔ Chinese language 华语

huāyuán garden 花园

huàzhuāng pǐn makeup
化妆品

huàzhuāng yòng zhǐ facial
tissue 化妆用纸

huī sè gray 灰色

huídá answer 回答

huìjiàn meet with 会见

huílái come back 回来

huìyì meeting; conference
会议

hújiāo pepper 胡椒

hú luóbo carrot 胡萝卜

húndùn wonton 馄饨

huǒ fire 火

huó live; exist 活

huǒchái matches 火柴

huǒchē train 火车

huótuǐ ham 火腿

huòzhě or (conjunctive) 或者

hùshi nurse 护士

hùzhào passport 护照

J

jī chicken 鸡

jí anxious; in a hurry 急

jiā add 加

jiǎ false 假

jiàgé price 价格

jiājù furniture 傢具

c = ts; q = ch; x = sh; z = dz; zh = j

Jiānádà Canada 加拿大

jiǎndāo scissors 剪刀

jiǎnchá examine 检查

jiāng ginger 姜

jiǎngjià bargain 讲价

jiàngyóu soy sauce 酱油

jiànkāng healthy 健康

jiànyì advice 建议

jiǎo foot (anatomy) 脚

jiào call 叫

jiāojuǎn film (rolls) 胶卷

jiāoshuǐ glue 胶水

jiàotáng church 教堂

jiāotōng traffic 交通

jiāowài suburb 郊外

jiǎozhǐ toe 脚趾

jiǎozi dumpling 饺子

jiàqī vacation 假期

jiǎrú if 假如

jiàshǐ pilot 驾驶

jiātíng family 家庭

jiāyòng diànqì appliance 家用电器

jiāyóu zhàn gas station 加油站

jiàzhí value 价值

jìdé remember 记得

jiè borrow 借

jiēdào street 街道

jiègěi lend 借给

jiéhūn marry 结婚

jiějie elder sister 姐姐

jiěmèi sisters 姐妹

jièmò mustard 芥末

jiémù program 节目

jiérì holiday; festival 节日

jièshào introduce 介绍

jié zhàng settle a bill 结帐

jièzhǐ ring 戒指

jǐge several 几个

jīhū almost 几乎

jìhuà plan 计划

jīhuì opportunity 机会

jìjié season (time of year) 季节

jīn gold 金

jǐngchá police 警察

jǐngchá jú police station 警察局

jīngcháng often 经常

jīnglǐ manager 经理

jǐngtàilán cloisonné 景泰蓝

jìngzi mirror 镜子

jìniàn pǐn souvenir 纪念品

jǐnjí urgent 紧急

jìnkǒu entrance; import 进口

jīnqiāng yú tuna fish 金枪鱼

jìnrù enter 进入

jīntiān today 今天

jìsuàn jī computer 计算机

jìsuàn qì calculator 计算器

jiǔ nine 九

jiǔ liquor 酒

jiǔbā bar 酒吧

jiùhù chē ambulance 救护车

jiǔjīng alcohol 酒精

jiǔshí ninety 九十

jì xìn mail a letter 寄信

jiōnⅥⅥ ⅥⅥⅥⅤⅥⅥⅠⅥ 俭价

juédìng decide 决定

jùjué refuse (v) 拒绝

jùlí distance 距离

jūnrén soldier 军人

júzi orange 桔子

K

kǎchē truck 卡车

kāfēi coffee 咖啡

kāfēi sè brown 咖啡色

kāi open 开

kāi guàn qì can opener
开罐器

kāi huì hold a meeting 开会

kāishǐ begin 开始

kāiwèi xiǎocài appetizer
开胃小菜

kǎlāōukèi karaoke 卡拉OK

kàn look at 看

kànjiàn see 看见

kǎo bake 烤

kǎo miànbāo toast (bread)
烤面包

kǎpiàn card 卡片

kě thirsty 渴

kè gram 克

kělián poor (pitiful) 可怜

kěnéng maybe 可能

késòu cough 咳嗽

kéyǐ O.K. 可以

kōng empty 空

kōngtiáo air conditioning
空调

kǒuhóng lipstick 口红

kòuzi button 扣子

kū cry 哭

kǔ bitter 苦

kuài fast 快

kuài piece 块

kuàijì shī accountant 会计师

kuàizi chopsticks 筷子

kùnnán difficulty 困难

kùzi pants 裤子

L

lā pull 拉

là spicy (hot) 辣

lái come 来

lājī garbage 垃圾

làjiāo jiàng hot pepper sauce
辣椒酱

lán blue 蓝

lánqiú basketball 蓝球

lánwěi yán appendicitis
阑尾炎

lánzi basket 篮子

lǎo old; well done (cooking)
老

láobǎn boss 老板

lǎoshī teacher 老师

lèi tired 累

lěng cold (adj) 冷

lěngdòng jī freezer 冷冻机

lí pear 梨

lí . . . jìn near to 离…近

liǎn face 脸

liáng measure 量

liǎng two (measure) 两

liàng bright 亮

liángkuài cool 凉快

liànxí practice 练习

lǐfà haircut 理发

lǐfà guǎn barbershop 理发馆

lǐfà shī barber 理发师

líkāi leave; depart 离开

líng zero 零

lǐngdài necktie 领带

língdiǎn à la carte 零点

língqián change (coins) 零钱

lǐngshì guǎn consulate
领事馆

língshòu retail 零售

lǐngzi collar 领子

línjū neighbor 邻居

línyù shower 淋浴

c = ts; *q* = ch; *x* = sh; *z* = dz; *zh* = j

lǐpǐn gift 礼品
lìrùn profit 利润
lǐtáng auditorium 礼堂
liú keep 留
liù six 六
liù shí sixty 六十
liú xiě bleed 流血
Liùyuè June 六月
lǐyóu reason 理由
lìzi example 例子
lóngxiā lobster 龙虾
lóushàng upstairs 楼上
lóutī staircase 楼梯
lóuxià downstairs 楼下
lù road 路
lǜ green 绿
lǚguǎn hotel 旅馆
luòhòu backward 落后
lǜshī lawyer 律师
lùxiàng dài videocassette 录像带
lùxiàng jī videocassette recorder 录像机
lǚxíng travel; journey 旅行
lǚxíngshè travel service 旅行社
lǚxíng zhīpiào traveler's check 旅行支票
lùyīnдài recording tape; cassette 录音带
lǚyóu shǒucè guidebook 旅游手册
lǚyóu zhě tourist 旅游者

M

mǎ horse 马
máfan trouble 麻烦
mǎi buy 买
mài sell 卖

māma mom 妈妈
màn slow 慢
máng busy 忙
mǎnyì satisfied 满意
māo cat 猫
máojīn towel 毛巾
máoyī sweater 毛衣
màoyì trade 贸易
màozi hat 帽子
mǎshàng immediately 马上
měi every 每
měigè each 每个
Měiguó America 美国
Měiguó rén American (person) 美国人
měilì beautiful 美丽
mèimei younger sister 妹妹
měiróng yuàn beauty parlor 美容院
měitiān daily 每天
méiyǒu without 没有
měiyuán dollar (U.S.) 美元
mén door 门
ménlíng doorbell 门铃
mēnrè humid 焖热
mǐ meter 米
miànbāo bread 面包
miànbāo chē van 面包车
miánbèi quilt 棉被
miǎnfèi free; without cost 免费
miánhuā cotton 棉花
miàntiáo noodle 面条
miǎo second (unit of time) 秒
miào temple 庙
mǐfàn rice 米饭
míngtiān tomorrow 明天
míngxìnpiàn postcard 明信片
míngzì name 名字
mō touch 摸

mógū mushroom 蘑菇
mǒu rén someone 某人
mùdì cemetery 墓地
mǔqīn mother 母亲
mùtou wood 木头

N

ná hold; take 拿
nǎilào cheese 奶酪
nǎiyóu cream 奶油
náli where 哪里
nàli there 那里
nán difficult 难
nán háizi boy 男孩子
nán péngyou boyfriend 男朋友
nán rén man 男人
nánfāng south 南方
nánkàn ugly 难看
něige which 哪个
nèige that 那个
nèikù underpants 内裤
nèiyī undershirt 内衣
nèn rare (cooking) 嫩
néng able; can 能
nǐ you 你
Nǐ hǎo. Hello. 你好。
nián year 年
niánqīng young 年轻
niàobù diaper 尿布
níngméng lemon 柠檬
niúnǎi milk 牛奶
niúpái steak 牛排
niúròu beef 牛肉
nóngmín farmer 农民
nuǎnqì jī heater 暖气机
nǚ chènshān blouse 女衬衫

nǚ fúwùyuán female service person (waitress, stewardess, etc.) 女服务员
nǚ háizi girl 女孩子
nǚ péngyou girlfriend 女朋友
nuǎnqì heat 暖气
nǚér daughter 女儿
nǚrén woman 女人

P

pà afraid 怕
pài send; appoint 派
páiqiú volleyball 排球
páishuǐguǎn drain (n) 排水管
pàng fat 胖
pángbiān side 旁边
pángxiè crab 螃蟹
pánzi dish; plate 盘子
pǎo run 跑
pǎodào runway 跑道
péngyou friend 朋友
piányi cheap 便宜
piào ticket 票
piàoliàng pretty 漂亮
pídài belt 皮带
pīfā wholesale 批发
pífū skin 皮肤
pígé leather 皮革
píjiǔ beer 啤酒
pímáo fur 皮毛
pīn spell (v) 拼
píng flat (adj) 平
píngcháng regular 平常
píngguǒ apple 苹果
píngzi bottle 瓶子
pīnyīn spelling 拼音
pútáo grape 葡萄

pútáo jiǔ wine 葡萄酒

pǔtōng cāng economy class 普通舱

Pǔtōnghuà Mandarin (dialect) 普通话

Q

qī seven 七

qiān thousand 千

qián money 钱

qiàn owe 欠

qiánbāo purse; wallet 钱包

qiānbǐ pencil 铅笔

qiáng strong 强

qiáng wall 墙

qiánmiàn front; ahead 前面

qiānzhèng visa 签证

qiǎokèlì chocolate 巧克力

qìchē automobile 汽车

qìchuǎn bìng asthma 气喘病

qǐlái get up 起来

qíncài celery 芹菜

qīng light (weight) 轻

qǐng please 请

qīng diǎn lighter (adj) 轻点

qīngjié jì detergent 清洁剂

qióng poor (not rich) 穷

qīpiàn deceive; cheat 欺骗

qīshí seventy 七十

qìshuǐ soda pop 汽水

qítā other 其他

qiūjì autumn 秋季

qìyóu gasoline 汽油

Qīyuè July 七月

qīzi wife 妻子

quánbù all; entire; whole 全部

quèrèn confirm 确认

qúnzi skirt 裙子

qǔxiāo cancel 取消

R

rè hot 热

rè gǒu hot dog 热狗

rén person 人

rènhé any 任何

rìchéng itinerary 日程

rìqī calendar date 日期

róngyì easy 容易

ròu meat 肉

ruǎn soft 软

ruǎn cípán floppy disk 软磁盘

ruǎnjiàn software 软件

rùchǎng fèiyòng cover charge 入场费用

ruò weak 弱

S

sān three 三

sān fēn zhī yī one third 三分之一

sānshí thirty 三十

Sānyuè March 三月

shāfā sofa 沙发

shālā salad 沙拉

shālā jiàng salad dressing 沙拉酱

shān mountain 山

shàngděng báilándì cognac 上等白兰地

shāngdiàn store (shop) 商店

shàngmiàn above 上面

shāngrén businessman 商人

shàngwǎng on-line 上网

shànzi fan 扇子

shǎo few; less 少

shāoshāng burn (injury) 烧伤

shéi who 谁

shēng liter 升

shēng cài lettuce 生菜
shēng de raw 生的
shēngrì birthday 生日
shénme something; what 什么
shénme dìfāng somewhere 什么地方
shénme shíhòu when 什么时候
shēntǐ body 身体
shèshì Centigrade 摄氏
shèxiàng jī camcorder 摄像机
shī wet 湿
shí ten 十
shì be 是
shì try; test 试
shì de yes 是的
shíbā eighteen 十八
shìchǎng market 市场
shíèr twelve 十二
shíjiān time (of day) 时间
shíjiān biǎo schedule; timetable 时间表
shìjiè world 世界
shíjiǔ nineteen 十九
shíliù sixteen 十六
shípǐn food 食品
shíqī seventeen 十七
shìqíng matter; affair 事情
shísān thirteen 十三
shísì fourteen 十四
shítou stone 石头
shīwàng disappointment 失望
shíwǔ fifteen 十五
shíyī eleven 十一
shì zhōngxīn downtown 市中心

shìpín gāomì guāngpán VCD 视频高密光盘
shǒu hand 手
shòu thin 瘦
shǒubèi arm 手臂
shōudào receive 收到
shǒudiàntǒng flashlight 手电筒
shòuhuò yuán salesman 售货员
shǒu jī cell phone 手机
shōujù receipt 收据
shǒujuàn handkerchief 手绢
shōurù income 收入
shǒutào glove 手套
shǒuxù fèi processing fee 手续费
shōuyīnjī radio 收音机
shóuzhǐ finger 手指
shǒuzhuó bracelet 手镯
shū book 书
shù tree 树
shuāng pair 双
shuāzi brush 刷子
shūcài vegetable 蔬菜
shūdiàn bookstore 书店
shūfu comfortable 舒服
shuǐ water 水
shuì sleep 睡
shuíguǒ fruit 水果
shuǐlóngtóu faucet 水龙头
shuìyī pajamas 睡衣
shùliàng quantity 数量
shuō say; speak 说
shūzi comb 梳子
sì four 四
sì fēn zhī yī one quarter 四分之一

---

c = ts; *q* = ch; *x* = sh; *z* = dz; *zh* = j

sīchóu silk 丝绸

sījī driver 司机

sīrén private 私人

sìshí forty 四十

sòng send; deliver 送

suàn count 算

suānnǎi yogurt 酸奶

sùdù speed 速度

suǒ lock 锁

sùshí zhě vegetarian 素食者

T

tā he; she; it 他；她；它

tàiyáng sun 太阳

tàiyáng yǎnjìng sunglasses 太阳眼镜

tāmén they 他们

tāng soup 汤

táng sugar 糖

tàng iron (v) 烫

tángguǒ candy 糖果

tángjiāng syrup 糖浆

tǎnzi blanket 毯子

tǎojià bargain (v) 讨价

táoqì pottery 陶器

táozi peach 桃子

tèbié especially; special 特别

tiān day 天

tián sweet 甜

tiānqì weather 天气

tiáogēng spoon 调羹

tiáowèi liào spice 调味料

tiělù railroad 铁路

tígòng offer (v) 提供

tíkuǎn jī automatic teller machine (ATM) 提款机

tīng listen 听

tíng stop (v) 停

tīngjiàn hear 听见

tíngzhǐ stop 停止

tǐyù chǎng stadium 体育场

tòng ache; pain 痛

tóngshì colleague 同事

tóngxué classmate 同学

tóngyì agree 同意

tōu steal 偷

tóu head 头

tóuděng cāng first class 头等舱

tóufa hair 头发

tóuyūn dizzy 头晕

tóuzī investment 投资

tǔdòu potato 土豆

tuī push 推

tuǐ leg 腿

tuì kuǎn refund 退款

tuījiàn recommend 推荐

tuō xié slippers 拖鞋

túshūguǎn library 图书馆

W

wàiguó de foreign 外国的

wàimiàn outside 外面

wàitào jacket 外套

wǎn bowl 碗

wǎn late 晚

wǎncān dinner 晚餐

wán le finished; ended 完了

wánchéng finished 完成

wàngjì forget 忘记

wǎngqiú tennis 网球

wǎngzhǐ homepage 网址

wánjù toy 玩具

wánměi perfect 完美

wǎnshàng evening; night 晚上

wáwa baby; doll 娃娃

wàzi socks 袜子

wēibō lú microwave oven
微波炉

wèidào flavor; taste 味道

wéijīn scarf 围巾

wèishénme why 为什么

wéixiǎn dangerous 危险

wèizi seat 位子

wèn ask 问

wēndù temperature 温度

wēnnuǎn warm 温暖

wèntí question; problem 问题

wǒ I; me 我

wǒde my 我的

wòfáng bedroom 卧房

wǒmén us 我们

wǔ five 五

wù fog 雾

wǔcān lunch 午餐

wú yòng de useless 无用的

wūdǐng roof 屋顶

wǔhuì dance 舞会

wùhuì misunderstanding 误会

wǔshí fifty 五十

wǔyè midnight 午夜

Wǔyuè May 五月

X

xǐ wash 洗

xiā shrimp 虾

xià yígè next 下一个

xiàjì summer 夏季

xiàn string 线

xiǎng think 想

xiàng similar to; resemble 像

xiàng toward 向

xiāngbīnjiǔ Champagne
香槟酒

xiāngcháng sausage 香肠

xiāngfǎn opposite 相反

xiāngjiāo banana 香蕉

xiàngliàn necklace 项链

xiǎngniàn miss (think of, remember) 想念

xiàng qián forward 向前

xiāngshuǐ perfume 香水

xiāngxià countryside 乡下

xiāngxìn believe 相信

xiāngyān cigarette 香烟

xiànkuǎn cash 现款

Xiānsheng Mr.; teacher; gentleman 先生

xiànzài now 现在

xiǎo small; little 小

xiào laugh 笑

xiǎo dìtǎn rug 小地毯

xiǎochī snack 小吃

xiǎofèi tip; gratuity 小费

xiǎohái child 小孩

xiàohuà joke 笑话

xiǎoshí hour 小时

xiǎoshuō novel (n) 小说

xiǎotōu thief 小偷

xiǎoxīn careful 小心

xiàwǔ afternoon 下午

Xīcān Western food 西餐

xiě blood 血

xiě write 写

xiè dùzi diarrhea 潟肚子

xiédài shoelace 鞋带

Xièxie nǐ. Thank you. 谢谢你。

xiěxíng blood type 血型

xiézi shoes 鞋子

xǐfà jì shampoo 洗发剂

Xīfāng West; Occident 西方

xīguā watermelon 西瓜**

xīhóngshì tomato 西红柿

xīlánhuā broccoli 西蓝花

xīn new 新

xìn believe; letter; mail 信

xìnfēng envelope 信封

xǐng awaken 醒

xìng surname 姓

xíngli suitcase; baggage; luggage 行李

xīngqī week 星期

Xīngqīèr Tuesday 星期二

Xīngqīliù Saturday 星期六

Xīngqīsān Wednesday 星期三

Xīngqīsì Thursday 星期四

Xīngqītiān Sunday 星期天

Xīngqīwǔ Friday 星期五

Xīngqīyī Monday 星期一

xīnwén news 新闻

xìnxī information 信息

xīnxiān fresh 新鲜

Xīn Xīlán New Zealand 新西兰

xìnyòng kǎ credit card 信用卡

xīnzàng heart 心脏

xiōngdì brothers 兄弟

xǐshǒu jiān washroom 洗手间

xiū fix 修

xiūlǐ umbrella 雨伞

xiūlǐ repair 修理

xiūxi take a rest 休息

xiū zhījia manicure 修指甲

xiùzi sleeve 袖子

xīwàng wish; hope 希望

xǐyī launder (clothing) 洗衣

xǐyī jī washing machine 洗衣机

xǐzǎo bathe 洗澡

xǐzǎo jiān bathroom 洗澡间

xīzhuāng suit (clothes) 西装

xuǎn choose 选

xuǎnzé choice 选择

xuē boot 靴

xuě snow 雪

xuéshēng student 学生

xuéxí learn 学习

xuéxiào school 学校

xúkězhèng permit; license 许可证

xūnròu bacon 熏肉

xúnwèn chù information desk 询问处

xūyào need 需要

Y

yā duck 鸭

yáchǐ tooth 牙齿

yágāo toothpaste 牙膏

yáqiān toothpick 牙签

yáshuā toothbrush 牙刷

yān smoke 烟

yán salt 盐

yāncǎo tobacco 烟草

yǎng itch 痒

yángcōng onion 洋葱

yángmáo wool 羊毛

yàngpǐn sample 样品

yángròu lamb; mutton 羊肉

yǎnjīng eye 眼睛

yǎnjìng glasses; spectacles 眼镜

yánsè color 颜色

yǎnyuán actor 演员

yāo waist 腰

yào want 要

yào medicine 药

yàofāng prescription 药方

yàofáng pharmacy; drugstore 药房

yāoguǒ cashew 腰果

yāoqǐng invite 邀请

yáokòng qì remote control
遥控器

yàoshi key 钥匙

yáyī dentist 牙医

yě also 也

yěcān picnic 野餐

yī one 一

Yìdàlì shì miàntiáo spaghetti
意大利式面条

yīfu clothing 衣服

yígè a; an; one 一个

yī guì closet 衣柜

yíhàn regret 遗憾

yǐhòu after 以后

yījià clothes hanger 衣架

yǐjīng already 已经

yín silver 银

yíng win 赢

yīngcùn inch 英吋

yǐngdié videodisc 影碟

Yīngguó United Kingdom
英国

Yīngwén English (language)
英文

yínháng bank 银行

yīnliàng volume (sound) 音量

yǐnliào beverage 饮料

Yīngtèwǎng Internet 英特网

yīnwèi because 因为

yǐnxíng yǎnjìng contact lens
隐形眼镜

yīnyuè music 音乐

yīnyuè jiā musician 音乐家

yīnyuè huì concert 音乐会

yìqǐ together 一起

yǐqián before 以前

yīshēng doctor 医生

yìshù jiā artist 艺术家

yìsi meaning 意思

yì xiē some 一些

yí yàng same 一样

yīyuàn hospital 医院

Yīyuè January 一月

yǐzi chair 椅子

yòng use 用

yǒngbù never 永不

yóu oil 油

yǒu have; there is; there are
有

yǒu shíhòu sometimes 有时候

yǒu xiào valid 有效

yǒu yìsi interesting 有意思

yǒu yòng de useful 有用的

yòubiān right (direction)
右边

yóuchāi mailman 邮差

yóufèi postage 邮费

yóujú post office 邮局

yóupiào postage stamp 邮票

yóutǒng mailbox 邮筒

Yóuyì Shāngdiàn Friendship
Store 友谊商店

yóuyǒng swim 游泳

yóuyǒng chí swimming pool
游泳池

yóuyǒng yī bathing suit
游泳衣

yú fish 鱼

yǔ rain 雨

yù jade 玉

yuǎn far 远

yuànyì willing 愿意

yuánzhū bǐ ballpoint pen
圆珠笔

---

c = ts; *q* = ch; *x* = sh; *z* = dz; *zh* = j

yuànzi courtyard 院子

yùdìng reservation 预定

yuè month 月

yuèduì orchestra 乐队

yuēhuì appointment 约会

yuèjīng dài sanitary napkin 月经带

yuèjīng yòng miánsāi tampon 月经用棉塞

yuètái platform 月台

yùmǐ corn 玉米

yùndòng chǎng stadium 运动场

yùndòng yuán athlete 运动员

yùndǒu iron (clothes) (n) 熨斗

yǔnnuò promise 允诺

yùnqi luck 运气

yùnsòng deliver 运送

yúsǎn umbrella 雨伞

yǔyán language 语言

yǔyī raincoat 雨衣

Z

zài again 再

zài at 在

zài . . . lǐ in 在…里

zài . . . límiàn inside 在…里面

zài . . . shàng on top of 在…上

zài . . . zhījiān between 在…之间

zài . . . zhōng among; during 在…中

zài dǐxià below; under 在底下

zài hòumiàn behind 在后面

zài pángbiān beside 在旁边

zài xiàmiàn below; underneath 在下面

Zàijiàn. Good-bye. 再见。

zāng dirty 脏

zǎo early; Good morning. 早

zǎocān breakfast 早餐

zǎopén bathtub 澡盆

zǎoshàng morning 早上

zázhì magazine 杂志

zěnme how 怎么

zhàngfu husband 丈夫

zhǎnlǎn exhibition 展览

zhànshí temporary 暂时

zhànzhēng war 战争

zhàogù care for 照顾

zhàopiàn photograph 照片

zhàoxiàng jī camera 照相机

zhèige this 这个

zhékòu discount 折扣

zhèli here 这里

zhēn needle 针

zhēnde true; real; really 真的

zhēnglùn argument 争论

zhēnjiǔ acupuncture 针灸

zhěntou pillow 枕头

zhǐ paper 纸

zhídá de hángbān nonstop flight 直达的航班

zhīdào know; be aware of 知道

zhídào until 直到

zhífēi de hángbān direct flight 直飞的航班

zhìliàng quality 质量

zhīpiào check (an order for money) 支票

zhíyè profession 职业

zhǐyǒu only have 只有

zhōng clock 钟

Zhōngguó China 中国

Zhōngguóhuà Chinese (language) 中国话

zhōngjiān middle 中间

zhòngliàng weight 重量

Zhōngwén Chinese (language) 中文

zhōngwǔ noon 中午

zhòngyào important 重要

zhōu state; province 州

zhōumò weekend 周末

zhù reside 住

zhuàn earn 赚

zhuǎnjiē qì adaptor (electrical) 转接器

zhūbǎo jewelry 珠宝

zhǔnbèi prepare 准备

zhǔnbèi hǎole ready 准备好了

zhuō bù tablecloth 桌布

zhuōzi table 桌子

zhǔrén host 主人

zhūròu pork 猪肉

zhúsǔn bamboo shoot 竹笋

zì word; Chinese character 字

zìcóng since; until now 自从

zìdiǎn dictionary 字典

zìmù subtitles 字幕

zǐsè purple 紫色

zìxíng chē bicycle 自行车

zìyóu freedom; liberty 自由

zǒngjī switchboard operator 总机

zǒngjīnglǐ general manager 总经理

zǒngshì always 总是

zǒu walk; go 走

zū rent; hire; charter 租

zuàn diamond 钻石

zǔhé yīnxiǎng xìtǒng stereo system 组合音响系统

zuì drunk; intoxicated 醉

zuì shǎo least 最少

zuǐbā mouth 嘴吧

zuìhòu last; final 最后

zuìjìn recently 最近

zuò make; do 做

zuò sit 坐

zuǒbiān left (direction) 左边

zuótiān yesterday 昨天

zuòzhě author 作者

c = ts; q = ch; x = sh; z = dz; zh = j

IMMIGRATION AND CUSTOMS FORMS

The following are the forms you'll have to fill out when either entering or exiting China.

ENTRY CARD	FOR FOREIGN TRAVELLERS
	PLEASE COMPLETE IN ENGLISH. FILL IN ☐ WITH ✓

		Date of Birth	YEAR	MONTH	DAY	OFFICIAL USE ONLY
Family Name						
Given Names			Male			
			Female			
Passport No.		Nationality				
Visa No.		**Your Main Reason for Coming to China (one only)**				
Place of Visa Issuance		Convention / Conference ☐	Business ☐			
Flight No. Ship Name Train No.		Employment ☐	Settle down ☐			
From		Visiting friends or relatives ☐				
		Outing /in leisure ☐	Study ☐			
		Return home ☐	Others ☐			
Intended Address in China						

I declare the information I have given is true, correct and complete. I understand incorrect or untrue answer to any questions may have serious consequences.	SIGNATURE	Date of Entry	YEAR	MONTH	DAY

证件种类　签证种类
出入境管理局　公安部　监制

DEPARTURE CARD
FOR FOREIGN TRAVELLERS
PLEASE COMPLETE IN ENGLISH. FILL IN ☐ WITH ✓

Family Name	
Given Names	
Passport No.	
Nationality	
Flight No. Ship Name Train No.	
Destination	
Address in China	

Date of Birth — YEAR MONTH DAY

OFFICIAL USE ONLY

☐ Male
☐ Female

Your Main Reason for Departure from China (one only)

Convention / Conference ☐	Business ☐
Employment ☐	Settle down ☐
	Visiting friends or relatives ☐
Outing /in leisure ☐	Study ☐
Return home ☐	Others ☐

I declare the information I have given is true, correct and complete. I understand incorrect or untrue answer to any questions may have serious consequences.

SIGNATURE

Date of Departure — YEAR MONTH DAY

证件种类

出入境管理局

公安部监制

HEALTH DECLARATION FORM ON ENTRY/EXIT

Entry-Exit Inspection and Quarantine of the P.R.China

**Notice:For your and others' health,please fill in the form truly and completely.
False information of intent will be followed with legal consequences.**

Name _____ Sex: ☐Male ☐Female

Date of Birth _____ Nationality/Region _____

Passport No. _____ Flight No._____

The contact address and telephone number _____

_____

1.Have you had close contact with poultry or bird in the past 7 days?

Yes☐ No☐

2.Have you had close contact with patients or suspects suffering from

Avian Influenza in the past 7 days? Yes☐ No☐

3.Please mark the symptoms and diseases you have with " √ " in the

corresponding " ☐ "

☐Fever ☐Snivel ☐Cough ☐Sore throat

☐Headache ☐Diarrhoea ☐Vomiting ☐Breath Difficulty

☐Venereal disease ☐AIDS/HIV ☐Psychosis

☐Active pulmonary tuberculosis

I declare all the information given in this form are true and correct.

Signature: _____ Date:_____

Temperature (for quarantine official only):_____℃

CHINA CUSTOMS
BAGGAGE DECLARATION FORM FOR INCOMING PASSENGERS

Please read the instructions on the reverse side and provide information or mark " √ " in the space

1. Surname

Given Name

2. Date of Birth ___ Year ___ Month ___ Day

3. Sex ☐ Male ☐ Female

4. No. of Traveler's Document

5. Nationality(Region) China ☐ (Hong Kong ☐ Macao ☐ Taiwan ☐)
Other Nationals

6. Purpose of the Trip
☐ Official ☐ Business ☐ Leisure ☐ Study
☐ Immigration ☐ Visiting Friends or Relatives ☐ Return Residents ☐ Others

7. Flight No./Vehicle No./ Vessel Name

8. Number of persons under the age of 16 traveling with you

I am (We are) bringing into China's Customs territory (having)

	Yes	No
9. (residents) articles valued at over RMB 5,000 from overseas.	☐	☐
10. (non-residents) articles valued at over RMB 2,000 that will remain in the territory.	☐	☐
11. over 1,500ml (12% volume) alcoholic drinks, over 400 sticks of cigarettes , over 100 sticks of cigars, or over 500g of tobacco.	☐	☐
12. Chinese currency in cash exceeding RMB 20,000 or foreign currencies in cash exceeding USD 5,000 if converted into US dollar.	☐	☐
13. animals and plants , animal and plant products , microbes , biological products , human tissues, blood and blood products.	☐	☐
14. radio transmitters, radio receivers, communication security equipments.	☐	☐
15. other articles which are prohibited or restricted from being brought into the territory in accordance with the law of the People's Republic of China.	☐	☐
16. unaccompanied baggage .	☐	☐
17. goods of commercial value, samples, advertisements.	☐	☐

I HAVE READ THE INSTRUCTIONS ON THE REVERSE SIDE OF THIS FORM AND DECLARE THAT THE INFORMATION GIVEN ON THIS FORM IS TRUE.

Passengers who are bringing any articles included in items 9-15 shall fill out this form in detail.

Description	Quantity	Value	Type/Model	Customs Remarks

PASSENGER'S SIGNATURE   Year   Month   Date

CHINA CUSTOMS

INSTRUCTIONS

- **IMPORTANT INFORMATION**

1. All incoming passengers, except those who are exempted from examination or control in accordance with relevant regulations and those under the age of 16 traveling with adults, shall complete truthfully the declaration form in an appropriate language as provided by the Customs and submit it to the Customs officer at the declaration desk.

2. In the Customs control area where "Dual Channel" system is available, passengers who are bringing any articles included in items 9-17 shall follow the "GOODS TO DECLARE" ("RED CHANNEL", marked " ■ "), while other passengers may choose to go through the "NOTHING TO DECLARE" ("GREEN CHANNEL", marked " ● ").

3. "Residents" listed in item 9 in the form refers to passengers residing in China's Customs territory. "Non-residents" listed in item 10 refers to those passengers residing out of China's Customs territory.

4. The value of articles included in items 9 and 10 shall be the Customs value verified and accepted by the Customs.

5. Passengers, who are carrying foreign currencies in cash exceeding USD 5,000 if converted into US dollar or having unaccompanied baggage, shall fill out two declaration forms, of which one will, after being endorsed by the Customs, be returned to such passengers for use at the time when the currencies are taken out of China's Customs territory or for use of going through Customs formalities of unaccompanied baggage.

6. False declarations may result in penalties by the Customs.

- **ARTICLES PROHIBITED FROM IMPORTATION IN ACCORDANCE WITH THE LAW OF THE PEOPLE'S REPUBLIC OF CHINA**

1. Arms, imitation arms, ammunition and explosives of all kinds.

2. Counterfeit currencies and counterfeit negotiable securities.

3. Printed matter, films, photographs, gramophone records, cinematographic films, tapes (audio and video), compact discs (audio and video), storage media for computers and other articles which are detrimental to the political, economic, cultural and moral interests of China.

4. Deadly poison of all kinds.

5. Opium, morphine, heroin, marihuana and other addictive drugs and psychotropic substance.

6. Fruits, solanaceae vegetables, live animals (except dogs and cats as pet), animal products, pathogenic micro-organisms of animals and plants, pests and other harmful organisms, animal carcasses, soil, genetically modified organisms, relevant animals and plants, their products and other quarantine objects from countries or regions with prevalent epidemic animal or plant diseases.

7. Foodstuff, medicines and other articles coming from epidemic stricken areas and harmful to man and livestock or those capable of spreading diseases.

CHINA CUSTOMS
BAGGAGE DECLARATION FORM FOR OUTGOING PASSENGERS

Please read the instructions on the reverse side and provide information or mark "√" in the space

1. Surname

Given Name

2. Date of Birth Year Month Day

3. Sex Male Female

4. No. of Traveler's Document

5. Nationality(Region) China (Hong Kong Macao Taiwan)

Other Nationals

6. Purpose of the Trip
- Official
- Business
- Leisure
- Study
- Immigration
- Visiting Friends or Relatives
- Return Residents
- Others

7. Flight No./Vehicle No./ Vessel Name

8. Number of persons under the age of 16 traveling with you

I am (We are) taking out of China's Customs territory

9. trip necessities (camera, vidicon, laptop, etc.) valued each at over RMB 5,000, which will be brought back at the end of the trip. — Yes No

10. Chinese currency in cash exceeding RMB 20,000 or foreign currencies in cash exceeding USD 5,000 if converted into US dollar. — Yes No

11. gold, silver and other precious metals. — Yes No

12. cultural relics, endangered animals or plants and products thereof, biology species resources. — Yes No

13. radio transmitters, radio receivers, communication security equipments. — Yes No

14. other articles which are prohibited or restricted from being taken out of the territory in accordance with the law of the People's Republic of China. — Yes No

15. goods of commercial value, samples, advertisements. — Yes No

I HAVE READ THE INSTRUCTIONS ON THE REVERSE SIDE OF THIS FORM AND DECLARE THAT THE INFORMATION GIVEN ON THIS FORM IS TRUE.

Passengers who are taking any articles included in items 9-14 shall fill out this form in detail.

Description	Quantity	Value	Type/Model	Customs Remarks

PASSENGER'S SIGNATURE   Year   Month   Date

CHINA CUSTOMS

INSTRUCTIONS

- **IMPORTANT INFORMATION**

1. All outgoing passengers, except those who are exempted from examination or control in accordance with relevant regulations and those under the age of 16 traveling with adults, shall complete truthfully declaration form in an appropriate language as provided by the Customs and submit it to the Customs officer at the declaration desk.

2. In the Customs control area where " Dual Channel " system is available, passengers who are taking any articles included in items 9-15 shall follow the "GOODS TO DECLARE" ("RED CHANNEL" , marked " ■ "), while other passengers may choose to go through the " NOTHING TO DECLARE " ("GREEN CHANNEL" , marked " ● ") .

3. The value of articles included in item 9 shall be the value shown on the lawful commercial invoices issued within China's Customs territory.

4. Passengers , who are taking articles Included in item 9 , shall fill out two declaration forms , of which one will , after being endorsed by the Customs , be returned to such passengers for use at the time when such articles are brought back into China 's Customs territory.

5. False declarations may result in penalties by the Customs.

- **ARTICLES PROHIBITED FROM EXPORTATION IN ACCORDANCE WITH THE LAW OF THE PEOPLE'S REPUBLIC OF CHINA**

1. Arms, imitation arms, ammunition and explosives of all kinds.

2. Counterfeit currencies and counterfeit negotiable securities.

3. Printed matter, films, photographs, gramophone records, cinematographic films, tapes (audio and video), compact discs (audio and video) , storage media for computers and other articles which are detrimental to the political, economic, cultural and moral interests of China.

4. Deadly poison of all kinds.

5. Opium, morphine, heroin, marihuana and other addictive drugs and psychotropic substances.

6. Manuscripts, printed matter, films, photographs, gramophone records, cinematographic films , tapes (audio and video) , compact discs (audio and video) , storage media for computers and other articles which involve state secrets.

7. Valuable cultural relics and other relics prohibited from exportation.

8. Endangered and precious rare animals and plants (including their specimens), and their seeds and reproducing materials.

CHINA ON THE INTERNET

The Internet has brought China into the homes and offices of people all over the world. Many Chinese cities have been quick to grasp the power of the World Wide Web to get the word out about investment and trading opportunities as well as tourist destinations and cultural events. And many other organizations have posted interesting and valuable information about China. Here is a smattering of web pages that introduce various aspects of China and things Chinese.

CHINESE GOVERNMENT SOURCES

The **China Internet Information Center** provides official positions of the Chinese government on a variety of domestic and international issues, as well as basic information about China and the Chinese government on-line (*http://www.china.org.cn/english/index.htm*). Other official government sites include those maintained by the **Ministry of Foreign Affairs** (*http://www.fmprc.gov.cn/eng/*) and the **Ministry of Commerce** (*http://english.mofcom.gov.cn/*).

The Chinese Embassy in Washington (*http://www.china-embassy.org/*) maintains a web site that provides information about China, its culture, economy, and political structure and the Embassy's own operations, including visa and passport policies and procedures. Other sites are maintained by sister organizations such as **China's Permanent Mission to the United Nations** (*http://china-un.org/eng/*) and its **Consulates-General** in **New York** (*http://www.nyconsulate.prchina.org/*), **Los Angeles** (*http://chinaconsulatela.org/en/aboutus_en.htm/*), **San Francisco** (*http://www.chinaconsulatesf.org/eng/*), and **Houston** (*http://www.chinahouston.org*).

Other Chinese embassies in the English-speaking world that are on-line are those in **London** (*http://www.chinese-embassy.org.uk/*), **Ottawa** (*http://www.chinaembassycanada.org/*), **Canberra**

(*http://www.chinaembassy.org.au/*), and **Pretoria**
(*http://www.chinese-embassy.org.za/*).

U.S.-CHINA RELATIONS

The **U.S. State Department's Bureau of East Asian
and Pacific Affairs** has a page of basic information on China
located at (*http://www.state.gov/r/pa/ei/bgn/18902.htm*).

The **U.S. Embassy in Beijing** (*http://www.usembassy-
china.org.cn/*) provides information on China's agriculture,
economy, environment, science, and technology, as well as
information on visas and services provided to U.S. citizens
visiting China. It also has contact information for the U.S.
consulates in Guangzhou, Shanghai, Shenyang, and Chengdu.

The **National Committee on United States-China
Relations** (*http://www.ncuscr.org/*) is a nonprofit
educational organization that encourages understanding of
China and the United States between citizens of both
countries. The committee was founded in the belief that
vigorous debate of China policy among Americans was
essential and that balanced public education could clarify
U.S. interests and strengthen American foreign policy.

MEDIA

Many Western publications that feature extensive China
coverage are on the Net. The weekly Hong Kong-based **Far
Eastern Economic Review** (*http://www.feer.com/*) is one of
them. The U.S.-China Business' Council's acclaimed **China
Business Review** (*http://www.chinabusinessreview.com*)
comes out every two months and is known for its in-depth
coverage of China's economy and commercial developments.
You can catch up on events in Hong Kong through the eyes of
its two principal English-language newspapers, the **South
China Morning Post** (*http://www.scmp.com/*) and the
Hong Kong Standard (*http://www.thestandard.com.hk*).
Both include extensive coverage of events in China.

For the Chinese government's point of view, there's
nothing as authoritative as the official **Xinhua News
Agency**, the voice of the Communist Party, which maintains

an English-language site on the Internet
(*http://www.xinhuanet.com/english/*). The official **People's Daily** is also on the web in English
(*http://english.peopledaily.com.cn*). Also available on the Net are the **China Daily** (*http://www.chinadaily.com.cn/*), the **Beijing Review** (*http://www.bjreview.com.cn*), and **China Central Television**, or CCTV
(*http://www.cctv.com.cn/english/index.shtml*).

DOING BUSINESS IN CHINA

The **U.S. Department of Commerce** has posted useful information for exporters to China on the Net at
(*http://www.export.gov/china/*). And the **U.S. Census Bureau** provides historical data on the U.S. trade balance with China at (*http://www.census.gov/foreign-trade/balance/c5700.html*).

The United States-China Business Council is the principal organization of U.S. companies engaged in trade and investment in China. The council provides business advisory services and policy advocacy, sponsors conferences and meetings, and issues publications about doing business in China. Its web site (*http://www.uschina.org/*) is an excellent source of information on China's business environment.

The Beijing-based **American Chamber of Commerce of the PRC** (AmCham China) is a central point of contact and exchange for members of the American business community in China; it promotes trade, commerce, and investment between the United States and China. Its web site (*http://www.amcham-china.org.cn/*) features position papers on bilateral issues and other information about the China market.

The **Hong Kong American Chamber of Commerce** has a web site (*http://www.amcham.org.hk/home.shtml*) that gives information on China in general in addition to material on living and working in Hong Kong. The **Hong Kong Trade Development Council** (*http://www.tdctrade.com*) is also an excellent source on these topics.

See also the web sites of the **Canada-China Business Council** (*http://www.ccbc.com/*) and the **Hong Kong Canada Business Association** (*http://www.hkcba.com/*) for private-sector information on Canada's commercial relations with China.

TRAVEL AND TOURISM

Major tourist destinations in China are described in a web site maintained by **China International Travel Service** (*http://www.cits.net/*).

You can find general information about traveling to China (customs, visas, medical care, crime, and security concerns), as well as any current travel advisories at the U.S. State Department's **China Consular Information Sheet** (*http://travel.state.gov/china.html*). Also visit **Tips for Travelers to the PRC** at (*http://travel.state.gov/travel/tips/regional/regional_1173.html*).

There are many web sites devoted to specific cities in China, some official and some not so official. **Beijing** and **Shanghai**, for example, are well represented on the Web. Visit the **Beijing Page** (*http://www.flashpaper.com/beijing/*). And check **Shanghai Panorama** (*http://shanghai.muzi.net/*).

Other Chinese localities presented on their own web sites include **Dalian** (*http://www.china-dalian.com/*), **Guangzhou** (*http://www.chinapages.com/guangdong/guangzhou/guangzhou.htm*), **Chongqing** (*http://www.chinatour.com/attraction/chongqing.htm*), and **Chengdu** (*http://www.regenttour.com/chinaplanning/ctu/index.htm*). And you can learn more about **Tianjin** here: (*http://www.chinatour.com/attraction/tianjin.htm*).

You can find out about touring **Taiwan** from any of a number of web pages. Taiwan's official Government Information office has a website: (*http://gio.gov.tw*). General information for visitors to Taiwan, including maps, attractions, and tours, is also provided from the the **Tourism Bureau** at (*http://www.tbroc.gov.tw/*).

And there is no dearth of **Hong Kong**-related web sites. For basic tourism information, visit the Hong Kong Tourism

Board site (*http://www.hkta.org*). General information about Hong Kong tourism can be viewed at (*http://www.tourism.gov.hk/english/welcome/welcome.html*).

ARTS AND CULTURE

China is a central focus for the **Asia Society**, whose programs are described on its web site (*http://www.asiasociety.org/*). The nonprofit organization is America's leading institution dedicated to fostering understanding of Asia, and its programs include art exhibitions and performances, films, lectures, seminars and conferences, publications and materials, and programs for students and teachers.

Washington's **Freer Gallery of Art** and **Arthur M. Sackler Gallery**, both parts of the Smithsonian Institution, have fabulous collections of Asian art that include a large number of priceless Chinese pieces. They also maintain a web page to prove it at (*http://www.si.edu/asia/start.htm*).

The **Shanghai Museum** (*http://www.shanghaimuseum. net/en/index.asp*) boasts a huge collection of bronze, ceramics, calligraphy, painting, sculpture, furniture, jade and ivory carvings, oracle bones, seals, coins, minority arts, and bamboo, wood, and lacquer ware. Both it and the **Beijing Art Museum** (*http://www.chinats.com/beijing/ beijing124.htm*) whose collection includes pieces from the Neolithic Age to the Ming and Qing Dynasties and the twentieth century, feature images of some of their best pieces on-line.

Taipei's **National Palace Museum**, which houses one of the world's finest collections of Chinese art, has a site (*http://www.npm.gov.tw/*) that presents fine pieces from its collection.

Other Chinese museums with their own sites include the **Beijing Museum of Ancient Architecture** (*http://www.china.org.cn/english/kuaixun/71652.htm*), an institution devoted to the collection, study, and display of China's ancient architectural relics. Another site (*http://www.warriortours.com/cityguides/xian.htm# xianyang*), provides links to several of the ancient city of

Xi'an's museums and cultural relics, including the **Shaanxi Provincial History Museum** and the **Mausoleum of Qinshihuang**, the first Emperor of the Qin Dynasty (221 B.C.–206 B.C.) the site of the famous terra-cotta warriors and horses.

You can get a virtual "taste" of China's **Forbidden City** (*http://www.chinavista.com/beijing/gugong/!start.html*), the former palace of emperors, a museum in its own right today. Also worth a "virtual visit" is the site of the **Ancient Beijing Observatory** (*http://www.china.org.cn/english/kuaixun/71861.htm*), a remnant of the Beijing city wall that displays astronomical instruments made during the Qing Dynasty.

Beijing Opera is the subject of several web sites, including the **Beijing Opera Page** (*http://www.geocities.com/vienna/opera/8692/index0.html*), and Cantonese Opera has several pages of its own on the Internet, among them **Cantonese Opera from Around the World** (*http://members.aol.com/canopera/commun.htm*).

CHINESE CUISINE

The countless varieties of Chinese food are celebrated on a web site (*http://www.travelchinaguide.com/intro/cuisine_drink/cuisine/eight_cuisines.htm*) that is organized by region, from Anhui to Zhejiang. Another site (*http://www.ethnicfoodsco.com/china/regionalchinesecuisine.htm*) gives an overview of regional fare and links to cooking techniques, culinary history, and even medicinal cuisine.

FURTHER READING

Want to do further reading on China? Of course you can search **Amazon** (*www.amazon.com*) and **Barnes and Noble** (*www.barnesandnoble.com*), which sell everything from soup to nuts. But also check out **China Books and Periodicals** (*http://www.chinabooks.com/*), a specialty shop that focuses its offerings exclusively on books and other products related to China.

Note: The Internet addresses listed in this section were valid as of the publication date of this book. Web sites may move from time to time, and often even disappear. If a link turns out to be out of date, use a search engine like Yahoo (www.yahoo.com), Google (www.google.com), or Lycos (www.lycos.com) to locate the site's new address.

READY REFERENCE KEY

Here are some phrases and words that you are likely to use often. For a more extensive list of phrases, refer to the appropriate chapter within the book.

SIMPLE WORDS AND PHRASES

Hello. (How are you?)	*Ní hǎo.* 你好。	
Do you speak English?	*Nǐ shuō Yīngwén ma?* 你说英文吗？	
Do you understand?	*Nǐ tīng de dǒng ma?* 你听得懂吗？	
I don't speak Chinese.	*Wǒ bú huì shuō Zhōngguóhuà.* 我不会说中国话。	
I don't understand.	*Wǒ bù dǒng.* 我不懂。	
Please speak a little more slowly.	*Qǐng shuō màn yìdiǎn.* 请说慢一点。	
Please repeat.	*Qǐng zài shuō yíbiàn.* 请再说一遍。	

BEING POLITE

please	*qǐng*	请
Thank you very much.	*Fēicháng xièxie.* 非常谢谢。	
Excuse me. (apologizing)	*Duìbuqǐ.*	对不起。

Excuse me. (getting attention)	*Láojià.*	劳驾。
Good morning.	*Zǎo.*	早。
Good night.	*Wǎn ān.*	晚安。

NEEDS AND WANTS

I need ____.	*Wǒ xūyào ____.* 我需要____。
I want ____.	*Wǒ yào ____.* 我要____。
We'd like ____.	*Wǒmén xiǎngyào ____.* 我们想要____。
I'm looking for ____.	*Wó zhǎo ____.* 我找____。
Please give me ____.	*Qǐng géi wǒ ____.* 请给我____。
Please show me ____.	*Qǐng géi wǒ kànkan ____.* 请给我看看____。
Please bring ____.	*Qǐng sònglái ____.* 请送来____。

TIME

| What time is it? | *Jídiǎn zhōng?* 几点钟？ |
| What day is today? | *Jīntiān xīngqī jǐ?* 今天星期几？ |

c = ts; *q* = ch; *x* = sh; *z* = dz; *zh* = j

It's noon.	*Shì zhōngwǔ.*	
	是中午。	
Three in the afternoon.	*Xiàwǔ sāndiǎn zhōng.*	
	下午三点钟。	
A.M.	*shàngwǔ*	上午
P.M.	*xiàwǔ*	下午
evening	*wǎnshàng*	晚上
Today is ____.	*Jīntiān shì ____.*	今天是___。
yesterday	*zuótiān*	昨天
tomorrow	*míngtiān*	明天
tonight	*jīnwǎn*	今晚
last night	*zuówǎn*	昨晚
this week	*zhèige xīngqī*	这个星期
next week	*xiàge xīngqī*	下个星期
last week	*shàngge xīngqī*	上个星期
It's early.	*Hái zǎo.*	还早。
It's late.	*Wǎn le.*	晚了。
It's too late.	*Tài wǎn le.*	太晚了。

ADJECTIVES

best	*zuì hǎo*	最好
better	*gèng hǎo*	更好
cheap	*piányi*	便宜
difficult	*nán*	难
easy	*róngyì*	容易

enough	*gòu le*	够了
expensive	*guì*	贵
fast	*kuài*	快
good	*hǎo*	好
large	*dà*	大
less	*shǎoxiē*	少些
long	*cháng*	长
more	*duōxiē*	多些
short (length)	*duǎn*	短
slow	*màn*	慢
small	*xiǎo*	小
too much	*tài duō*	太多

DIRECTIONS

I'm lost.	*Wǒ mí lù le.*	我迷路了。
Where is ____?	____ *zài nǎli?* ____在哪里？	
Shall I go ____?	*Wǒ yīnggāi xiàng* ____ *zǒu ma?* 我应该向____走吗？	
▨ to the left	*zuó*	左
▨ to the right	*yòu*	右
▨ straight ahead	*qián*	前
How far away is ____?	____ *yǒu duōyuǎn?* ____有多远？	
Please show it to me on the map.	*Qǐng zài dìtú shàng zhǐ géi wǒ.* 请在地图上指给我。	

INDEX